The Power of Contestation

The Power of Contestation

Perspectives on Maurice Blanchot

Edited by
Kevin Hart and Geoffrey H. Hartman

The Johns Hopkins University Press
Baltimore and London

The Johns Hopkins University Press
2715 North Charles Street
Baltimore, Maryland 21218-4363
www.press.jhu.edu

Library of Congress Cataloging-in-Publication Data
The power of contestation : perspectives on Maurice Blanchot / edited by
Kevin Hart and Geoffrey H. Hartman.
    p.   cm.
Includes bibliographical references and index.
ISBN 0-8018-7962-0 (hardcover : alk. paper)
1. Blanchot, Maurice—Philosophy. I. Hart, Kevin, 1954– II. Hartman,
Geoffrey H.
PQ2603.L3343Z7955 2004
843'.912—dc22
2004004587

A catalog record for this book is available from the British Library.

Literature represents a power of a particular sort that does not concern possibility . . . art is infinite contestation, contestation of itself and contestation of other forms of power—not simple anarchy, but the free search for the original power that art and literature represent (*power without power*). —MAURICE BLANCHOT

Contents

Acknowledgments

The editors would like to thank Jennifer Nichols for her invaluable help as a research assistant while this collection was in its final stages of preparation. Kevin Hart would also like to thank Villanova University for inviting him to be Visiting Professor of Christian Philosophy in the 2001 academic year. It was at Villanova that much of the work on this collection was done.

The Power of Contestation

Introduction

Kevin Hart and Geoffrey H. Hartman

"Maurice Blanchot is not one of the most widely read French writers," Georges Bataille conceded when preparing a short text on his friend in 1953 or 1954.[1] Almost immediately, though, he made a very bold claim: Blanchot is "the most original mind of his age . . . he has revealed to us the strangest perspectives, the most unexpected things within the horizon of human existence" (67). Bataille wrote those words for an English literary journal, but like another project he intended to devote to his friend, the manuscript was never completed.[2] The piece first appeared in a special issue of the French review *Gramma*, "Lire Blanchot I," in 1976, by which time his claim had come to seem less outrageous. In the fifty years since Bataille composed those few pages, Blanchot's reputation as an original thinker and writer has steadily grown, both inside and outside France, partly as a response to works he had already published by the mid-1950s, partly as a consequence of his later works, and partly due to the influence of both on French writers who have become major figures in their own right. It is impossible to imagine the ferment of French thought that took place around and after the popular revolution of May 1968 without reference to him. Had Blanchot not written narratives such as *Thomas l'obscur* (1941;

rev. 1950) and *L'arrêt de mort* (1948), and collections of essays such as *L'espace littéraire* (1955) and *L'entretien infini* (1969), it is doubtful whether Gilles Deleuze and Michel Foucault, Roland Barthes and Jacques Derrida, would have explored the issues they did and in quite the ways they chose. Edmond Jabès might not enjoy the same high regard among his peers without Blanchot's firm support for the first volume of *Le Livre des questions* (1963), while it would be hard to conceive Georges Bataille or Emmanuel Levinas without the profound friendship that they shared, in different ways, with Blanchot.[3]

Bataille's evaluation of Blanchot appears to have been written just before the publication of *L'espace littéraire*, and with foreknowledge of its contents. It is in that obsessive book that Blanchot develops an intense meditation on the relations of writing and death, on reading and the resuscitation of the dead.[4] We find there the theses of the death of the author and the impossibility of reading, which Barthes and Paul de Man respectively would explore years later.[5] The question that twists and turns throughout these studies of Mallarmé and Rilke, Kafka and Hölderlin, appears to be more philosophical than literary: Is human being wholly determined by a relation with the possible? In their different ways Hegel, Nietzsche, and Heidegger have answered in the affirmative, Blanchot notes, and each of them has placed death at the center of his answer. "Death, in the human perspective, is not a given, it must be achieved. It is a task, one which we take up actively, one which becomes the source of our activity and mastery. Man dies, that is nothing. But man *is,* starting from his death."[6] There is nothing strange in figuring human existence in terms of death as a possibility: that, Blanchot argues, is precisely what modern philosophy has been telling us since the *Phänomenologie des Geistes* (1807). No meaning without death, says Hegel; one should die in a good and proper way, in the immanence of life, declares Nietzsche; while Heidegger concludes that, in the moment of death, Dasein grasps the possibility of the impossible. What makes Blanchot so extraordinary, Bataille would add, are his two responses to this shared assumption of modern philosophy. First, we maintain a relation with death not only of possibility but also of impossibility; second, this relation of impossibility is discerned not through our rapport with the divine, with being, or with truth but with our capacity to make art.

Blanchot organizes his thoughts about the impossible by way of the image. This is territory that Jean-Paul Sartre had long since made his own: the works of his first maturity as a philosopher were *L'imagination* (1936) and *L'imaginaire* (1940). Impressed by Edmund Husserl's insight that consciousness is intentional—always a consciousness of something—Sartre argued that the imagination also has an intentional structure. It does not derive from internal mental objects, as the classical conception of the imagination would have us believe. That doctrine, he convincingly showed, is riddled with contradictions.[7] Rather, the imagination is always and already outwardly directed, forever in touch with the world. Sartre did not stop at this phenomenological claim. What chiefly interested him is that the imaginative act creates other possible worlds that can, and often do, contrast sharply with the actual world in which we live. This fact testifies to the primacy of human freedom: a theme that Sartre was to make distinctively his own in the years during and after the Second World War. In "Les Deux versions de l'imaginaire" (1951) Blanchot also rejects the classical understanding of the image and, like Sartre, does so from within the broad horizon of phenomenology: he had read Heidegger's *Sein und Zeit* (1927) shortly after it was published and remained deeply impressed by it. Yet Blanchot's line of attack comes from a slightly different angle, compared to Sartre's, and proceeds in a quite different manner.[8] He begins by noting that the classical doctrine assumes that an image derives from an object that precedes it both in time and in the order of being. "After the object comes the image," says Blanchot.[9] Could anything be more simple or more commonsensical? The very next sentence takes us into a very complex world, however. And here we see one of Blanchot's characteristic moves as a critic, one that he shares with the later Heidegger though not with Sartre. He develops his thought by seizing on a perfectly ordinary word, "after" (*après*), and giving it an extraordinary meaning:

> "After" means that the thing must first take itself off a ways [*s'éloigne*] in order to be grasped. But this remove [*éloignement*] is not the simple displacement of a moveable object which would nevertheless remain the same. Here the distance [*l'éloignement*] is in the heart of the thing. The thing was there; we grasped it in the vital movement of a comprehensive action—and lo, having become image, instantly it has become that which no one can grasp, the unreal, the impossible. It is not the same thing at a distance [*éloignée*] but the thing as distance [*éloignement*], present in its absence, graspable because ungraspable, appearing as disappeared. It is the return of what does not come back, the strange heart of remoteness as the life and the sole heart of the thing. (255–56)

So there are *two* versions of the imaginary: one that is classical and another that calls that entire way of thinking into question. Hegel is right to prize the labor of the negative, Blanchot thinks: finitude is the very condition of understanding. Unless the thing before me is finite, I cannot make an image of it. Or, with respect to human beings, it is our mortality that forms the necessary condition for an image being made of us. The first account of the image is therefore a consequence of the negativity of death. Yet this negativity is not completely used up in a relation of possibility with death. The image itself cannot be grasped: "it has become . . . the impossible." There are no consoling religious or humanist conclusions to be drawn from this; we are exposed to a loss of reality, not an intensification of it. As Blanchot says, looking wryly at Genesis 1:27, "*man is unmade according to his image.*"[10]

Where Sartre argues that the image is outwardly directed, Blanchot insists that it belongs to what he calls *le dehors,* the outside—the non-realm of the impossible. This is not another world that, because it has been created by a novelist or poet, bespeaks the glory and the misery of human freedom; it is a non-place that fascinates the artist in the act of composition, freezes him or her in its dark gaze, and brings him or her to the point of abandoning the work in hand. It is not another world that contrasts with the one in which we live, not even the disturbing fictional world we encounter in Sartre's novel *La Nausée* (1938); it is an interruption of the unity of "world" by what escapes the duality of being and non-being: the play of images, the murmur of words, the rhythm of music. The notion of the outside allows us to render more precise Rilke's thought that death need not be figured solely in terms of negation.[11] Death can also be contemplated by way of the neutral, neither being nor non-being, in which case it is not recognized as an event, let alone a true event. Blanchot calls this aspect of death *le mourir,* dying. It is disclosed to human beings (but without disclosure, Blanchot would add in his characteristic syntax), meaning that it is not registered as psychological experience but as akin to ontological attunement, what Heidegger had called *Stimmung* in his lectures of the 1920s.[12]

The attunement or mood that comes about when men and women confront non-being is anxiety, Heidegger had shown in his brilliant inaugural lecture at Freiburg, "Was ist Metaphysik?" (July 24, 1929). For Blanchot, however, the approach of the outside gives rise to a mood of fascinated, indefinite weariness. Nothing can begin or end in this "vague and vacant outside," this "neutral existence, nil and limitless," this "suffocating condensation where being ceaselessly perpetuates itself in nothingness," for beginnings and endings require negation.[13] There is only the return of what has never taken place.

Completed books, brought to a high polish and valued for buttressing national culture or a philosophical ideal, tend to bypass or repress the outside. Only strange narratives that respond to the murmur of dying like Hermann Broch's *Der Tod des Vergil* (1945) or Samuel Beckett's *L'innommable* (1953) and fragmentary works like René Char's "Partage formel" do not shy away from it.[14] There is an analogy between the tomblike completed book and death, Blanchot suggests, and there is also an uncanny rapport between writing and dying, a relationship that can never be encompassed in the present. "To write is no longer to situate death in the future," he says, but is "to know that death has taken place even though it has not been experienced."[15] In other words, writing a poem or a story does not gather the self into a unity but rather fragments it and, indeed, makes one realize that this fragmentation has always and already occurred.

Blanchot's understanding of the image converges with Levinas's as elaborated in "La Réalité et son ombre" (1948) although the two friends differ over the consequences to be drawn from the nature of the image. Levinas published his essay in Sartre's journal, *Les Temps Modernes,* as though to underline his disagreement with the famous author of *L'imagination* and *L'imaginaire,* and the essay appeared with a preface by the editorial committee, who sharply criticized it along Sartrean lines.[16] For Levinas, the shadowy nature of the image means that art is to be distrusted; it seduces us away from our ethical responsibilities. He will have nothing of Heidegger's elucidations of poems by George, Hölderlin, Rilke, and Trakl or his insistence that "poetically man dwells."[17] It is criticism, not poetry, that is of use to us because it deals in concepts, not images, and thereby keeps us in the real world where other people have a claim on us. Yet when Levinas considers Blanchot's meditations on the outside, which are rooted in specific literary texts and are in some ways close to the later work of Heidegger, he merely notes that his friend "abstains from ethical preoccupations, at least in explicit form."[18] Is there an *implicit* concern with ethics in the Blanchot of *L'espace littéraire,* something wholly absent in the Heidegger of *Erläuterungen zu Hölderlins Dichtung* (1944), for example? There is. Where Heidegger regards art as the lighting up of beings, Blanchot conceives it as "a black light," Levinas observes. It is "a night coming from below—a light that undoes the world, leading it back to its origin, to the over and over again, the murmur, ceaseless lapping of waves, a 'deep past, never long enough ago'" (137). Poetry (a broader category than verse) makes us insecure in the world, points us to the essence of nomadism, and consequently does not deny the other person a welcome in my home or in my country. For Blanchot, as Levinas reads him, art "must herald an order of justice" (137); the poetic word truly belongs to ethics, not aesthetics.

To summarize: literature for Blanchot indicates our relation with death; more, it discloses that death is itself divided into the negative and the neutral; and this neutral aspect of death—namely, dying—reveals that our response to the world cannot always take the form of possibility or power but is marked by a passivity beyond all the usual oppositions of activity and passivity. When these things become clear, we begin to understand Bataille's large claim for Blanchot. He has challenged the entire basis of modern philosophy, and made thinking about art primary for pondering the human condition. No longer are reflections on art to be addressed only once metaphysics, epistemology, ethics, and religion have been satisfactorily worked out. On the contrary, the sheer fact that we have art is taken to shake the ground of the sort of systems we find in Kant and Hegel. Also, as our understanding of Blanchot increases, we can make sense of Levinas's claim that *L'espace littéraire* is "situated beyond all critique and all exegesis."[19] It is not a judgment of the value of Blanchot's writing as literary criticism. Not at all—or not at all directly. It is a statement that places his writing with respect to the very practice of commenting on fiction and poetry. "And yet it does not tend toward philosophy" (127), Levinas adds, meaning that Blanchot "does not see, in philosophy, the ultimate possibility; nor, as a matter of fact, does he see in possibility itself—in the "I can"— the limit of the human" (127).

For Levinas in 1956 Blanchot is certainly an original mind, for he radically rethinks what is inherited from literature and philosophy. Everything that has been thought on the basis of the Same, the One, or the Possible—that is, Levinas implies, *everything*—is to be rethought beginning from the Other, the Plural, the Impossible. Ten years later, in 1966, when reflecting on *L'attente l'oubli* (1962), Levinas stressed once again that there is more than literature in his friend's work. This new text—a unique attempt to combine fiction and fragment—may appear as literature stripped to the bone, yet it overflows with prophetic meaning.[20] It "preserves that moment that is located between seeing and saying, that language of pure transcendence without correlation . . . pure extra-vagance, a language going from one singularity to another without their having anything in common . . . a language without words that beckons without signifying anything, a language of pure complicity, but of a purposeless complicity."[21] If the author of *L'espace littéraire* abstained from overt "ethical preoccupations," the man who signs *L'attente l'oubli* several years later seems to be enacting in his writing the very ethics that Levinas has been at pains to affirm in *Totalité et infini* (1961) and thereafter.[22]

Thus Levinas in 1956 and 1966. If we move forward in another even step to 1976 we find, in the same number of *Gramma* in which Bataille's unfinished essay appeared, Derrida's first study of Blanchot. One of the speakers in this long text, "Pas," observes that, were it fitting to praise Blanchot, and were his most recent work, *Le Pas au-delà* (1973), not to render the metaphor utterly inappropriate, "I would say that never as much as today have I imagined him to be so far ahead of us. He waits for us, still to come, to be read and re-read by those who do so now they know how to read, and *thanks* to him."[23] We have passed from the descriptive claim that Blanchot's writing is "beyond all critique" to the evaluation that as a thinker the man is "far ahead of us." "Pas" itself mimics the form of Blanchot's conversations between unnamed speakers in *L'entretien infini* (1969), and is the first of Derrida's texts to compliment Blanchot by allowing his writing to be marked by the older man's.[24] Blanchot's conversations are themselves influenced by Heidegger's "Aus einem Gespräch von der Sprache" (1953–54), and in general Blanchot has helped to mediate the reception of Heidegger in France. Unlike Jean Beaufret, though, he never simply transmitted the thought of the master from Germany. Derrida, the preeminent French philosopher to have inherited Heideggerian questions and motifs, testifies eloquently both to Blanchot's faithfulness to Heidegger and to his originality with respect to the philosopher: "When Blanchot constantly repeats—and it is a long complaint and not a triumph of life—the impossible dying, the impossibility, alas, of dying, he says at once the same thing and something completely different from Heidegger."[25] And he adds, "It is just a question of knowing in which sense (in the sense of direction and trajectory) one reads the expression the possibility of impossibility" (77). Do we take Heidegger's words—"*the possibility of the impossibility of any existence at all*"[26]—to mean that human beings grasp impossibility as a possibility in our last moments, as Heidegger taught? Or do we take them to affirm that impossibility has a modality of its own, neither of being nor non-being: an endless dying that forever haunts our meanings and values but that cannot be reduced to them? The answer, Derrida implies, is yes to both questions.

Derrida's first text on Blanchot was published in 1976, as we said a moment ago. Unlike Levinas, he did not contribute to the special number of *Critique* in June 1966 that was consecrated to Blanchot.[27] Since 1962 Michel Foucault had been on the journal's editorial committee, a sign of the respect with which he was held in Paris, especially for the then recent *Folie et déraison: Histoire de la folie à l'âge classique* (1961); and when Jean Piel had the bold idea of a Blanchot issue the task of finding suitable contributors fell to Foucault and Roger Laporte. Perhaps Derrida was not invited to submit an essay or perhaps he was overcommitted with writing projects. Either way, he did not feature in the special number of *Critique,* even though his admiration for Blanchot had always been high, and even though Blanchot had recognized the richness and sharpness of his thought after reading "Violence et métaphysique: Essai sur le pensée d'Emmanuel Lévinas" (1964). For his part, from the mid-1950s Foucault had been entranced by Blanchot's essays and narratives. "At that time, I dreamt of being Blanchot," he confided to a friend.[28] In *Les Mots et les choses* (1966) he figured his favorite modern writer as an exemplary witness to a historical mutation that was occurring, a new *episteme* characterized by the erasure of the human subject. And when the Blanchot special edition of *Critique* appeared in bookshops shortly after *Les Mots et les choses,* many people took Foucault's contribution, "La Pensée du dehors," as a way into a book as baffling as it was brilliant. They were not wholly mistaken, especially if they focused on the section of the essay entitled "L'expérience du dehors."

In thinking of literature as experience, Foucault believed, Blanchot was leading us away from the philosophy of subjectivity that had run from Descartes to Husserl and beyond.[29] What is valuable in regarding literature as experience is not so much what it tells us about fiction and poetry, as conventionally understood, as what it reveals about experience: such was Foucault's judgment. Beginning with Stéphane Mallarmé and Franz Kafka, then becoming increasingly more finely determined in Bataille, Klossowski, and Blanchot, literature frees itself from the grip of modern philosophy, and in particular from the demand to refer everything to the statement "I think." When approached on its own terms, literature indicates another path, one marked by "I speak," which, rather than indicating a pure interiority, leads us to the outside.[30] Literature for Blanchot and Foucault does not signify lived experience, *le vécu,* but rather experience as an exposure to peril, *l'expérience.* To respond to the murmur of the outside is to undergo a strange trial, for the person fascinated by it slides from the possible to the impossible, from the power of being able to say "I" to the powerlessness of becoming a neutral "one."

Testimonies within France have continued to make Bataille's claim for Blanchot's significance less wild than it once seemed. The last decade has seen a late flowering of research and popularization alike consecrated to his thought and its ramifications. If one culminating point was the broadcast of the documentary "Maurice Blanchot" in the series "Un siècle d'écrivains" on France 3 in 1998, another was a major conference on his narrative and critical writing, "Maurice Blanchot: Récits critiques," held at the Université de Paris in March 2003.[31] After his death, *Magazine Littéraire* was quick to devote a dossier to him, appropriately entitled "L'énigme Blanchot."[32] In one of the best studies of Blanchot to have come out of France in recent years, *L'être et le neutre* (2001), Marlène Zarader tells us that he is "more than one player among others in modernity, because he brings to the point of incandescence the whole epoch's temptation."[33] Changing her metaphor, she goes on to add that "Blanchot's work today serves as a *mirror*—with all the limits (notably, the effects of circularity) that are indissociable from it. The epoch does not cease to contemplate itself there" (20). She quotes Foucault's essay in *Critique*, "La Pensée du dehors," in which he declares that Blanchot is not so much a *witness* to a thought—let us say, all too quickly, the thought of experience—as the very thought *itself.* This is not to suggest that Blanchot was permanently exposed to view in French intellectual culture, as Sartre was. Not at all: he was never a visible public presence. He never appeared on "Apostrophe," never gave any lectures, and never received a prize. Active in May 1968, he was not recognized on the streets. How could he have been? The only photographs of the man appeared years after.[34] (In order to dispel the suspicion that Blanchot might not even exist, Denis Hollier impishly reassures us that he saw him once "pale but real, in a committee, in May 1968.")[35] Foucault stresses that Blanchot is "not hidden by his texts, but absent from their existence and absent through the marvelous force of their existence."[36] The man whom Bataille called "the most original mind of his age" is also, as Foucault says, an "invisible presence" (19). That is one reason Bataille's claim can still seem so odd to people who, conditioned to the culture of fame, expect great minds also to be familiar faces.

Blanchot was born in 1907, two years after Sartre, and like him never occupied a university chair. He did not teach in lycées like the young philosopher but always lived by his pen, writing first for rightest papers like *Journal des Débats, Le Rempart,* and *L'Insurgé,* and then, from the mid-1940s, for *L'Arche, Critique,* and especially the *Nouvelle Nouvelle Revue Française.* Unlike Sartre, Blanchot has never produced a "big book" like *L'être et le néant* (1943) or *Critique de la raison dialectique* (1960). All his critical volumes from *Faux pas* (1943) to

L'amitié (1971) are collections of review essays—sometimes heavily revised, sometimes not. *L'espace littéraire* and *L'entretien infini* might appear to be tightly structured but they are not treatises, and the latter work begins by meditating on the "exigency of discontinuity" that is a part of modern thought as Blanchot understands it.[37]

The description "novelist-philosopher" might at first seem broad enough to include both Sartre and Blanchot, and yet the latter abandoned the novel after *Le Très-haut* (1948), preferring the very French genre of the *récit*, to which he has given a distinctive half-twist. When he distinguished the *roman* and the *récit* in the 1920s, Ramon Fernandez noted that the former shows events taking place in time while the latter presents events that have already occurred.[38] The genre of the *récit* encourages analysis or meditation rather than action, and strictly speaking it is "impossible to prevent the thing being told from being *terminated* and its representation from having become independent and obeying only the laws of combination of the impersonal mind" (67). Readers of *L'arrêt de mort* and *Celui qui ne m'accompagnait pas* will readily agree that Blanchot has taken the quality of the incessant in the *récit* to an extreme that is, if not explicitly invited by the genre, then more or less tolerated by it. After Blanchot, the *récit* seems exposed to the endless murmur of the outside. But what of the other half of the description, novelist-*philosopher*? For all his familiarity with even the most demanding of European philosophers, Blanchot discreetly distances himself from philosophy. Which is not to say that he rejects the philosophical. Rather, he has to subscribe to a thinking that takes its cue from the Other rather than the Same. This thought, Blanchot has steadily maintained, has social implications, which he has indicated by the teasing expression "communism . . . beyond communism" and has sketched in terms of everyday life.[39] Without rejecting the older Sartre's *gauchiste* speculations on method, or indeed his role as a committed intellectual, Blanchot seeks another way of coming to terms with our responsibility for one another.

Only in his later writings, beginning with "Discours sur la patience" (1975), does Blanchot identify himself closely with Levinas's ethics as grounded in the transcendence of the other person with respect to me.[40] In following Levinas, however, Blanchot is not simply adhering to one philosophical position among others. He does not propose to theorize *about* the other person, to make a contribution to what analytic philosophers call "the problem of other minds," but to think solely on the basis of speaking *to* another person. The word "philosophical" then indicates a movement of thought that begins by granting a privilege to the Other instead of the Same. That it cannot enjoy any mastery is happily admitted. Consider one of the things that Blanchot most admires in Levinas:

> One is always struck by one of his typical procedures: to begin, or to follow out, an analysis (most often, phenomenologically inspired) with such rigor and informed understanding that it seems precisely in this way that everything is said and that truth itself is disclosed—right along, that is, until we get to a minor remark, usually introduced by, e.g., an "*unless*" to which we cannot fail to be attentive, which fissures the whole of the preceding text, disturbing the solid order we had been called upon to observe, an order that nonetheless remains important.[41]

Of this failure to gather everything into a statement, to furnish knowledge in the present, Blanchot says, "This is perhaps *the* movement that could properly be called philosophical, not by stroke of force or belabored assertion, but a movement that was already Plato's expedient in his dialogues (his probity, and ruse as well)" (48). This leaguing of close reading and the philosophical has marked all those, including the writers of this introduction, who have learned from Blanchot, either directly or indirectly.

We have reported at length on testimonies to Blanchot's intellectual standing in France, and it is worth adding some words about a slightly different matter: his influence there. For his younger contemporaries especially, Blanchot was seen to offer alternate paths in the 1950s for literary, philosophical, and political thought, beyond those sanctioned by the massively influential Sartre. We stress the plural—"paths"—because his influence has been covert, intense, and remarkably varied. On the one hand, he has stimulated philosophers who believe it is necessary to traverse phenomenology, people like Derrida, Lacoue-Labarthe, and Nancy; on the other hand, he has been equally admired by Deleuze and Foucault, who begin by rejecting phenomenology and trying to rid themselves of all traces of transcendental thought. He has worked a change for practitioners of prose fiction such as Marguerite Duras, Louis-René des Forêts, and Roger Laporte, as well as poets like René Char, Michel Deguy, and Edmond Jabès. Turning to politics, we find that Blanchot threw himself into struggles for the extreme right when young and for the extreme left when older. In the 1930s he wrote in support of national revolution and against Hitlerism, and in 1936 he rejected the Blum administration so fiercely as to advocate terrorism as a method of public salvation.[42] If his later political influence seems to have been concentrated on the rue Saint-Benoît group—Robert Antelme, Marguerite Duras, and Dionys Mascolo, among others—it must also be acknowledged that it has spread far beyond this particular left-wing enclave. In the Second World War Blanchot worked with the Résistance, and was almost executed by a firing squad: an incident beautifully evoked in *L'instant de ma mort* (1994); in 1960 he was responsible for a crucial draft of the explosive "Declaration sur le droit à l'insoumission" during the Algerian war; and he played an exacting role on the Comité d'action étudiants-écrivains in May 1968, which included writing some of the most trenchant political tracts of the day and perhaps of any day. The "invisible presence" is also, as Blanchot's biographer has put it, an "invisible partner" of many literary, philosophical, and political movements in the twentieth century.[43]

Just two examples will suffice to suggest the sort of sway that Blanchot has had on the generation that followed him, the very thinkers that, since the late 1960s, have helped to redraw the humanities in English-speaking countries, especially the United States. For the young Foucault, it was Merleau-Ponty rather than Sartre who was initially of interest, while for the slightly older man the *Critique de la raison dialectique* was no more than the terminal moraine of Hegelianism.[44] Someone seeking to depart from the philosophy of subjectivity would hardly find Sartrean authenticity to his taste, and Merleau-Ponty's phenomenology of language did not go as far as Foucault wanted. Yet Blanchot's strong interest in madness, as evidenced in "La Folie par excellence" (1951), and his emphasis on losing "the power to say 'I'" could only be attractive to the Foucault of *Folie et déraison* and *Les Mots et les choses*.[45] Similarly, the young Derrida found Sartre's interpretations of the major intellectual currents of the age weak and flawed, and his phenomenological ontology less than satisfying. Nonetheless, when reading Sartre while a student at the École Normale Supérieur, he "discovered Blanchot, Bataille, Ponge—whom I think one could have read otherwise. . . . Things changed when, thanks to him but especially against him, I read Husserl, Heidegger, Blanchot and others."[46] Doubtless the way in which Blanchot interlaced literature and the philosophical seemed to Derrida more rigorous and more subtle than the analyses gathered together in either *Qu'est-ce que la littérature?* (1948) or the various volumes of *Situations*. And doubtless the intriguing ways in which Blanchot folded together motifs of both Heidegger (non-being) and Mallarmé (absence) made him a thinker whose work would be as provocative as it was valuable for Derrida's own writing.

The reception of recent French thought in the United States has usually been told in terms of "structuralism" and "poststructuralism." What happened, so the story goes, is that an international conference was held October 18–21, 1966, at the Johns Hopkins University in Baltimore to welcome and weigh the structuralism that Claude Lévi-Strauss and others had made prominent. This colloquium, "Critical Languages and the Sciences of Man," had the express ambition of bringing "into an active and not uncritical contact leading European proponents of structural studies in a variety of disciplines with a wide spectrum of American scholars."[47] Americans and Europeans assembled as planned, and things got off to a good start. Halfway through, the event was proceeding very nicely, with Barthes, Goldmann, and Lacan reading impressive papers—and then, on the final day, the young Derrida delivered his talk, "La structure, le signe et le jeu dans le discours des sciences humaines." As Derrida's dense reading of Lévi-Strauss and Rousseau was slowly taken in over the conference's final hours and in the weeks and months following it, structuralism began to seem less and less viable. Interest shifted to something that people started to call "poststructuralism." Hence the joke: structuralism lasted just three days in America! Popular as this version of events has been in and around universities, it offers too stripped-down an account of American-French intellectual relations to be of much help in understanding what happened in the mid-1960s and thereafter. For one thing, as early as 1956 Paul de Man (who participated in the conference at Johns Hopkins) had argued that formalism was a dead end.[48] He was sharply critical of Barthes's paper, "Écrire: Verbe intransitif?," in the discussion period, and he disagreed also with Jean Hyppolite's reading of Hegel.[49] When disseminated by Derrida in America, some deconstructive seeds fell on fertile ground, but some had been sprouting there anyway.[50] For another thing, Lacan and his American supporters had read Derrida's "L'écriture avant la lettre" in the December 1965 edition of *Critique,* and sensed the importance of the piece. Here was a new way of thinking about writing that Lacan was eager to claim as arising ultimately from his own work.

Never a structuralist and only rarely a commentator on it, Blanchot did not feature in the colloquium at Johns Hopkins. Only Georges Poulet referred to him.[51] Just four months before the conference, however, de Man had published "La circularité de l'interprétation dans l'œuvre critique de Maurice Blanchot" in the special issue of *Critique* that we have already discussed. For a critic who was seldom, if ever, satisfied by the work of others or himself, the essay is notable for the approval expressed about its subject's approach to reading and for the tone of general admiration. Yet it would be de Man's essay on Derrida, not Blanchot, that would set the agenda for a generation of English-speaking critics; and in the late 1970s and 1980s many people would venture to read Blanchot chiefly because Derrida spoke of him so often and with such esteem.[52] Those indebted to Blanchot—Barthes, Derrida, and Foucault in particular—were translated quite rapidly, published by large publishing houses, and given pride of place in the proliferating courses on literary theory, which had become the new prestige subject in literary studies. *Madness and Civilization,* a translation of the shorter version of *Folie et déraison,* appeared as early as 1965 with Pantheon, which followed up with *The Order of Things* in 1970. Barthes's *Elements of Semiology* was published by Cape in 1967, and Hill and Wang followed the year after with *Writing Degree Zero* and then, in 1974, with *S/Z.* Derrida's *Of Grammatology* appeared in 1976 with the Johns Hopkins University Press, while *Writing and Difference* came out in 1978 with the University of Chicago Press.

The reception of Blanchot in the English-speaking world has been quite different. "Of the small number of unimpeachably major, original voices in modern French literature, that of Maurice Blanchot has waited the longest to find an audience in English." So declared Susan Sontag.[53] Several years earlier, Geoffrey Hartman had made what he called "an extravagant claim": "When we come to write the history of criticism for the 1940 to 1980 period, it will be found that Blanchot, together with Sartre, made French 'discourse' possible, both in its relentlessness and its acuity."[54] Talked up though he was, Blanchot was not taken up in the academy: there was no method that could be discovered and applied. Although *Thomas the Obscure* (a translation of the *récit,* not the novel) came out as early as 1973, it was with a very small press, David Lewis, Inc., and it gained only a cult readership. Other works of fiction, from *Death Sentence* (1978) to *The One Who Was Standing apart from Me* (1993), were published by Station Hill Press, again a niche publisher rather than a mainstream press. Only in 1982, when the University of Nebraska Press brought out *The Space of Literature,* was Blanchot taken up by a prestigious university publisher. Even so, he has had to wait longer than those he bewitched in the 1950s and 1960s to be translated in impressive bulk. It was in the mid-nineties, twenty years after the irruption of "poststructuralism," that Stanford University Press and the University of Minnesota Press produced major collections of his essays, and in the same period two anthologies of his work were published: *The Blanchot Reader* (1995) and *The Station Hill Blanchot Reader* (1998). A similar story of initial enthusiasm and later approval from above can be told of special numbers of English journals: in 1976 *Sub-Stance* devoted an issue to Blanchot, although it was not until 1998 that *Yale French Studies* did the same.

So Blanchot has become of interest in the English-speaking world well after the king wave of poststructuralism crashed over colleges and universities. He is being read in English a full generation after Barthes, Derrida, and Foucault, and with all the vigilance that they have passed on, "and *thanks* to him," as Derrida put it. Sometimes he is read with their constructions of his ideas in mind, and at other times as offering futures for thought that were not taken up in the 1970s and 1980s. Contemporary talk about community and subjectivity, about literature and the sacred, about experience and speech, about the Holocaust and "being Jewish" is increasingly being done with Blanchot as a vanishing point. Formidably difficult, his writing has nonetheless attracted intrepid and knowledgeable elucidators. Two of the contributors to this collection, Gerald L. Bruns and Leslie Hill, have helped to bring our man's work more surely into focus, although each would readily admit that the very idea of neatly translating Blanchot into a series of well-formed propositions is doomed to failure.[55] His narratives ask us to reset our assumptions about reading and writing, while his essays give us hints on how to do just that. Each sentence in those works is completely clear and often beautifully cut, with many facets reflecting a strange light. The difficulties tend to come when one passes from sentence to sentence, and then they come in numbers.

Archilochus is of help to us: his fragment lets us see that Blanchot is a hedgehog rather than a fox, that he knows one big thing, not many little things. We can call that "one big thing" the outside, the impossible, or the neutral, and we can approach it by way of dying or writing or the everyday. We have several names at our disposal because Blanchot turns out to be a rather foxy hedgehog. When priming our contributors we asked them to be guided by the word "contestation," partly because it involves the outside (or, if you like, the impossible or the neuter), and partly because it invites us to consider experience from various perspectives: political, of course (as the French *contestaire* suggests), but also ethical, literary, philosophical, and religious. We can be more precise about the book in general by giving preliminary answers to several questions: What is contestation? What is contested? How? Why?

In his essay in this collection Philippe Lacoue-Labarthe reminds us that "contest" belongs to a string of words that includes "attest," "detest," "protest," and "test," and that these all press upon "contestation." In the seventeenth century, the word signified a solemn asseveration; in the eighteenth, the action of calling to witness. Before either of these senses were in circulation, back in the sixteenth century, "contestation" already denoted contention, conflict, controversy; the sense of a claim or a point being contested has remained in French and English. Yet the word is inflected differently when used by Blanchot. Many readers come across it for the first time when reading Bataille's *L'expérience intérieure* (1943), so let us begin there. Bataille introduces the word in the first part of the book, "Principles of a Method and a Community," and, as we will see, contestation is linked to both method and community. Here is the first instance of the word in the book:

> I come to the most important point: it is necessary to reject external means. The dramatic is not being in these or those conditions, all of which are positive conditions (like being half-lost, being able to be saved). It is simply to be. To perceive this is, without anything else, to contest with enough persistence the evasions by which we usually escape. It is no longer a question of salvation: this is the most odious of evasions. The difficulty—that contestation must be done in the name of its authority—is resolved thus: I contest in the name of contestation what experience itself is (the will to proceed to the end of the possible). Experience, its authority, its method, do not distinguish themselves from the contestation.[56]

Bataille adds a footnote to the last use of "contestation" which reads, "As I write in Part 4, the principle of contestation is one of those on which Maurice Blanchot insists as on a foundation" (12). The implication is that "contestation" is one of his friend's signature words, although it is just as likely that the word was shared between the two men. (They were introduced by Pierre Prévost at the end of 1940, and "links of admiration and agreement" were "immediately formed."[57] A full year after they became friends, Bataille started to write *L'expérience intérieure*.) There are important things to notice in the passage just quoted—the relationships of contestation and experience, contestation and authority—but before we discuss them it is worth while to see how the concept of contestation was at work in Blanchot before Bataille used the word.

In the 1930s Blanchot was a revolutionary of a particular kind. Anticommunist and anticapitalist, he passionately argued for a spiritual revolution. Unlike the Marxist revolts earlier in the century, it would not bring about more disorder but would generate a true, abiding order. It would be a true revolution since, as he said in 1931 with regard to Mahatma Ghandhi, "all revolution is spiritual [*spirituelle*]."[58] By 1937 we can discern the outline of his general cast of mind. It can be put in a word: refusal. Consider the conclusion of his farewell essay for *Combat* in December 1937, "On demande des dissidents":

> In reality what counts is not being above parties, but against them. It is not to take up the vulgar slogan: neither right not left, but to be really against the right and the left. It is evident in these circumstances that the true form of dissidence is that which abandons one position without ceasing to observe the same hostility towards the opposite position or rather which abandons it in order to accentuate this hostility. A true communist dissident is the one who leaves communism, not in order to move closer to capitalist beliefs, but to define the true conditions of struggle [*lutte*] against capitalism. In the same way, the true nationalist dissident is the one who neglects the traditional formulas of nationalism, not in order to move closer to internationalism but to combat [*combattre*] internationalism in all its forms, including the economy and the nation itself. These two specimens of dissidence seem to us to be equally useful. But they also seem equally rare. Dissidents wanted.[59]

Lutte and *combattre* are his chosen words here, not *la contestation*. All the same, it is clear that the young right-wing Blanchot figures politics as a matter of contesting both the left and the right. Notice that the movement of refusal, here, does not pass beyond all distinctions. The communist dissident is valued for adopting a more radical position than the party allows, while the nationalist dissident is prized for seeking a vantage point from which to criticize internationalism all the more fiercely. The end of contestation, as it works here, is secretly contained within communism and nationalism respectively. Later, he will tell us that contestation has no end outside itself, while also insisting that it indicates a communism beyond any communist state in existence. Is this a contradiction? We must cover more ground before we are in a position to answer.

Bataille refers us to the fourth part of *L'expérience intérieure*, and two passages are of immediate interest there. The first is the report of a conversation between Bataille and Blanchot in which Blanchot asserts that inner experience must "be contestation of itself and non-knowledge" (102). And the second draws out what is implicit in the first, that there can be no end to contestation:

> What I call contestation does not simply have the character of an intellectual proceeding (of which I speak with respect to Hegel, to Descartes—or in the principles of the introduction). Often this character is even wanting (in the writings of Angèle de Foligno, as far as it would appear). "Contestation" is still a movement essential to love—that nothing can satisfy. What is presumptuous in the little sentence, often cited, of Saint Augustine, is not the first affirmation: "Our heart is uneasy" but the second: "until the moment when it rests in Thee." For there is deep down in a man's heart so much uneasiness that it is not in the power of any God—nor of any woman—to allay it. (123)

Two philosophers and two mystics are named here. Descartes and Hegel are introduced in order to be dismissed for their intellectualism: neither method-ological skepticism nor the dialectic should be confused with the movement of contestation. Angela and Augustine are merely found to be wanting, for their mysticism falls short of inner experience precisely because it has an end in God. Believers will object that Bataille misunderstands the very idea of God, who, being omnipotent, can never lack the power to do something. And it might be added that the endlessness of contestation is not incompatible with belief in the deity. St. Paul might be counted a witness to this when he speaks of continually "reaching forth unto those things which are before" (Phil. 3:13), thus, as Gregory of Nyssa observes, figuring God in terms of infinity. There can be no resting place in the endless divinity; God grants peace of heart: the two statements do not contradict each other.

In his admiring review of *L'expérience intérieure,* which remains one of the most insightful pieces written on the book, Blanchot presents Bataille's rejec-tion of eternal rest in God very sympathetically: "If the questioning [*la con-testation*] arms itself with this reassuring perspective, challenges the vague and superior authority (God) that has given it its form, suppresses any hope in life and outside of life, it is the very fact of existence that is now called into question."[60] Elsewhere, he is not so certain; and as Kevin Hart shows in his essay in this collection Blanchot discerns a movement of contestation in some of the Christian mystics, though by no means in all of them. Meister Eckhart and St. John of the Cross are to be prized in this regard. With Eckhart, "notions of salvation, hope, and bliss no longer count from the viewpoint of faith's supreme experience, which is beyond all measure and all end" (27). And if we read the review of *L'expérience intérieure* carefully we can see that Blanchot says that inner experience "would in every respect be similar to mystical ecstasy if it were disengaged from all the religious presuppositions that often [*souvent*] change it and, by giving it a meaning [*sens*], determine it" (39). Often is not always. Blanchot does not set inner and mystical experience in opposition; rather, he suggests that in principle contestation can work in and through both.

Blanchot is also more nuanced than Bataille in his phrasing when it comes to the intellectual resources on which one draws when seeking inner experience: "This struggle [*contestation*] is carried on by reason" (38), he says, while pointing out that it does not fulfill reason's usual ends. At first we might think that this is reason turning on itself in order to show that all knowledge claims are at heart unreliable. Yet if Blanchot is a skeptic he does not naturally fall into a group with Pyrrho (and the yearning for ataraxia) or with Descartes (and the longing for apodictic truth). In 1930, ten years before he met Bataille, Blanchot submitted a thesis, "La conception du dogmatisme chez les sceptiques," for the Diplôme d'Études Supérieures, which was duly conferred by the Sorbonne. Fifty years later, in 1980, we find a trace of that early work in an essay on Levinas. "Contradiction is also the essence of skepticism," he writes, "just as it combats every dogmatism openly, by exposing its unsatisfactory or onerous presuppositions (origin, truth, value, authenticity, the exemplary or proper, etc.), so does it do so in an implicit way, referring itself back to a 'dogmatism' so absolute that every assertion is threatened (this is already to be observed in the ancient skeptics and in Sextus Empiricus)."[61] Properly understood, skepticism "affirms nothing that is not overseen by an indefatigable adversary, one to whom he does not concede but who obliges him to go further, not beyond reason into the facility of the irrational or towards a mystical effusion, but rather towards another reason, towards the other as reason or demand" (42). So if the line separating contestation from mystical ecstasy is divided and equivocal, another line distinguishing it from skepticism is also less than firm and straight.

Mysticism and skepticism: the third "ism" that is drawn in the wake of contestation but that never quite converges with it is nihilism. The Blanchot of *L'entretien infini* (1969) was seeking to understand nihilism and found that it kept escaping all his best attempts to capture it. "Is this not to formulate a radical nihilism?" one of his unnamed speakers asks in a dialogue in response to the thought that "there is no limit to the destruction of man." To which the other voice replies, "If so I should be quite willing, for to formulate it would also perhaps already be to overturn it. But I doubt that nihilism will allow itself to be taken so easily."[62] Later, in another part of the text, we are told something else: "The overman is he in whom nothingness makes itself will and who, free for death, maintains this pure essence of will in willing nothingness. This would be nihilism itself" (148). Thus spake Blanchot. A decade later, when meditating on Levinas, Blanchot denounces a "maniacal and pathetic sort of nihilism . . . for which, once and for all, nothing is of *value*."[63] What is objectionable about this construction of nihilism is that it would be "a kind of rest or security"; it is at fault for "always stopping prematurely" (42). Like mysticism and skepticism, nihilism as it is usually formulated tends to be a failed contestation.

The word that links and separates contestation from the mystical, the skeptical and the nihilistic is experience, understood as *expérience*. As early as his review of *L'expérience intérieure*, Blanchot strives to make this plain: "The experience . . . does not distinguish itself from the struggle [*la contestation*] of which it is the dazzling expression in the night" (39). Indeed, it is "questioning [*la contestation*] expressing itself in an original situation, in an experience that one can live" (40). The event is not without anguish since, after all, taboos are violated in questioning everything. And yet the event cannot be solitary:

> Questioning [*La contestation*] is the calling into question of a particular and limited being, and it is also, consequently, an effort to break this particularity and these limits; isolation is a posture of a being that does not allow him to slip outside of being; it is appropriation, awareness of particularity; it is the will and glory of being in this particularity. To the individual thus closed in on himself, experience offers a subject with which he can communicate; this subject cannot be completed or grasped by action, for with it there would be no communication but simply servile taking of possession, pleasure, that is to say reinforcement of the egoistic "I." (40)

In its most general sense, experience is a relation with the Other, whether this exteriority be construed as the outside or another person. Even the solitary act of writing presumes the possibility of contact with another person since, as Blanchot suggests in an early essay, there is something faintly absurd in composing a sentence that declares how lonely one is.[64] How can we characterize this relation with the Other? It is neither a matter of dialectical appropriation, which would reinforce the "I" rather than call it into question, nor is it a matter of fusion, which would absorb the "I" in a supposedly higher mystical or political state. Let us consider each alternative before attending to Blanchot's proposal of a third way.

First of all, Blanchot wishes to distance himself from the Hegelianism that stands behind the alternative of dialectical appropriation, the most memorable image of which is given in the struggle between the Lord and the Bondsman in the *Phänomenologie des Geistes*. To be sure, the contestation that Hegel envisages accounts for the birth of self-consciousness and the stark impossibility of existing simply by oneself, but it understands contestation by way of the Bondsman's "fear of death, the sovereign master."[65] Far from calling the "I" into question, Blanchot maintains, the thought of one's finitude further entrenches a sense of self. I am most radically contested, he argues, not by my death but by the death of another person. The thought is best evoked in one of his meditations on Bataille: "To remain present in the proximity of another who by dying removes himself definitively, to take upon myself another's death as the only death that concerns me, this is what puts me beside myself, this is the only separation that can open me, in its very impossibility, to the Openness of a community."[66] Second, Blanchot needs to remove himself from the danger that lingers around the latter alternative: the fusion of the self with the Other. In fact there are two dangers here. One is mysticism, which Blanchot regards, somewhat hastily, as an immediate absorption of the self into the Godhead. And the other is fascism. We recall the various social temptations that fascism posed in the France in which Blanchot grew to maturity: the "collective subject" of Maurice Barrès, the "beautiful community" of Charles Péguy, and the "Integral Nationalism" of Charles Maurras.[67]

Blanchot seeks a third position, a fresh understanding of what is involved in experience, which he describes as a "relation without relation." Here, he thinks, is an opportunity to think experience outside the unity presumed by the "I" or imposed by the Other. Even before trying to make decent sense of this relation of the third kind—something ventured by Jill Robbins in her contribution to this volume—we can sketch answers to the three remaining questions posed earlier, "What is contested?," "How?," and "Why?" It is the sufficiency of the self that is contested, first of all, and it is done with community in mind. More generally, as Blanchot comes to see in the essays that compose *L'entretien infini,* there is something to be contested that is more deeply rooted in the human mind than a substantial sense of self. We refer to unity. Everything that answers to unity—"the idea of God, of the Self, of the Subject, then of Truth"—will be interrogated by writing understood as "plural speech."[68] Writing is not reconceived in order to bring forth new styles of poetry or fiction; rather, its horizon is social. It indicates "possibilities that are entirely other: an anonymous, distracted, deferred, and displaced way of being in relation" (xii, vii). We might be tempted to call this a "vision of society" were Blanchot not hostile to optic metaphors and were the image given to us not so minimal.

The relation without relation takes hold, Blanchot thinks, in terms of speech rather than sight. "What is present in this presence of speech, as soon as it affirms itself, is precisely what never lets itself be seen or attained: something is there that is beyond reach (of the one who says it as much as of the one who hears it)."[69] This "something" is the unknown, *l'inconnu,* and it impinges on us only in conversation. Since the person with whom I am talking escapes unity, whether understood in terms of appropriation or fusion, there is no concept under which he or she falls: such is Blanchot's justification for figuring one's fellow human as unknown and regarding the human relation as irreducibly strange. Yet we do know something about the relation between the two speakers, Blanchot thinks, and this generates a concept of its own. The relationship between another person and myself is a "double dissymmetry"; it is neutral but not neutralized. In other words, the inter-subjective space is, from my perspective, curved upwards in favor of him or her, and, from the other's perspective, rises upward toward me. Each of us is bound to the other by a responsibility that can never be recalled to a fixed limit. For Blanchot, this discontinuity or infinite distance between us is prior to any sense of ourselves as individual subjects, and indeed prevents a subject from closing around itself. The contestation of the self occurs because there is community, even if it is the small community of friends or lovers.

Earlier we flagged an apparent contradiction in Blanchot's account of contestation, and now is the time to return to it. He maintains, on the one hand, that radical self-questioning has no end outside itself yet, on the other hand, that it leads to a communism beyond communism. Plainly, he is not suggesting that contestation is linked to any already constituted community or indeed to a community that will be established in any future present.[70] A political order can always be questioned; the community is never fully present. That questioning, though, turns on the death of the other person, and if it is always the other person's mortality that I have in mind, the preciousness of his or her life, then contestation will ultimately affirm a society in which the other is prized over the self. For Blanchot, this prizing of the other person is embedded less imperfectly in communism than in liberal democracies. Religious people in particular will object at once and claim that the affirmation of a communism beyond communism is more surely contained in a theocracy such as the Kingdom of God than in the decidedly secular terms that Blanchot has chosen. In defense, it might be replied that Blanchot finds the affirmation of the other person in the Hebrew Bible, even though he takes the chief legacy of the Jews to be speech with the Most High rather than the revelation of monotheism. To which it can be replied in turn that Blanchot comes close to allegorizing the Jews out of history, and that he suborns religion to ethics.[71]

Michael Holland begins our book with a characteristically acute and informative essay, "An Event without Witness: Contestation between Blanchot and Bataille," which situates the word "contestation" in the social and political world of France in the 1930s and beyond. Contestation for Bataille and Blanchot is one of the main ways by which they reoriented themselves after the Occupation; it allows them to exceed the political groupings—nationalism and socialism—that were in play before the Second World War and, more intriguingly, it allows them to begin the intense conversation that started from the moment they met in 1940. In Roman and medieval law, contestation—*litis contestatio*—once signified the imminent resolution of conflict; in modern times the meaning of the word has changed, for now it denotes an opposition to the law. This opposition to established political order, as separately lived by Bataille and Blanchot, has exposed them "to an ordeal of passivity, despair, and nothingness" which they experience in quite different ways. Holland closely examines three periods in Blanchot's intellectual development: his involvement with right-wing politics in the 1930s, his account in the 1950s of author and reader being violently contested by the work, and his broodings on the neuter after 1968. For Blanchot, early and late, contestation is "an event without witness"; Holland concludes by noting that his writing becomes increasingly preoccupied with the impossibility of witnessing to the absolutely singular and absolutely shameful event of the last century: the Holocaust.

The question of testimony, coupled with the question of responsibility, is also taken up by Geoffrey Hartman in his probing essay, "Maurice Blanchot: The Spirit of Language after the Holocaust." "What is the motivating *spirit* of Blanchot's literary corpus seen as a whole?" Hartman asks. The young Blanchot, contributor to journals of the far right before the war—journals marked by an *antisemitisme de peau*—also contributed to a mentality that allowed the Holocaust to happen. How, though, did Blanchot break with the "spiritual revolution" of his years before the war? For that to happen, Hartman speculates, Blanchot had to affirm "a counter-spirit, drawn from the same source . . . yet antithetical and without hope for retroactive justification." So Blanchot develops a counter-spiritual language, one that eschews the word "spirit." Nowhere is this better seen than in his later writing, such as the fragmentary *L'écriture du désastre* (1980), a perpetually interrupted meditation on Auschwitz, atheism, writing, and the neuter. Not to be read without caution, Blanchot's counter-spiritual writing is both ascetic and seductive, and perhaps most seductive in its asceticism. Yet the dangers it poses are well worth encountering, for a work like *L'écriture du désastre* at least can stand the test of Adorno's demand "that no word intoned from on high—moral, spiritual, theological—should remain untransformed after the Holocaust."

If we think of Blanchot by way of the two principal friendships of his life, we can see a movement away from the Christian framework presumed and criticized by Bataille to the affirmation of "being Jewish" that is always to be found in the work of Levinas. Blanchot's readings of Levinas, especially in *L'entretien infini*, are among the most important and suggestive engagements that we have had with that philosopher. Like Hartman, Jill Robbins attends to the roles of response and responsibility in Blanchot's work, but unlike Hartman she restricts herself to the Blanchot of *L'entretien infini*, the writer who, while affirming the fragmentary, also wrote at length and in detail on other people's books. "Responding to the Infinity between Us" examines contestation from an unusual angle, by considering the ways in which conversation is itself a mode of contestation. A true conversation, for Blanchot, does not take place between two selves but rather is an endless questioning of the status of the self as a subject. It is to be thought by way of interruption and asymmetry rather than continuity and reciprocity. Genuine conversation is a speaking without power.

Adorno has already been mentioned, yet until Vivian Liska wrote "Two Sirens Singing," the next chapter in our collection, no one had meditated on the relations that hold these two major thinkers together and apart. At first glance, Adorno and Blanchot appear to be very distant from one another: the one sharply condemning the "jargon of authenticity" in the young Heidegger, and the other learning deeply from *Sein und Zeit*. Yet both these "extreme contemporaries" develop profound cases against totalitarianism, both ponder the value of interruption, and both brood on the Holocaust: "writing lyrical poetry after Auschwitz is barbaric," said Adorno; "no matter when it is written, every *récit* from now on will be from before Auschwitz," adds Blanchot. One of the most beautiful passages in all Blanchot is his short piece "La Chant des sirèns" in *Le Livre à venir* (1959), and certainly one of the most arresting moments in *Dialektik der Aufklärung* (1944), which Adorno wrote with Max Horkheimer, is the analysis of "Odysseus or Myth and Enlightenment." The different treatment of Odysseus in these two books provides Liska with an opportunity to inaugurate a badly needed conversation between Blanchot and Adorno. For both writers, the Sirens' song is at once nonhuman and at the core of the human; it promises the possibility of another mode of being, one in which self and other, distance and proximity, past and future coexist without merging.

That Blanchot drew deeply from *Sein und Zeit* is clear to anyone who reads his first collections of criticism: *Faux pas* (1943), *La Part du feu* (1949), and *L'espace littéraire* (1955). It is also plain to readers of *L'attente l'oubli* (1962), Blanchot's remarkable attempt to present narrative in a fragmentary manner, that he remained entranced by the style and tone of Heidegger's later writings. Some passages from what would become *L'attente l'oubli* were offered by Blanchot to a volume that marked Heidegger's seventieth birthday: and this supplies a starting point for "A Fragmentary Demand" by Leslie Hill, author of *Maurice Blanchot, Extreme Contemporary,* the title of which we have already heard when thinking about Vivian Liska's essay. The fragmentary becomes for Blanchot one of the main ways in which unity is contested. In choosing *these* fragments, though, Hill is able to guide us through a thicket of difficult questions: What is Blanchot's relation to Heidegger? What relations are there between literary and philosophical discourse in Blanchot's writing? And what is the politics of the fragmentary?

The self-questioning of art is one of the themes that Hill explores with respect to Heidegger. For Gerard L. Bruns, it is Jean-Paul Sartre who is the appropriate conversation partner for Blanchot. Art is not simply produced, as Sartre would like us to think, but rather is something that is brought into being by contestation. Such is Bruns's initial move in "Anarchic Temporality"; having made it, he goes on to explore the passivity and anonymity of the artwork according to Blanchot with Marcel Duchamp and Mallarmé in mind. Writing turns the author away from the possible toward the impossible. In reflecting on that turn, Bruns draws our attention to a thread that many readers of Blanchot do not notice: the relation between writing and friendship. Like the work of art, friendship is not a product made by two self-sufficient subjects but is a contestation of identity and fusion. The image of conversation between friends recalls the analysis provided by Jill Robbins that we mentioned earlier.

Can death be a friend? Blanchot thinks so, and in his powerful last testament *L'instant de ma mort* (1994) he tells us and also shows us. Philippe Lacoue-Labarthe's attention is drawn, however, to (as his title has it) "The Contestation of Death." Yet contestation and friendship do not arrange themselves as contradictories for Blanchot, and this becomes clear when reading Lacoue-Labarthe's exacting reflections on the experience of death and "experience without experience." Michael Holland has already given us a historical account of the expression *la contestation.* Now, Lacoue-Labarthe recalls for us the different ways in which death has been contested from Plato to Montaigne, from Malraux to Blanchot. Lacoue-Labarthe places *L'instant de ma mort* under the authority of three motifs that govern Blanchot's work from the very beginning: politics, the experience of death, and literature (or, as he came to prefer, writing). And he shows with great subtlety that those three motifs remain firmly in place in Blanchot's final work of any length.

Toward the start of this collection, Geoffrey Hartman asks us to contemplate a movement from Blanchot's investment in a spiritual revolution to his elaboration of a counter-spirit so radical that it does not countenance the use of the word "spirit." In the concluding essay Kevin Hart approaches Blanchot's writing by way of what his title names "The Counter-spiritual Life." In his description of the exile and the return as mediated of what was once supposed to be immediate to consciousness, Hegel offers us an account of the life of the Spirit. This is, to be sure, an intellectualist account of experience in which the objects experienced are held to be present to consciousness in and through representations. Bataille elaborates his account of "negative inner experience" alongside the Hegelian dialectic, and it is certainly not intellectualist in character. Far from concluding with absolute knowledge, it opens onto a *perte de connaissance* and is dedicated to *non-savoir,* non-knowledge. The experience imagined here is what Hart calls "counter-spirit," and it is his contention that, beginning in the 1940s, Blanchot mediates on this counter-spiritual life and its relations with the life of Spirit. Three main motifs are examined: inner experience as a quasi-mystical ecstasy, literature as the experience of non-experience, and contestation as a new way of being in relation with others. It would be a mistake, Hart thinks, to regard these motifs as distinct stages in Blanchot's intellectual development. For when Blanchot figures the counter-spiritual life by way of politics, he does not thereby deny literature as the experience of non-experience. It would be more accurate to regard each motif as emerging from the contestation of any one of the others.

CHAPTER ONE

An Event without Witness

Contestation between Blanchot and Bataille

Michael Holland

> Où chercher le témoin pour lequel il n'y a pas de témoin?
> —MAURICE BLANCHOT, "Le Dernier à parler"

In an essay to mark the death of Georges Bataille, Michel Foucault analyzes the notion of what Bataille calls "inner experience," before adding: "I believe that it is this philosophy of non-positive affirmation which Blanchot has defined by means of the principle contestation."[1] The following year, Foucault returns to the issue: "There is something which is preoccupying me at the moment: it is the meaning of that most important of terms, contestation, which we find in Bataille, and to some extent in Blanchot. This notion of contestation is one of the most problematical, difficult and obscure of notions, belonging to a tiny current of philosophy whose source, at least, could be traced to people like Blanchot and Bataille."[2] Foucault's emphasis on the notion of contestation here is strange. While it might be possible to detect in the early sixties the first signs of the *political* current destined, a few years later, to propel the notion of contestation to the fore, it is hard to locate the philosophical current he refers to. And why does he hesitate over which author exactly is its source?

Things become clearer if we investigate where it is that, according to Foucault in 1963, Blanchot invokes "the principle of contestation." It is likely that he is looking no further than the article Blanchot himself had published less than a year earlier to mark the death of his friend. For Blanchot, Bataille's notion of "inner experience" is "the manner in which radical negation which has nothing left to negate *affirms* itself. That is what we have just attempted to explain by stating that experience is indistinguishable from contestation. But of what sort therefore is the affirmation which it falls to such a moment to establish?"[3] To which Foucault in effect replies, following on from the passage quoted above: "This is not a matter of generalized negation, but of an affirmation which affirms nothing: which breaks entirely with transitivity."[4] In fact, this is a restatement of Blanchot's reply to his own question. Inner experience offers thought:

> an affirmation which, for the first time, is not a product (the result of double negation), and thus escapes all the movements, oppositions and reversals of dialectical reason. It is a difficult event to circumscribe. Inner experience affirms, it is pure affirmation, it does nothing but affirm. It does not even affirm itself, for then it would be subordinate to itself: it affirms affirmation. It is in that sense that Georges Bataille could accept to say that it contains within it the moment of authority, after having devalued all possible authorities and dissolved the very idea of authority. It is the decisive Yes.[5]

It seems clear now that Foucault's use of the term "contestation" in 1963 and 1964 is first and foremost a response to what Blanchot wrote in 1962. But if that sheds important light on the close affinities between the two thinkers, clarification stops there. A term usually signifying political opposition acquires a meaning that confines it entirely to the reality of the mind, where its activity, though affirmative, is not positive, and can only be referred to by means of a paralyzing tautology which both Foucault and Blanchot preserve intact, or else transform into series of paradoxes.

The difficulty in circumscribing the *event* to which contestation gives rise, and which Blanchot acknowledges, would seem to condemn further commentary merely to generate further tautology, relieved only by further paradox, in an immobile parody of rational thought which can only gesture in the direction of the nonpositive affirmation to which contestation without negation corresponds. However, neither Foucault nor Blanchot will linger at such an aporia. Each in his way is drawn back, because of the death of Bataille, to something crucially at issue for them in their relationship to Bataille's thought. But that issue is resolved for neither of them in what they write at the time. It simply surfaces in a signifier: "contestation," which remains suspended while they move on.

In what each of them says, however, there is a sign that Blanchot's relationship to the notion is not purely circumstantial, but that it has a history. Both the uncertainty of attribution on Foucault's part and Blanchot's allusion to Bataille's *acceptance* of the notion of authority recall the fact that, at the time of writing *L'expérience intérieure,* Bataille was in close dialogue with Blanchot, and that out of their exchange came some of the key notions to be found in that work, one of which was *la contestation.*

The term "contestation" makes its appearance at the very beginning of Bataille's essay. What he calls "inner experience" is the putting into question (to the test), in fever and anguish, of what a man knows about the fact of being."[6] As such, it is the drama of being itself: "To become aware of it is single-mindedly to contest, as consistently as is required, the subterfuges by means of which we usually escape. There is no longer any question of salvation, which is the most hateful of subterfuges. The difficulty—namely that contestation must be exercised in the name of an authority—is resolved as follows: I contest in the name of contestation, which is experience itself (the will to go to the utmost possible extreme). Experience, its authority, and its method are indistinguishable from contestation."[7] It is clear at once that the term "contestation" is being made here to carry almost the entire weight of Bataille's argument. But there is more: not only does Bataille endow it with a more original meaning than the relatively simple one that is usually attached to it; its meaning gives rise to the tautology that both Blanchot and Foucault replicate, and which effectively makes it inaccessible to rational thought. A little further on, however, Bataille confronts the issue of intelligibility head-on. Acknowledging the analogy between his experience and that of the mystics, he nevertheless refuses both their asceticism and the silence it entailed: "Neither able nor willing to have recourse to asceticism, I must link contestation to the *liberation of the power of words.*"[8]

This leads him to relate his experience closely to what forms the core of Western rationality: the spirit of contestation, he argues, was Descartes's "tormenting spirit" (*génie tourmenteur*) (124). But for Bataille, the intuition into the existence of God which founds the Cartesian project is "essentially what is dying in me" (*essentiellement ce qui meurt en moi*) (124). Contestation has destroyed its ultimate object. All that remains is *le non-savoir:* "The spirit of contestation finally ends up formulating its last and ultimate affirmation: '*I know only one thing: that a man will never know anything.*'"[9] It is here that Bataille's experience comes closest to that of the mystics, and where their silence finds its philosophical equivalent in tautology. But at this very point, Bataille decisively reorients the "project" which is originally that of Descartes: "I am dragging around my concern to write this book like a burden. In fact I am acted *upon*."[10] The notion of contestation is now beginning to acquire an originality which breaks the bounds of the saturating tautology which is the trace it leaves behind in Bataille's language (and subsequently in Foucault's and Blanchot's). What tautology attempts unproductively to enclose within a single act of language is allowed by him to take place simultaneously in two. Though obliged to resort to the language of Cartesian rationalism for which contestation is *active* (both project and process), Bataille simultaneously appeals to another language altogether, in which, "even if absolutely nothing corresponds to the idea I have of interlocutors or readers," he will be acted *upon (agi)* by language: "The *third party,* the companion, the reader who acts on me is language; it is he (it) which speaks in me, which keeps alive in me the language that is addressed to him. And language is no doubt a project, but more than that it is that *other,* the reader, who loves me and already forgets me (kills me), and without the present insistence of whom I could do nothing, I should have no inner experience."[11] In this language, the *authority* vested in God has been replaced by the *power* of words. Hence the powerlessness of the rational subject does not result simply in oblivion (fusion with the other): it allows the subject to be swept up into a process of communication where, ceasing to be an agent, he is acted upon, not simply by another agent-subject (which would remain within Descartes's frame) but by language itself: "There is no longer subject = object, but a 'yawning gap' between the one and the other and, in the gap, the subject, the object are dissolved, there is a passage, a communication, but not from one to the other: the *one* and the *other* have lost their separate existence."[12] Language as "communication" allows something to happen between writer and reader, when subject to inner experience, which is not achieved otherwise, not even in experience itself, where subject and object (other subject) are simply lost to each other. Contestation thus *gives rise to* communication in the very process of destroying all existing means of communication.

This certainly allows contestation, as Bataille uses the term, to escape the thrall of tautology; it nevertheless appears highly rarefied compared to its political equivalent. However, while explicitly turning away from the world of events toward his inner world, Bataille grounds his book in the simplest of concrete realities: the discussions that took place, in the period leading up to the publication of *L'expérience intérieure* in 1943, between him and Maurice Blanchot. In the light of the German occupation of France, the absence of a political dimension to contestation appears as no more than a reflection of contemporary circumstances. But it was those circumstances which brought about the meeting between Bataille and Blanchot, and that historical event, whose political significance lies in the fact that each of them, separately, found himself forcibly *reduced to silence* in the domain of politics where each had been active, provides the constant focus of Bataille's analyses. Indeed, alongside the purely speculative dimension, the book contains what amounts to a *chronicle* of the successive stages in its realization. And present, all along this chronological axis, is the dialogue with Maurice Blanchot. Indications such as "Conversation with Blanchot" (67), "Blanchot asked me" (75), culminate in the oft-quoted passage to which Blanchot himself alludes in 1962:

> In a manner quite independent of his book [*Thomas l'obscur*], verbally, yet so that he in no way betrayed the sense of discretion which makes me thirst for silence when I am in his company, I heard the author posit the foundation of all "spiritual" life, which can only:
>
> — have its principle and its end in absence of salvation, in the abandonment of all hope,
> — affirm in relation to inner experience that it is the authority (but all authority must be expiated),
> — be contestation of itself and *non-savoir*.[13]

Having made "reader" and "interlocutor" synonymous (75), his claim that "the reader is language, it is he who speaks in me, who maintains a living language in me addressed to him," now acquires a concrete dimension. The identity between Blanchot's words and key notions in *L'expérience intérieure* means that, in the conversations between him and Blanchot, Blanchot's language effectively "entered" his own. And this is no marginal borrowing: the principle of contestation is both central to Bataille's experience and "one of those on which Maurice Blanchot insists as fundamental."[14]

This transforms Bataille's argument from being one whose rarefied terms seem to condemn it to remain detached from the real, into one whose focus is a practice of language grounded in real dialogue. Foucault's uncertainty over attribution now acquires its significance: the notion he briefly focuses on is both Bataille's and not Bataille's: it was brought to their discussions by Blanchot. Yet it is not simply Blanchot's either: without Bataille's work, it would have vanished without a trace.[15] The linguistic status of the term in Bataille's writing is therefore unusual: as the dominant term in a set of notions by means of which he gives conceptual expression to his experience, it is at the same time what he calls a "sliding word" (*un mot glissant*) (280). This suggests that conceptual expression is secondary to some other dimension of language. And as he makes clear, that other dimension is what he calls "language" (*le discours*) when it takes the form of communication with another. It is thus more important, for him, to open up the language in which he writes of his experience to the language of another, than simply to present to others his own version of what is his experience. At the same time, this does not simply give the other's discourse sovereignty over his own. A clear indication of this is to be found at the point where, after having accommodated Blanchot's principles and placed them at the heart of his thinking, he cites him again, but this time to *resist* the terms of his argument: "Blanchot asked me: why not pursue my inner experience as if I were the *last man?* Yes, in a way . . ."[16] This reservation, which concludes the central section of his book, "Torture" (*Le Supplice*), arises out of a refusal on Bataille's part to relinquish the orientation toward *another,* which is what gives his experience its justification: "Inner experience is conquest and as such it is for the other [*pour autrui*]" (76). To be the last man would mean that no human other remained. But this also underscores the fact that the other (*ce lui obscur*) is not Blanchot. That is because, as Bataille presents experience, neither he nor any individual other is in a position (the position of the Cartesian subject) to have and share a language. Rather, in the separate "yawning gaps" which are all that survive the dissolution of the self-other relation, language itself, thanks to its own power, establishes a mode of communication between a *writing* "self" and a *reading* "other." It is at this level that the other (Blanchot) "speaks in me," that his language becomes mine. But at that level, he is already dispossessed of it (no longer Blanchot) because he is nothing but language ("the reader is language"). Language has taken back its own: a word uttered by one rational subject to another in the language of Cartesian reflection is repeated, *by* and *as* language across the "yawning gap" of unintelligibility into which the Cartesian subject (the original subject of contestation) has dissolved, and which is thereby transformed into communication between two "subjects" whose only existence is *in* this in-between (as "*inter*locutors").

A word such as "contestation" thus epitomizes the language that Bataille is seeking in writing *L'expérience intérieure* but never attains: the language that would encompass and transcend the languages the book essays and dramatizes: confessional discourse on the one hand, with its metaphors and its fictions, its hyperbole and its delirium ("I am *open*, a yawning gap . . ."); rational discourse on the other, with its concepts and its reflexive detachment vis-à-vis the discourse of confession ("there is no longer subject = object, but a 'yawning gap' "). Naturally drawn into the language of reflection, the term "contestation" ("Descartes's tormenting spirit") can achieve no more at that level than tautology ("I contest in the name of contestation"). Enlisted in the service of confession, on the other hand, it quickly leads to what Bataille calls "the last and ultimate affirmation" of *non-savoir,* which is to say the affirmation of ignorance, the "last affirmation" of the "last man"—one version of *nihilism.*

The word "contestation" thus exists in a limbo, which is none other than that third dimension within which Bataille places the language of communication to which his book aspires. Somewhere between the two languages of his book, and outside of them, the word deploys a dimension of "communication" between "subjects" whose identity remains "obscure." But why that word and not "the last man"? To what extent is the power of words the power of "contestation"?

Prior to the moment at which the word "contestation" enters the language they share, neither Bataille nor even Blanchot makes significant use of it. Nevertheless, what it has come to signify in the twentieth century—opposition to established political order—determines a major aspect of the writing of both men during the 1930s. It can thus be said that when the word is uttered between them, what it makes explicit has been implicit in their respective discourses up to that point. This is significant in two respects. First of all, it situates the encounter thanks to which both Bataille and Blanchot reorient themselves as writers after the Occupation, in relation to a common political practice (implicitly "contestation") that exceeds the division between right and left, nationalism and socialism, which kept Bataille's activities and those of Blanchot radically apart in the 1930s, and indeed made the two men, potentially at least, political enemies. Retrospectively, the antidemocratic language that emanated from both *Contre-Attaque* and *Combat* or *L'Insurgé* following the election of the Front Populaire displays one common feature: a comprehensive attack on all forms of the now-defunct bourgeois Republic. For both men, this force carries the name "Revolution." There is a further dimension to this, however: by the later 1930s, what "contestation" refers to shifts site in the language of both men. No longer a matter of individual action, it is located within the political sphere itself, and presented as an unstoppable process of *self-destruction* to which the democratic Republic is succumbing. For Bataille, "the democratic regime, struggling with fatal contradictions, will not be able to be saved";[17] while for Blanchot, "it is not only the regime, but France itself which seems to be ranged against France."[18] Correspondingly, the forceful expression of a principle of contestation, now denied an outlet, is increasingly infiltrated by something utterly opposed to it, and which Bataille and Blanchot each independently characterize in terms of anguish and despair in the face of nothingness.

In Bataille this dimension to revolutionary contestation has been present since the early 1930s. Observing in 1933 the withering of revolutionary forces under pressure from the totalitarian state, he relocates the *source* of revolutionary sentiment in a "blind chaos" where it is "pain," "misery," "anguish," and "despair" which prevail, turning it into "a perishable force augmented by consciousness of possible death."[19] In the same period, Blanchot's notion of revolution is simpler—a glorification of national energy: "Our greatest hope today is that, for the sake of the freedom of the nation, there arise the magnificent promise of revolution."[20] But for each, his notion of revolution, whether simple or complex, remained an active one in the early 1930s. As the decade progressed, however, something latent in Bataille but hitherto absent in Blanchot entered the political discourse of both writers: a recognition that the pure power of revolutionary contestation, now unused by virtue of the fact that the bourgeois state was foundering in its own internal contradictions (contesting itself out of existence), is not only a force born of anguish, despair, and consciousness of death (Bataille's premise) but, as such, is the very opposite of a force. From Bataille's perspective, this is reflected in a declaration of November 1938: "The *Collège de Sociologie* considers the general absence of a powerful reaction to the war as a sign of the *devirilization* of man."[21] In Blanchot's writings in *L'Insurgé*, the claim that there are two Frances, "that France which lies" (*cette France qui ment*) and "la France authentique,"[22] gradually gives way to the acknowledgment that "la France authentique" has been entirely replaced by what he calls "l'Anti-France,"[23] which he describes as "a nation laid low by a strange moral and social inertia."[24] As a result, the best that can be hoped for the French is that "the imminence of disaster may transform their cowardice into anguish and make their confidence rot into despair,"[25] since the call to destroy France in the name of "the true traditions of *la France profonde*"[26] has been undermined by the recognition that France is "nothingness itself" (*le néant même*).[27]

When Bataille and Blanchot meet, therefore, the circumstances (occupation by the Germans) constitute for each of them no more than the realization of what each separately had foreseen: the destruction of the French state. And though much more would need to be undertaken so as to trace their dual itinerary, it is nevertheless possible to argue that, when the term "contestation" emerges between them, what makes their dialogue possible is the fact that, for each of them separately, what the term traditionally defines: namely active opposition to a political system, has exposed each of them to an ordeal of passivity, despair, and nothingness, and that the absolute *nihilism* which begins to loom in their political consciousness as an inevitability has had the last remaining barrier to it forcefully removed with the overthrow of France by the forces of totalitarianism. In this language of nihilism (to which Blanchot and Foucault will return twenty years later), contestation simply persists as tautology, its all-pervasive negation transformed into unthinkable repetition by the persistence of rational discourse beyond the point of its demise. But for Bataille, that repetition is doubled by another sort, even if it is elusive: the search for a language which, beyond the collapse of rational discourse where both of the original subjects of language have been suppressed, will occupy a position *en tiers* and restore the possibility of communication. In *L'expérience intérieure*, the terms in which Bataille describes that language are so enigmatic as to be barely meaningful, all the more so since nothing about the language of the book bears the traces of this *langage en tiers*. Nothing, that is, *except* the word "contestation." And it is now clear that if that word repeats itself not only as tautology but in two absolutely different modes of language, both Bataille and Blanchot have their own version of that language. In order to see what those two very different languages have in common, but also what divides them, it is necessary to look into the history of the term "contestation."

For much longer than the period during which it has signified the *pursuit* of conflict, "contestation" referred to the very opposite: the process whereby, in what Roman law calls *litis contestatio* (joinder of issue), conflict was *resolved* by recourse to witnesses.[28] And in the history of contestation, it is the role of the witness (*testis* and at the same time *terstis, le tiers*)[29] which casts decisive light on the emergence of the term into the dialogue between Bataille and Blanchot in 1940. In *litis contestatio,* contestation exists only in the civil sphere, and its reality is contained entirely in what Poste's translation of Gaius calls *exclamation:* contestation is essentially a *call* or an *appeal:* "*be* a witness." There is, however, more than one dimension to contestation thus understood. Encompassing the appeal that any individual may make to any other to act as a witness in his cause is the need for the witness to establish his trustworthiness by means of an oath. More often than not, this takes the form of what Thomas Aquinas calls "simple contestation of God," as when a man says "God is my witness."[30] Every witness who answers the call of contestation implicitly or explicitly calls upon God as his witness, contests God. In the medieval version of contestation, therefore, a continuum of speech and hearing, a great sweep of verbal communication, circulates as the voice of justice throughout Christendom, ensuring the triumph of social stability over strife. But as the Middle Ages becomes the modern era, contestation will come increasingly to signify not the availability of the witness but his absence. In two distinct phases, the appeal to witnesses will become stifled. Why does this happen?

The first sign of change in the significance of the term is in itself a mild one. From having been an intransitive notion, designating a mutual appeal to witnessing, contestation begins to refer to a state of disputation or disagreement. As if reflecting the emergence into the Christian worldview of schism and dissent, contestation becomes an acknowledgment that dispute cannot so easily be resolved by appeal to witnesses, that difference of opinion has now become an established mode of social existence. At one level, this shift of emphasis is a gradual one: the spirit of contestation as *litis contestatio* continues to prevail at the level where conflict is resolved by law. At the same time, whole areas of human relation hitherto encompassed by the law are now becoming the site of intense debate, of *antinomy.* The schismatic process that finally splits Christendom into two worlds, Catholic and Protestant, is accompanied by the increasing predominance of contestation considered as transitive: contestation *between.* And if that term moves so easily from its medieval meaning to this first version of its modern meaning, it is quite simply that, as the schism at the heart of Christendom becomes established, the God whom the Christian "contested," in Aquinas's sense, is increasingly the focus of contestation considered as endless dispute.

However, the true shift that occurs between the medieval and the modern notions comes with a further change in the significance of the term. Contestation *between,* which endures up to and beyond the age of Absolutism, exists in a controlled and productive state, and indeed coexists with the increasing emphasis on eye-witnessing which develops with the intrusion of skepticism into religious belief, and accompanies the rise of the scientific mind.[31] At the same time, the second phase in the development of its meaning begins to happen. While Orest Ranum can claim that " 'contestation' seems never to be in the vocabulary about sedition and revolt in the dictionaries and legal sources of the seventeenth century," Donma Stanton points out that popular revolt in the provinces in the later seventeenth century often bordered on sedition. And as Michel Bareau and Judith Spencer indicate, at the siege of la Rochelle, "the Protestants are perceived as 'contestataires,' and denounced for running a State within the State."[32] It is this intrusion of the political into the religious which characterizes the shift from the first to the second phases in the modernization of the notion of contestation. And it reaches a climax when the forces of sedition and unrest, dubbed "contestataires," finally turn their energies against the figure in whom power was vested, namely the king.

This is nowhere more evident than in that act which Michelet said "contained the Revolution": the passing of the decree by which the Third Estate declared that it would henceforth be known as the National Assembly. On 23 June 1789, in what Sandy Petrie calls "a stark conflict of performative speech," "to the National Assembly's declaration of existence was opposed the king's declaration of its non-existence."[33] This dispute over where authority was vested saw a pure example of early modern contestation overspill to invade the seat of authority itself. This was possible because contestation was now no longer a matter of words alone: both the Third Estate and the monarch backed up their claim with armed force. For the first time, contestation considered as dispute *between* parties became a trial of force, and it is that which pushes contestation to the brink and transforms it into what it signifies today. But the decisive factor in this change is neither language nor force, but one of ultimate witness: to what authority does each party to the contestation between king and National Assembly *appeal?* For the king, that could be nothing less than God Himself. From the point of view of the National Assembly, on the contrary, "Royal authority was recognized to be the simple effect of national acquiescence before it" (28). And their appeal to the people to abandon that acquiescence does not acknowledge God as ultimate authority and witness: in a founding tautology,[34] the people have replaced God. The triumph of the speech act which becomes "the Revolution itself" is thus not only that of the people over the monarch, but that of Christendom over its own God. In destroying the monarchy, the Revolution radicalizes the notion of contestation by sweeping away altogether the divided remains of the Christian God, whose *visual* oversight of human affairs had come to replace the continuity of witnessing as appeal around which the Christian world was structured. Henceforth, contestation will be primarily a *political* movement in which language and violence are loose and uncontrollable because there is now no ultimate witness. At one level, by sweeping away the ocularcentric frame within which witnessing had become confined, the speech act that coincides with the Revolution could be said to restore the primacy of the word in which Christian witness originally resided. However, the *People* to whom the Revolution appeals as witness in replacement for God comes into political existence as no more than language. The Word, made flesh, is just a word. And what that word encompasses is a blind amalgam of force and language, whose elevation to the status of witness dislocates the entire frame within which the Christian world existed.

The more familiar perspective on this modern version of contestation portrays the people as a slumbering giant, whose acquiescence is the precondition of social peace, but which is capable, when discontented, of abominable acts of destructive violence. However, that conservative republican perspective conceals something much more disturbing: the fact that the entire political system that emerged from the French Revolution, when contestation acquired its modern significance as pursuit of conflict, is grounded in a permanent act of contestation in that modern sense, which is to say, a pursuit of conflict to its ultimate extreme. Born of the Terror, in which to be denounced was to be destroyed, Western politics, both foreign and domestic, has consistently and continuously contested the very right to existence of enemies who must be eliminated in a violence without need of witness for its justification. This is most evident on the external front. When he defines his notion of the General Strike, Georges Sorel repeatedly invokes the notion of the "Napoleonic battle," "which definitively crushes those it vanquishes" (*celle qui écrase définitivement le vaincu*).[35] And this anticipates Carl Schmitt's definition of modern wars, which are always wars to end all war, and which "transcend . . . the limits of the political framework" to turn the enemy into "a monster that must not only be defeated but also utterly destroyed."[36] But as Schmitt also argues, the construction of politics around the distinction between friend and enemy, which accompanies the emergence of modern, "revolutionary" contestation, introduces violence without witness into the domestic sphere by defining the political enemy ultimately as "the other, the stranger; and it is sufficient for his nature that he is . . . existentially something different and alien, so that in the extreme case conflicts with him are possible. These can neither be decided by a previously determined general norm nor by the judgment of *a disinterested and therefore neutral third party*" (27; my italics). Which leads him to the ultimate claim for which, retrospectively, his "concept of the political" appears simultaneously both lucid and (given his sympathies) very chilling: "The friend, enemy, and combat concepts receive their real meaning precisely because they refer to the real possibility of physical killing" (33).[37] Schmitt's claim that Western politics engages in acts of pure violence against the enemy in which the very structure of witnessing ("the judgment of a disinterested and neutral third party") has ceased to govern human affairs accurately defines the mode of contestation (as pursuit of conflict) that emerges from the early modern notion with the French Revolution. Like the violence that Christendom visited upon its infidel enemy during the Crusades, politics as contestation knows no bounds, other than the utter annihilation of what it contests. It is essentially nihilistic.[38]

In the years leading up to the invasion of France by Germany, the contestation out of which the politics of the Republican state were constituted by an appeal to the authority of the people had broken its bounds. Having neglected the true border between friend and enemy since 1933, and now in imminent danger of being overrun by a foreign power, the state was perversely at war with the nation (Blanchot) or the community (Bataille) that it claimed to represent, intent on its annihilation while the people looked blindly on. If both Bataille and Blanchot suddenly cease their contestation *of* the French state, therefore, it is because of the terrible truth about their own project that France's slide reveals to them: namely that contestation (which they call Revolution) is not only the substance of what they are contesting (as counterrevolutionaries they find themselves contesting contestation); it is revealed in the French state in its true nature, which is not that of a heroic political project but that of a state of violence perpetually divided against itself, constantly undermining itself as project out of sight of anyone. The *insight* into this, which deflects both men's writing activity onto another dimension, is at one level a descent into the night of blindness. When Bataille evokes *death* and Blanchot *nothingness* as the only prospect for France, each, it might be said, is witness to the utter failure of witnessing in modern contestation. And it is from that perspective that Bataille's claim "I contest in the name of contestation" appears in all of its impotence: an act of blind reflexivity caught in the sterile loop of tautology. Yet as Bataille contests, he is, by virtue of his role in that loop, endlessly restoring to contestation that dimension that modern politics denies: the *appeal* to a witness. This allows us to read Bataille's project for a language that would be *en tiers* in all of its extraordinary significance. With no indication that he is understanding the term "contestation" in any way according to its original significance, the passive survival of witnessing contained in the language of tautology ("I contest in the name of contestation") is complemented in Bataille's thinking by an appeal to a language that will actively restore that dimension which modern contestation has extinguished. Moreover, in his reflections in response to Blanchot's offer of the notion of the *last man*, his thinking is extended. If he refuses to be the last man, it is because that would confine him to the nothingness that is engulfing everything: "I should be left faced with infinite annihilation" (*je demeurerais devant l'anéantissement infini*).[39] Therefore if for him "in experience the subject remains come what may" (*le sujet dans l'expérience en dépit de tout demeure*), it is not merely as a last surviving "I," an absurd witness without witness: "To the extent that he is not a child in the drama or a fly on someone's nose, he is *consciousness of the other;* becoming *consciousness of the other,* and like the ancient chorus, the witness and the vulgarizer of the drama, he loses himself in human communication, projects himself as a subject outside of himself, is engulfed by a limitless host of possible existences."[40]

In the clearest of terms, Bataille here restores the appeal to witnessing which was once inherent in contestation. Yet having accepted the term that Blanchot offered him, he brings out its full significance only to reject Blanchot's position. In order to see the full implications of this, it is necessary to bring in a dimension of the witnessing inherent in the original notion of contestation which has so far remained unexamined. This is the role of the witness as *martyr,*[41] and it returns us to the unbroken circuit of witnessing which is the foundation of Christendom. When a witness in *litis contestatio* appeals to God as his witness that the testimony he is providing is true and worthy of credence, implicit in his appeal is an understanding that if God may be "contested" in this way, in return, the witness must be recognized by God.[42] Christian witness has, however, nothing to do with the evidence of the eyes, nor is it even primarily a matter of voice. The martyr is in a "liminal situation," caught between the competing claims of earthly authority and divine authority.[43] Such a situation only becomes martyrdom as it is usually understood when it becomes impossible for the witness as martyr to reconcile those competing claims. In such circumstances, he succumbs to the division he can no longer bestride and is, at one level or another, torn apart. In the Christian world, which witnessing sustains, testimony presupposes not only witness as a mode of appeal but also and more fundamentally the situation of the witness as martyr. When a witness (*testis*) places himself in the position of a disinterested third party (*terstis*), the way he thereby assumes the division that is threatening the social order is a reflection of that lifelong adoption of the "liminal" position which Christianity requires of the witness as martyr.

By 1940, when Bataille and Blanchot first meet, and during their exchanges bring the word "contestation" back to the fore, the social order has collapsed. At one level, this leaves them witness to absolute disaster: the *néant* that Blanchot saw France becoming has now materialized. But this *néant* is not simply a void or an absence. Beyond the ultimate blind-spot of the system's collapse lies the blind struggle to turn the power of contestation against itself by which the Republic produced social order. Christian martyrdom, for which God is witness, endures in the Republic whose appeal is to the people, as the conflict in each citizen between authority and acquiescence.[44] With the Revolution, the martyr position vanishes from its original site as the appeal to God and is replaced by an appeal to the people. It thus becomes internal to each citizen, who as a member of the people is both pure power of contestation and renunciation of contestation in favor of social peace. The friend-enemy relation now takes place under the all-seeing eye of the law as a conflict between two modes of contestation within the same subject. It is that condition which is revealed to Bataille and Blanchot respectively in the late 1930s, as they realize that the Republic can be left to contest itself. Their step back both reveals the fact that the Republic is doomed and exposes them to the ultimate consequence of its collapse: namely that each citizen is henceforth left to endure his divided condition alone. By 1940, therefore, Bataille and Blanchot are not only witness to destruction without witness (*le néant*) but subject to the absolute division of the martyr (Bataille's "yawning gap"). The "liminal situation" has lost all grounding in reality, and in the absence of any transcendence other than language, the (political) subject is exposed to division in a free state.

Extraordinarily, all of the elements of this "postmodern" condition are present in Bataille's description of his experience. Out of the experience of martyrdom in the raw he appeals to the only transcendence remaining, language, to restore the role of the witness as both *terstis* and *testis* which modern contestation had extinguished. Yet that experience defines itself in opposition to Blanchot. And in the latter's review of *L'expérience intérieure*, his opposition is reciprocated. Initially, Blanchot gives a straight account of the thinking contained in Bataille's book: "Experience, it must be said straight away, is indistinguishable from contestation, of which it is the dazzling expression in the night." Experience is "the total division which is like the ultimate extreme of negation," and it takes place as "a state which is positive in character, which is authority, and which a being affirms in separating from himself."[45] So far, he is doing little more than fill in the detail of his own argument, which is present in Bataille only allusively, and having been brought to this point, we might assume that he would go on to explain what is the most obscure aspect of the thinking that Bataille attributes to him: that "all authority must be expiated." But at the point where he comes up against his own idea of expiation, his commentary makes a significant detour: "Experience is therefore essentially paradox; it is contestation expressing itself in an original situation, in a situation that can be lived."[46] Rather than explore that "original situation" as concrete, *lived* reality, however, Blanchot retreats behind a term: "paradox," whose generality would appear to lie at an absolute remove from the lived experience it reflects, and whose pure movement, he goes on, "wrenches man away from his self-satisfaction and *puts him in communication with nothing*" (my italics).[47]

The moment described here by Blanchot corresponds to the moment at which, by Bataille's account, the authority with which the subject of contestation affirms his experience as pure division is *expiated*. In Bataille, this results in an appeal to a third party, the other as witness. But that is precisely what the Old Testament notion of expiation corresponds to: an act in which a third party (the scapegoat) enters the breach that has opened up in man's relation to God. Why then does Blanchot shy away from the term? The answer goes to the heart of the difference over the role of witnessing which divides Blanchot and Bataille at the time. In Bataille, that third party, though of uncertain status, is nevertheless an interlocutor, indeed a new version of language itself, described as the "reader" of the "yawning gap" which has destroyed the subject, and which the latter's division can therefore be said to *inscribe*. For Blanchot too, language occupies the role of third party, but its otherness is that of the witness as martyr. Destined to assume the division that is to be expiated by dying like an animal, language lives on as the endless self-contestation of paradox. Communication thus remains a *human* relation for Bataille. For Blanchot, on the contrary, it marks the annihilation of the human: as communication, it leads to *nothing*.

The Heideggerian *Stimmung* which this assertion introduces into the exchange between Bataille and Blanchot is a radical rebuttal of the terms in which Bataille presents Blanchot's understanding of contestation, and is on a par, I would suggest, with Bataille's refusal to accept that he should live his experience as if he were the *last man*. The point at issue, in this contestation regarding "contestation" which divides the two friends, is ultimately that of witness. And it signals a parting of the ways for them, almost at the exact moment their paths cross. This is indicated in the different pathways through language that each man proposes at this time. For Bataille, the appeal to an entirely new and original mode of language marks a return, as it were instinctively, to the premodern form of contestation which sustained the Christian worldview. He contests insofar as the "yawning gap" of Godless martyrdom becomes a renewed circuit of appeal in and through the transcendence of language. For his part, Blanchot affirms the relation between contestation and communication ("Contestation, experience, communication are terms which bear a close similarity—if not more"),[48] but he presents what they bring about as in effect without appeal: the "passion of paradox" which he equates with contestation and presents elsewhere in *Faux pas* is the only remaining option for reason.[49] Hence if language takes on the role of third party, it is, as the notion of *expiation* indicates, as sacrificial victim: the scapegoat who pays the price of my abuse of authority by being destroyed.

Yet things are not as simple as that would suggest. It is undeniable that the "passion of paradox" will powerfully determine Blanchot's writing henceforth, and prove highly contagious in the writing of many who have sought to approach his writing critically. And as such, it would seem no more than the sterile automatism of a language in which communication is communication with nothing. But that *passion* is also a *patience*. And in Kafka, whose style he describes as almost a pure manifestation of contestation,[50] Blanchot discerns a patience which he comments upon as follows: "If one compared that patience to the dangerous mobility of Romantic thought, it would appear as its intimate core, but also as its inner pause: expiation at the very heart of sin."[51]

The paradox that so pervades Blanchot's critical writing can perhaps now be seen for what it is: a patient ordeal of expiation, in which language responds to the appeal to witness contained in the contestation of its own authority as sole remaining transcendence, by subjecting itself to the endless division of martyrdom. But this is not the only dimension to the language of contestation in Blanchot. As with Bataille, language has another mode. But unlike for Bataille, whose relation to that mode is one of appeal, the language that is the other of rational language exists for Blanchot in practice: it is the language of his fiction. And while remaining absolutely separate from rational language, it too is the scene of an ordeal of expiation. Writing in 1946 of Hölderlin, the poet whom the gods punished by making him destroy everything that he holds dear, Blanchot says: "That judgment is not merely a punishment for an excess of language; rather, expiation and language are the same thing: the poet destroys himself. Ruin, contestation, pure division, really *jedem offen* as the poem says, open to all; because he is no longer anything but absence and division, it is as such that he speaks."[52] For Blanchot, therefore, contestation restores the appeal to witnessing which it originally contained by establishing two languages, each of which is the site of the expiation of authority which experience as contestation endlessly endures.

But that is just the beginning: as the path of Blanchot's writing diverges ever more decisively from that of Bataille, drawn away from the Christian frame within which the latter is content to remain, and toward the Judaism of his friend Levinas, so the two languages of expiation will gradually converge, until, as he announces in 1962, the need for expiation will be overcome. This is not a *rapprochement* with Levinas. In an article entitled "Etre juif" (Being a Jew), with an avowed *brutality* which preserves the moment of contestation at its most destructive, Blanchot repudiates the Old Testament God in favor of what he calls the true gift of Israel: namely "the revelation of speech as the place where men are held in a relation to what excludes all relation,"[53] before continuing: "Speech gives rise to an original relation, one in which the terms present *have no need to expiate the relation,* but ask for and are given welcome precisely for what they do not have in common" (my italics).[54] At the same time, this overcoming of expiation does not return Blanchot to the witnessing to which Bataille appealed. Between 1941 and 1948, no doubt in response to

Nietzsche's assertion that the last man is "the most despicable" (*der Verächt-lichste*),[55] his fiction is the site of an increasingly destructive descent into abjection and animality,[56] whose metamorphoses mirror in the mode of the sacrificial beast of expiation the patient passion in which his critical language expiates itself as paradox.

Eventually, this ordeal too will come to an end. In his last work of narrative fiction, the last man at last appears: "Docile, almost obedient, saying very little that was negative, *not contesting*, and, in everything that needed doing, ready to offer naive assent" (my italics).[57] Fiction has opened onto a "Oui" which is no longer that of contestation. What is more, it is also without witness: "Even a God needs a witness. The divine incognito must be seen through here below. I had described at length what his witness might be. I became as it were ill at the thought that I would have to be that witness. But slowly—suddenly—the thought dawned that this story was without a witness: I was there—the 'I' was already no longer anything but a Who? an infinite number of Who?s—so that there should be no one between him and his destiny."[58] Blanchot is poised here on the threshold of a "parole" in which the *tiers* will be neither expiatory victim nor witness, but a response to the experience of contestation as *an event without witness*. And in the years to come, his writing will turn ever more exclusively toward the historical event of the Holocaust, as he seeks to place the language which he calls the true gift of Israel at the disposal of "those witnesses who never encounter an audience capable of listening to them and hearing them,"[59] or in Shoshana Felman's words, "to give reality [his] own vulnerability, as a condition of exceptional availability and . . . attention [to] the impossibility of witnessing."[60]

CHAPTER TWO

Maurice Blanchot

The Spirit of Language after the Holocaust

Geoffrey H. Hartman

Interpreters of Blanchot evade their duty unless they bring us nearer to four things: Blanchot's politics, the writing style of his extraordinary novels, his literary theory, his remarks on Judaism and the Holocaust. A fifth, perhaps quintessential matter, which I will not handle directly, is the sensitivity to theology or myth which one feels just under the surface of everything he writes.

"No word intoned from on high," Theodor Adorno wrote, "not even a theological one, can be justified, untransformed, after Auschwitz."[1] Sublime as well as rabid utterances, motivated by a self-styled "spiritual revolution," nationalistic, Christian, or post-Christian, had justified persecution and genocide. Difficult as the transformation is that Adorno calls for, to keep silent because of skepticism or despair is not a way out. The silences of speech always occur within the context of speech, and, like a Joker, remain part of the pack.

Blanchot's career began before the war as a contributor to extreme right-wing journals.[2] These were often characterized by an *antisemitisme de peau,* a crude, as if instinctive prejudice, but more significantly by what Charles Maurras distinguished as *antisemitisme de raison,* supposedly not a blind but a reasoned hatred, in reality a mixture of age-long Christian contempt and ignorant clichés about the Jews. (The claim of rationality, in fact, helped hatred to turn deliberate and systematic.) Blanchot, except during the time of Léon Blum's government, cannot be accused of anti-Semitism: indeed, he clearly and clairvoyantly opposed the "Hitler terror" against the Jews.[3] Yet, during the 1930s, in spite of every political contingency, he remained a strident partisan of the necessity for a "spiritual revolution" in France. In 1938 Blanchot moderated his political journalism and turned more to literature and literary theory— though it is difficult to determine a precise turning point.[4] Silent about what brought the change about, Blanchot eventually became a thinker evoking an exemplary "passivity" strongly associated with "literary space." At some point during that development he also began to restitute what might be called the cultural space of Judaism, as well as its life-space oppressively narrowed by Christianity, then totally eliminated by the genocide.

I will not try to unify a writing career which began in 1930. The notion of such a unity would be contested by Blanchot himself. But I will emphasize the implicit or explicit conception of language—less abstractly, of writing and the irreducibility of the writer to the person—Blanchot held from early on and deepened after his turn from political journalism to literature. Avoiding personal reference, and expressing himself through extensive theoretical explorations, literary reviews, enigmatic short novels, and the prose fragment, he shifts the focus from the abuse of particular words and expressions to a fundamental misconception—and hence a necessary reconception—of language, its relationship to the "genre humain".[5] "It is from speech always already destroyed [i.e., not given for the first time like the Pentateuch's original Tablets of the Law] that humans learn to draw the demanding character [*exigence*] of the words that speak to them: there is no truly firsthand understanding, no initial and intact speech. It is as if one never spoke except a second time, having refused to understand and having kept one's distance from the origin."[6]

This definition, which might be called meta-rhetorical, makes no distinction between distances instituted by the intellect, or those in the very nature of language, or a dissociation that is an aftereffect of trauma. Blanchot holds that the "exigence" of words born a second time comes about through the destruction of their first, illusory, pseudointimate status, of their instrumental or magical promise to unify or even incarnate thought.[7] Writing participates in a complex movement of erosion that constitutes the soul and life of words, making things appear insofar as they have disappeared, drawing light from that extinction, from the element of obscurity itself.

The clarity of things seems always to defeat the obscurity of language, yet it is only this obscurity which allows us to enhance sight and perception, to see with a kind of second sight the remarkable realities words point to. Utilitarian sediments or overlays disappear, "Washed in the remotest cleanliness of a heaven / That has expelled us and our images," as Wallace Stevens said in the "It Must Be Abstract" section of "Notes toward a Supreme Fiction." The danger Blanchot describes, most obsessively in his first book, *Thomas l'obscur* (1942), is the idealist's temptation to confuse this brilliant outside clarity with his own thought: an anxiety reaction to thought being invaded, even obliterated, by a phenomenal splendor. Thomas envisions the world of sense perception as his will and representation, at once bewitched by such idealism and treating it as a "repulsive fantasy." A sentiment of non-existence (also non-authenticity) tempts the human to regard itself from the point of view of the cosmos, that is, as not there, as in effect already absent, dead though conscious. This perspective allows Thomas and Anne (the two protagonists) to value Being instead of beings, and to de-instrumentalize their own existence. They glimpse a vision of their own body and the "great day" that embraces them, indeed all mankind.[8] The last chapter of *Thomas the Obscure* is an extraordinary poetic hymn that seeks to stand outside psychologism and invokes an impersonal memory. "Memory seemed to them that desert of ice which a magnificent sun was melting and in which they seized once more, by somber and cold remembering, separated from the heart which had cherished it, the world in which they were trying to live again."[9]

Blanchot's protracted and frustrating book *L'espace littéraire* (1955) also wishes to tame, through a turn to literary theory, the chiaroscuro or non-phenomenality of words, to present language as a necessary form of askesis through which we continue to suffer a sense of non-being vis-à-vis the now discreet, now terrifying clarity of the world of things. Other theoretical or mixed reflections follow suit. The relation of words to things becomes more than a philosophical problem: it is a part of whatever Blanchot writes. What escapes naming, even while being named, is not only a phenomenal *éclat* but its obverse. "Things," he tells us, "belong to a different order [than names]; they are what is most familiar, letting us live in their environment without being transparent. Things are lit up, but they do not allow the light to pass through, even were they themselves made of grains of light." Consequently, despite the splendor I have already mentioned, what also escapes naming ("but without making noise, not even the bustle of an enigma") is the relation of non-relation we have to things, and which Blanchot links to the "it," the "neuter" (ne-uter) or "outside" (*dehors*).[10]

In *L'attente l'oubli* (1962), to cite his most denuded work, Blanchot leaves behind the struggle between the "innocence" of images purged of instrumentalized meanings and the impossible attempt to make words equal the fascination of those images. The narrative (hardly a narrative) is stripped of everything except a virtual story in which a writer and a woman attempt to talk with each other.[11] Snatches of dialogue, at once affirming and denying their relationship, find neither a real beginning nor a resting point. Each person's solitude is absolute and yet (despite occasional gestures of passion or impatience) accepted as the human norm, or even as fulfilling a law.

Without any concrete allusion justifying a transcendent or intertextual setting, one might still imagine this book as Blanchot's "conversation with the dead" and counting, among the dead, not only the author deprived of selfhood but also a figure like Simone Weil. There is no metamorphosis, as there might be in a fantasized trance state, where the self is nonidentical; yet the mention of old and new gods suggests a transposition to the East.[12] At one point the (anonymous) man is asked to show his power, to resolve (as a writer?) what the last line of the novel calls "la retenue des choses en leur état latent" (the decorum of things in their latency). Mallarmé had defined Hamlet in a marvelous phrase as "Le Seigneur latent qui ne peut devenir." Is the temptation here similar to that of Christ, as Milton imagined it in *Paradise Regained,* a Christ asked by Satan to manifest his divinity as purely his own? It seems that Blanchot conceives the writer as one who stays permanently in the position of an *attente* that approaches revelation, or else nirvana, asymptotically. "Le nouveau vague," as the resultant style might be called, is peerless in contemporary French literature.[13]

Blanchot's word presentation has not been closely studied. It reveals an author who is resolutely nonautobiographical.[14] Given the complexities of the political and ideological picture in the 1930s—"un canevas idéologique, lâche et distendu"[15]—even a sustained memoir might falsify the past. It is tempting, though, to link Blanchot's retreat (into literature) to a double refusal: of an exploitative and instrumentalized language, and of a violently regenerative politics[16] achieved through that kind of language. While Blanchot's imagination responds to Heidegger's attempt to gain a "clearing" for Being obfuscated by beings, at the level of words he consistently dismantles fascism's claim to be a spiritual movement that enforces its demand for discipline and purification by a decisionist (pseudoperformative) use of language.

Yet if Blanchot's change is motivated by an opposition to the political exploitation and simplification of language, why does he remain uncommunicative about the origins of his change? Does he occult uncomfortable personal facts? Or is his reticence the result of a larger discovery, made in the very *process* of writing: through its pressure on personal identity?[17] "Every writer," he says characteristically in *L'espace littéraire*, "every artist knows the moment when he is rejected and as if excluded by his work in progress. It pushes him aside, the circle is closed in which he has no longer access to himself, yet in which he remains enclosed, because the work, unfinished, won't let him go."[18]

It is not surprising from what has already been said that Blanchot as literary critic develops an impersonality theory as radical as Mallarmé's. He sharpens the paradox whereby the self produced by the work also disappears into it: the author, according to Blanchot, has no more of an independent existence than an actor does, "that ephemeral personality who is born and dies every evening, having exposed himself excessively to view, killed by the spectacle."[19] The recession (a kenosis or emptying) of the self is emphasized more than self-fashioning; in accord with what Martin Jay has characterized as "down-cast eyes" in modern French thought,[20] Blanchot asserts that "to speak is not to see" and that the writer ought to be at once "a free and speaking subject" and "to disappear" as a subject, becoming "the patient whom dying traverses and who does not show himself."[21]

There is no way to reconcile this double obligation. It repeats a split in the concept of *pathos*. The split points to a style that actively elicits the reader's (viewer's) compassion for human suffering (*pathē*) or to a style expressing the highest degree of impassibility.[22] And though both of these discourse styles can be Hegelian—prefigurative of secular or spiritual fulfillment despite their open, fluid dialectic—it is, surprisingly, the one taking passivity as its task[23] and presupposing a traumatic epistemology, that gradually but surely dominates Blanchot's writing.

The notion of literary impersonality has complex antecedents in that of philosophical suicide: Novalis's sentiment is well known, that the first authentic philosophical act is annihilation of the self (*Selbsttötung*), a sentiment echoed by Carlyle in *Sartor Resartus*.[24] Walter Benjamin placed modernity itself under the sign of suicide, where that concept—as well as the enigmatic deed—points to an impasse, close to Durkheim's *anomie*.

The impasse is linked to modernity's desire for greater realism. That desire arouses an acute awareness that contemporary life cannot be mastered by artists who feel violated by it, that a realistic representation has to conspire with the fatal thing portrayed. This instigates, in reaction, a withdrawal from art as realistic exposure at the very moment art is most valued for that kind of exhibition.

Thus Blanchot's resolute antirealism describes the author or his characters in a submythical manner as patients "whom dying traverses." This "exteriority" jeopardizes the coincidence of meaning and intention, or self-expression and validation.[25] Given such intricacy, it is not possible to reduce Blanchot's version of impersonality theory to a simple, biographically inspired occultation.

After the Holocaust, moreover, impersonality theory is not identical with itself. Survivors like Primo Levi and Robert Antelme, while accepting the necessity to speak about their experience, are more completely aware than any previous "modernist" could have been about events so shaming to the person of the victim and his regard for humanity that speech is inhibited at its source. This shame blocks what Aristotle described as art's intrinsic desire for imitation, for achieving a resembling portrait.[26] Aware of this dilemma, Blanchot insists that while testimony is an obligation, the life of those who survived the Holocaust is a "rupture with the living affirmation: the attestation of the goodness of life (life which is not narcissistic but for the other) has been so decisively impacted that nothing remains intact. From that point on, it could be that all narration, even all poetry, has lost the basis on which a different language [*un langage autre*] might be erected, because of the extinction of the happiness of speaking latent even in the most mediocre silence."[27] Blanchot nevertheless struggles to open the way to that "other language" without falling into what Adorno denounced as "verruchte Affirmation," a shameful attraction to the contaminating event.

Blanchot's relation to Judaism must have begun after meeting Emmanuel Levinas at the University of Strasbourg in 1925 or 1926, which led to an abiding friendship. But we have only Levinas's affectionate and general words about Blanchot at that time; and there is no indication that there was an active interchange between the two on matters of religion. So far as I can tell, Blanchot's nonpolitical interest (in Judaism rather than Jews) begins with a presumed identity between that religion and the written word. That the word is not an image, even if it increases the fascination and lure of images because of its very difference, helps to attract him to the anti-iconic aspect of Judaism. Yet he generally does not focus either on Judaism or on the Holocaust, though he is unusually emotional in the way he describes the latter—"Humanity had to die as a whole by the ordeal it underwent in those who embody life itself, almost an entire people that had been promised a perpetual presence."[28] Nor does he connect the topics "Judaism" and "literary space" in a sustained way. His turn toward the theme of Jewishness, "être-Juif," is gradual rather than abrupt. What he *is* drawn to might be called its philology or *Sprachphilosophie,* its engagement with words that claim a divine primary source yet incite an endless secondary conversation about Torah.[29] As in Edmond Jabès, though with less pathos, there is an attempt to respect the pressure as well as liberty of words, their interminable, enigmatic, and non-narrative presence.[30] Measured against "the Law," whether as a religious or self-constituted absolute, words are "faux pas" without the possibility of justification, even while they seek to turn "le mot juste" from just a word into the just word. Yet the "infinite conversa-tion" ("entretien infini") stretching across the centuries that characterizes the Jewish commentary tradition (*midrash*) may have inclined Blanchot toward the figure of a community—though too avowed, perhaps.

One of Blanchot's earliest explicit linkages of Judaism and writing comes in a 1963 review of Jabès's *Book of Questions,* where the "rupture" that inter-rupts the non-silence of the spheres—the ceaseless murmur or mutter ("re-ssassement éternel") of the impersonal, unknown background of existence—is equated with a "rupture . . . called Judaism" central to history.[31] In another essay Blanchot quotes Hegel on the abyss Judaism posits between man and God, but adds: "words cross that abyss. Distance is not abolished, it is not even diminished; on the contrary, it is preserved and kept pure by the rigor of words that support the absoluteness of difference. . . . To talk to someone . . . is to recognize him as unknown and to welcome him in his quality of stranger, without obliging him to break with his difference."[32] Since experiments in music, film, and painting, as well as literature, that gather momentum in the postwar years and that extend modernism and influence the discursive system of criticism could also be aligned with sentiments like these, the link to Juda-ism is interesting rather than definitive. As late as *The Writing of the Disaster* (1980) there is no attempt to present Judaism as a system of thought; all but a few references are indirect.[33]

The same reticence holds for Christianity. Where we would expect Blan-chot's thoughts on passivity to touch on Christian passion and its mystical aura, he withholds such a derivation.[34] What we do find are remarks about the pressure of writing and reading on self-identity—on an official self that accepts or exploits the stability of normative, including grammatical, structures. In an early and unsubtle pronouncement Blanchot declares: "In authentic language, speech has not only a representational function but a destructive one. It makes the object *disappear,* it renders it absent, it annihilates it."[35] Blanchot never takes for granted the passage from self to other, from "moi" to "il" or "il y a," even in fiction where the "event" that would justify it remains fictive and cannot become present as more than a shared illusion. The decisive "event," unless it is the writer's anticipation of death itself, that is, of his life (or second life, "survie") after death, cannot effect the linguistically subtle yet radical interchange of "je" and "il," nor embody the kind of presence we generally express by dating an event.[36] Indeed, the very concept of agency disappears by 1980 behind a "disaster" which is the subject of *The Writing of the Disaster.*

Despite Blanchot's intense awareness, then, of the Holocaust, disaster is never given a precise historical location; instead, it is associated with "the detour of writing" and literary space as an immemorial adventure. Blanchot is always turning from "rupture," in the sense of a deliberate and potentially violent act, to "rupture" as a break with such a rupture. The space and time of writing define a negation to the second power (their rupture with a politics of rupture, with the worldly power—*puissance*—of words, as well as their ability—*pouvoir*—to create their own world); and this double negation, far from empowering a dialectical (positive and progressive) synthesis, undoes words as instruments of ego or will.[37] Blanchot's break with a 1930s kind of journalistic agitation, which had itself aimed at a violent departure from the French Republican past, could have been the historical point of connection with his turn to the strange, passive temporality of literary space.

This temporality defuses discursive structures or linguistic formations that sustain the illusion of speech as instrument or act—*act* in the strong sense of exerting, as well as contesting, power, or else helping a wounded self to recover. Countering that most common of therapeutic perspectives, Blanchot aligns literature instead with the *pâtir* in "passion" and "patience," and with "pas" as ambiguously a step (forward) and a sign of the negative. (The title of Blanchot's *Le Pas au-delà* could mean "The Step Beyond," i.e., transcendence, but that meaning is subverted by other possibilities, such as "The 'Don't Go Beyond.'") The negative turn so pervasive in his phrasing always retards an *élan vital,* particularly when prophetic or futuristic. The fall from sense into obscurity, or a vacuum that suctions off whatever identity has been achieved, is not more than a verbal step away. To the point where his method of "entre-dire" (a back-and-forth of anonymous voices or narrators, at once tender and irreconcilable) is always shadowed by an "arrêt qui interdit," a "death sentence" (to cite the title of an early novel), whose effect is to question or arrest fluid discourse, at least to inhibit its movement toward incarnation and beyond the detaining words.[38] Levinas writes there is no philosophy without death (remembering perhaps the opening of Franz Rosenzweig's *Star of Redemption*); for Blanchot, there is no writing without an accompanying consciousness of death. But how can artists tolerate an interruption Blanchot describes as if it were literally a dying, "the heart ceasing to beat, the eternal, pulsing drive to talk arrested"?[39]

The past seems to have no presence for Blanchot except as a reminder of mortality. A sense of the mortal rather than culpable informs all of his work. The living person seems already touched by death, or has passed through it. There is a sense of revenance, of uncanny and unpredictable returns. (Of this Blanchot gives a more vivid impression in his fiction, which affirms the imaginative appeal of passing, without sacrifice of consciousness, from life to death: "C'est toute vivante qu'Anne entendait passer à la mort."[40] She could be said to traverse dying, rather than vice versa. Though there is a presence of the past called history, the truth of the past is closer to "the passion of patience, the passivity of a time without present . . . [which is the writer's] sole identity."[41]

What Blanchot calls "disaster," without fixing its historical referent, presupposes a failure linked to the human condition: its vacillating over/under/ estimation of words, its consciousness that aspires to be unconditioned, omnipotent, equivalent to the world looking at itself. His clearest—if still enigmatic—narrative, *L'arrêt de mort,* though dominated in its vacillating course by the theme of a Nietzschean will to power, is associated with the Munich crisis of 1938 and turns away from the world of politics to a far more intimate action that occurs mainly in anonymous rooms whose features are reduced to a bed, a door (perhaps open, perhaps locked), a wall, a window. The will to power is converted into a will to die, a heroic wish to "see" death, to pass through it consciously rather than simply to give up. There is also a wish, equally strong and strange, to break the glass between self and other. Or, more precisely, not to break it, despite deathly fears of coldness, opacity, personal alienation. The narrator sees in the other (a woman, Natalie) the apparent independence of his own thoughts. "I saw her pass before me, coming and going in a place extremely near and infinitely separated and as if behind a window. . . . She bore herself in my presence with the freedom of a thought; she was in this world, but in this world I did not yet encounter her because she was my thought; and what intrigue formed between them, what complicity full of horror. I will add that she looked at me as someone whom she knew well and was friends with, but it was a recognition from behind the eyes, blind and without a sign, a recognition coming from the mind, friendly, cold and dead."[42]

The turn to literature, then, to its fictional authenticity or "errance," is not a quest for anamnesis leading to a recovered original and higher truth but a purification *from* essence, from this will to power so intimately entwined with notions of the living word and a real, incarnate, rather than phantom, existence. Words for Blanchot are alive, and demand to be restored to their full value. So Anne, in the later version of *Thomas l'obscur,* profoundly tormented (as is Thomas himself) by a sentiment of nonexistence, acts as if it cannot be overcome except by a voluntary death, one that would restore "the true significance of the words to give oneself: she gave Anne."[43] (This totally nonerotic giving of the self is more absolute than any previous religious conception of the womanly as a divine lure toward askesis and self-abnegation.) Thomas passes through a similar phase, when he is shown reading, and finds *he* is being observed by words: "already the words took hold of him and began to read him. He was seized, molded by intelligible hands, bitten by a tooth full of sap; he entered with his living body into the anonymous form of the words, giving them his substance, forming their relationships, offering the word being his being."[44]

It will take a lifelong quest, essay after essay, quasi-novel after quasi-novel, to disentangle this mixture of hubris and hysteria, of ancient myth and monomania. The sentiment of nonexistence, reinforced by the mediocrity of the exchangeable rooms, *non-lieux* in which the "action" of the novels takes place,[45] moves to the side of a struggle against selfhood, a struggle to suspend its power and accept the ambiguity of otherness—of people as well as things—as infinitely near yet infinitely strange. The relation between self and other passes through the negative intercourse of a speech that cannot bestow mutual identity, and invents in reaction (though still within the system of public discourse) the fiction of succeeding at this through a political *coup* or historical dialectic. In Blanchot's later writings the self is not even *haïssable,* as in Pascal: always falsely present, it fades into literature's poetic rather than historical memory.

Literature acts as the guardian of a "remembrance without remembrance of the origin. . . . memory as abyss."[46]

Understanding Blanchot is not made easier by the fact that the contextual vagueness of *The Writing of the Disaster* is counterpointed by an abundance of topical essays. These are mainly literary reviews with a great diversity of dates and names. Yet Blanchot remains reticent about "the gravity of history," the relation of all those dates to a private life that seems to have its own eras.[47] Similarly, while his criticism is full of names, these are always a shorthand for texts.[48] Hence the reader is left with an enigma concerning how this literary journalism is a way of telling the time of history, whereas the opposite had been the case in the early political journalism.[49] What is the motivating *spirit* of Blanchot's literary corpus seen as a whole? Can we get a historical answer as to what animated the idealist-terrorist of the 1930s, as to what life (death)-force or fire-portion ("la part du feu") exalted him and led to a culpable mentality, inseparable in retrospect—for many of us—from the consuming fires of the Holocaust?

I want to carry this question forward, one that comes from me rather than explicitly from Blanchot. Not only is the Holocaust undeniable, but the forceful spirit once active in the young Blanchot also appears incapable of being either denied or reclaimed. To break with that spirit, I speculate, required a counter-spirit, drawn from the same source (the rapture that produced the desire for rupture) yet antithetical and without hope for retroactive justification. Blanchot's later writing *is* this counter-spirit: it does not lessen what Levinas calls "suffering as an event." Nothing is overturned in the name of a violent separation of past and future, or of a decisive revolution. Blanchot's "disaster" is not datable because it does not install itself in history with absolute or quasi-apocalyptic specificity ("that rupture of violent power which wants to create an era and mark it as such"). Blanchot elides parousia and salvation as reference points, or discloses that a vehement temporal demarcation is itself the disaster.[50]

For Blanchot, then, writing cannot reference its own authenticity.[51] It has no essence except the inessential, the errant, the gratuitous, the strangeness at the heart of even the most intimate relationship. It is always outside or beside itself ("dehors"), nonidentical in its sameness, a "fureur d'écrire" as in Sade's self-defeating violence of "tout dire."[52] This is the true anguish (even when Blanchot seems to accept it theoretically), a negativity stronger than terror or nihilism, or their familiar obverse, decisionist language,[53] or the contrariety of dialectics. Such "dwelling in the negative," however, does not allow the solitary to be alone: he is constrained to consume himself as a writer, even when he has nothing to write. "It appears comic and wretched that [this] anguish, which opens and closes heaven, needs to manifest itself through the activity of a man sitting at his desk and tracing letters on a sheet of paper."[54]

"Opens and closes heaven" may allude to ecstatic "primal scenes" (*scènes primitives*), mixed images of abandon and abandonment that underwrite a "communauté inavouable" created by such "expérience intérieure." Blanchot calls it a community, because, however private, these ecstatic imaginings must be shared, in the sense that the writer by himself cannot contain them, indeed cannot claim to be present for them, or even hold them fast in memory, having been "altered" as an individual by them, that is, opened to alterity.[55]

No wonder that writing approaches a religiosity—avowed or not—in Blanchot: perhaps the atheological intensity of a Bataille, perhaps a residue of Blanchot's early political exaltation. Solitude, *désœuvrement,* a sense of absurdity, and the inexorable presence of what Blanchot describes as a "mute beast" keep the author at his task.[56] Even hope in the past, to bring in Benjamin's paradoxical concept, guarding against simplistic theories of progress and happiness—even hope in the past is not a motive, or would be unfaithful to an obliviousness ("an extra-temporal memory or a memory without a past, which could never have been experienced in the present")[57] that does not allow us to act in hope. "When we are patient, it is always in relation to an infinite misery [*malheur,* literally "bad luck" or "mis-fortune"], which does not impact on us in the present except by linking us to a past without memory. Misfortune of the other and the other as misfortune."[58]

That phrase, "a past without memory," is hard to accept. Blanchot does not say that a past *with* memory does not also exist—a past that is the basis of conscience and culpability. But he evokes a *dépassement* (the only one he admits to) of that past by a time without end or limit. During this time, time does not pass, that is, pass into something else. Time is not the mercy that limits eternity but the perpetuity of "malheur"—even when it does not overturn an unreasonable joy in the daily act of being alive ("la folie du jour").[59] "It is the horror of a suffering without end, a suffering that time can no longer redeem, that has escaped time and for which there is no longer recourse; it is irremediable."[60]

Through his literary turn Blanchot bypasses, in effect, the historian's or philosopher's remembrance of things past in favor of a thinking that commits itself to a language conveying that unspecific, primordial suffering in un-mediated time. For it is language as a temporal medium that opens the ego-enclosed self to the otherness of the other (*autrui*), releasing a feeling so insup-portable—as joy, or more likely as anguish—that violence against the other would ensue if the turn to language were not already a break with violence (although that break is not absolute, since language itself remembers, as it were, its own break with the phenomenal world), and in that way an antitheti-cal source of happiness. The characters in Blanchot's novels are often physi-cally close, corps à corps, yet *gisants* rather than locked in sexual or psychologi-cally mortal combat.

It is here that the link to Levinas becomes apparent. Levinas does not neglect the factor of language. However, no one has seen as clearly as Blanchot its human significance as a temporal medium. Perhaps medium is too cold a word, but mediation would be too warm. It is Levinas who, after Heidegger, takes up the question of how we enter into relation with time, given that the present is always foreshortened by a future, an *à venir* whose horizon is death. Levinas talks of the future more readily than Blanchot: his idea of transcen-dence, in fact, the ability to go out of oneself, beyond oneself, is linked to an affirmation of the future despite our consciousness of the inevitability of death, despite death's total, mysterious otherness that reduces the individual to solitude and passivity.[61]

The solution Levinas finds to the paradox of the human condition, its death-in-life, is to link the possibility of transcendence within time to the presence of the other person, "autrui." It is only by a face-to-face with others that we become present, that we take hold of time. This face-to face, as Hegel taught in the influential section of the *Phenomenology* concerning the feudal commerce of lord and liege man, constitutes a recognition scene, a condensa-tion of time that brings death from an abstract future into the immediacy of the present. Yet the impasse of that face-to-face, an impasse that could prove fatal, passes into a humanizing recognition. Levinas interprets this recognition as a choice affirming rather than denying otherness, or using one's power to renounce the violence intrinsic to denial. "The situation of face-to-face," he writes, "should be the very fulfillment of time; the encroachment of the pres-ent on the future is not the deed [*le fait*] of an isolated subject but of the intersubjective relation."[62]

For Levinas, then, there is no dialectical resolution to this fundamental encounter with otherness. It does not prompt, as in Hegel, a struggle for mastery that results in a reversal or a new contractual relation. Instead, the encounter recognizes the mystery of otherness—a mystery simply because it obliges us to accept an extraordinary passivity, to moderate both the ideal of virility and the demand for reciprocal status. As "in the absolutely original relationship of erotic love," there is imbalance and vulnerability, and they should not be reversed into mastery.[63] But that "absolutely original" as an unqualified qualifier is also applied by Levinas to the transphenomenal foundation of the ethical. In Levinas the empirical other is not to be confused with the infinitely other, who is the noumenal as well as numinous basis of all ethical relation and thinking.

To concentrate on the moment of writing is, for Blanchot, to experience Levinasian time; but his emphasis falls less on the possibility of transcendence, or "fecundity," than on "the fulfillment of one's solitude."[64] Writing is the site of a basic recognition of otherness; the writer experiences his work as a disengagement (Blanchot says *désœuvrement*) instead of a form of empowerment or cultural accrual (*œuvre, chef-d'œuvre*). In *Thomas l'obscur* Blanchot already concentrated on the nonperformative "act" of writing: on what happens between the writer and words as complex as fictional characters. He discovers in the process of writing a self that is without identity except through the Other who "escapes my power."[65]

Blanchot intimates through formulations like this an intolerable dichotomy, an entrapment in the vocabulary of power as force. His "moi sans moi," a dispossessed self, remains subject to the *regard* (gaze and regard) of the Other. Writing, instead of staying firmly on the side of mastery and justification, takes away the writer's crutch: his belief that what he does is an action, a "work," an affirmation of the world and his function in it. Precisely, in fact, because the writer creates (written) surfaces by which he is shielded from a gaze that could penetrate them—for what is identity except this opaqueness?—he cannot "read" his own self and so experiences it as nothingness or passivity.[66]

If this kind of analysis remains phenomenological, it is phenomenology striving to become ethics and being waylaid by words. Like Levinas, Blanchot describes language as a medium having access to immediacy: not just, however, through a momentary and deceptive clearing away of false mediations (language as skepticism) but through language *clearing itself away* and so revealing something infinitely "there," in which "relation itself . . . has all at once burnt up in a night without darkness: there are no more terms, there is no more rapport, there is nothing beyond—God himself is annihilated there."[67] This too, then, this very "there is nothing beyond," still hints at an attempt to go beyond Hegelian Christianity, to escape from mediation, from an endlessly dialecticized immediacy. "Judaism," Blanchot remarks, "is the sole thought that does not mediate."[68]

Impressed by its iconoclasm and outsider status, Blanchot absolutizes Jewish fate as "breaking with the star."[69] In disaster writing, words are intrinsically anti-idolatrous, errant, Abrahamic. "Look toward heaven, and count the stars," God says to Abraham in Genesis 15; "So shall thy seed be." For Blanchot such words have meaning purely as a figure: especially after the Shoah, in which the David star became a badge of doom, they cannot find a correspondence in reality. "The word," Blanchot writes, "is the promised land where exile fulfills itself as a dwelling place, since it is not a matter of being at home but always Outside, in a movement by which the Stranger liberates himself without renouncing his strangeness. To speak is definitively to seek the source of meaning in the prefix which the words 'exile,' 'exodus,' 'existence,' 'exteriority,' 'estrangement' discharge into various modes of experience, a prefix which designates distance and separation as the origin of all 'positive value.'"[70] Like Benjamin's allegory, writing exits empty handed. Or rather, in this "white night" of the soul, empty hands continue to write, skeptical of a greater fulfillment.

But is this an ethical as well as existential outcome? Blanchot, I have said, assumes that writing is the opposite of mastery: contrary to expectation, it puts the writer into a magnetic field whose core is absolute passivity, loss of rapport, and the absence of mediations needed to restore that rapport.

Here an important concept enters: that of the "exteriority" (in addition to the impersonal or kenosis effect) of writing. A verbal surface that resists deciphering because of its exteriority—actually, its elusive interiority[71]—means having one's being outside (like "things"), or commodifying the Other who evades appropriation, who cannot be internalized without traumatizing the self. This condition is viewed as an "infinite misfortune." It cannot compete with the phenomenality of sense perception. Nor can it be idealized *après coup* as the loss of a prior and potentially privileged moment, a Nervalian or Proustian *temps perdu*. To access such a moment, such a memory, is not even desirable, nothing like a fulfilling mystical union. There are moments of gaiety, or extreme light-heartedness in Blanchot, when his mind passes the fiction on itself that it could recover "the glaze of naturalness." But a vision of bad luck predominates, even of trauma as bad luck, as a historical "stroke" to which no meaning can be given. Though the individual may escape becoming a casualty, he cannot but feel "the misfortune [*malheur*] of the other [*l'autrui*] and the other as misfortune."[72]

Contra Hegel, such wounds of the spirit do not heal. And, however close Blanchot is to Levinas, this wounding, which seems to be the source of serious writing, is, in him, much less sure of its "fecundity" than in the "other humanism" of Levinas. Levinas's "exteriority" is linked to the possibility of inspiration or transcendence.[73] The Bible, for example, in this Jewish thinker, exceeds under the pressure of midrash "what it originally wants to say . . . what it is capable of saying goes beyond what it wants to say . . . it contains more than it contains . . . an inexhaustible surplus of meaning remains locked in the syntactic structures of the sentence, in its word-groups, its actual words, phonemes and letters, in all the materiality of the saying which is potentially signifying all the time. Exegesis would come to free, in these signs, a bewitched significance that smoulders beneath the characters or coils up in all this literature of letters."[74]

For Blanchot also—whatever the differences between him and Levinas—the morality of interpersonal relations enters primarily through language, and in the context of a link between extreme receptivity and "impersonification" (to borrow Mallarmé's word). One is tempted to think of a traumatism, an extreme dissociation that permits the overwhelmed self to save a scrap of its substance only by entering language in the third person ("il") or as impersonal pronoun (the "it" of "il y a"). In this mode it is closer to the linguistic than the ethical, or identifies the one with the other. Blanchot often echoes Levinas,[75] who defines this state as an *absence* of the ego in the *presence* of an unqualified sense of responsibility: "this responsibility—responsibility which I have for the other, for all, without reciprocity—displaces itself, does not belong any more to conscience, is not the engagement of an activist reflection, is not even a duty which would impose itself from outside or inside. *My* responsibility for the Other supposes an overturning such that it cannot register itself except by a change in the status of the 'mine' [*moi*], a change of time, and perhaps language."[76]

Levinas's statement, when filtered through Blanchot, becomes a remarkable conceptualization of what it feels like to enter a mind that knows there is disaster, but cannot correct or alter anything through customary expressions of solace and rationalization. *The most it can do is to accept the "I" that seeks to think pain, not only think about it.* The suggestion is that thought avoids pain—the pain of empathy, of Levinasian responsibility—by becoming teleological and giving it meaning. Blanchot's most spiritual *pensée* (but the word "spirit" for him has still too activist a connotation), is that we should think without aiming for meaning ("penser sans but") as one dies neutrally, simply ("mourir sans but"). Or, most starkly: "penser: mourir."[77] Yet what responsibility does Blanchot take *explicitly* upon himself?

Blanchot appropriates the moral philosophy of a Jew who has not allowed the Holocaust to turn him against philosophy. With Levinas, Susan Handelman has written, "the witness of the Holocaust now enters the 'reason' of philosophy."[78] Blanchot, however, remains historically unspecific about the disaster. How do we judge a concept of responsibility that does not return to the world but focuses on the self-other relation in the most unmediated way? By shedding the empirical self, Blanchot could be evading the guilt he incurred. In the very name of responsibility, he affirms a "moi sans moi"[79] as the seat of a suffering, that, inexpressive itself (lying, as Wordsworth once said, "too deep for tears"), is yet the basis of all expression, of all writing.

We must question this turn in Blanchot as long as our concept of suffering remains activist, achievement-oriented: the Hegelian tradition, with its "dialectical necessity of fulfillment," prescribes that the negative be avowed, not only endured. Because Blanchot (like Paul de Man) contributed, however rarely, to an atmosphere that made persecution normal, we expect avowal or explicit acknowledgment. Only an *act* of this kind, we believe, can have redemptive or remedial force.

Yet in clarifying the structure of responsibility Blanchot takes a different path. Where we could view his silence as a form of mastering (i.e., evading) the past, he implies over and again that the past cannot be mastered. The patience, suffering, and labor of the negative, which Hegel describes so movingly in his Preface to the *Phenomenology,* has no progressive historical visibility. There is nothing to see except the repetitive sufferance of the self-other relation. Even that "scene" is not passive enough insofar as it becomes manifest, "phenomenal" in the colloquial sense, unable to forgo a need to appear, to be on stage, thus creating our *société du spectacle.*

Blanchot's recessiveness, then, is based on a sustained critique of Hegelian teleology and such contemporary developments as Sartre's philosophy of engagement.[80] Needless to say, Blanchot does not dichotomize worldliness and art, as if the one could only live at the expense of the other. His analysis of language is no more "aestheticizing" than Wittgenstein's. But the issue of subjectivity, of the relation between the self and the collective, is included in his radically moral concern with a fascination played out in literature. The self is "dis-identified" by a force, the Other, that works in and on the self "transdescendentally." The Other, by virtue of its impact on the self, is no longer separate from it. The result is that the Other exerts quite nakedly an invasive, oppressive, even persecutory pressure. Ego is crushed or elided. Thus responsibility becomes the impossible task of achieving an absolutely receptive state, or substituting the Other for myself. (Levinas famously calls it being a "hostage" to the Other; and it reminds a literary reader of the Petrarchan lover's experience of love.)[81] Blanchot characterizes this substitution of a spiritual for the empirical self as a reversal (*renversement*).

He calls it that because it values "the 'I' excluded from mastery and its status as [destituted] subject in the first person" and because time changes direction: "le temps a radicalement changé sens."[82] The double-entendre here, since "sens" also denotes meaning, indicates that meaning itself has changed its sense, for it is no longer archeological or teleological. Time, that is, loses its potentially redemptive aspect; it is not a present extended between meaningful beginning and meaningful end, or a history of disasters in whose aftermath we live, and which gives us importance by that fact. We glimpse a temporal state without such forcible punctuation, and so without the possibility of a *récit*. The reversal, in any case, cannot be the effect of an act of will,[83] for it moves us away from agency, from the world-stage on which human power is displayed and realized. Trying to describe the reversal, Blanchot cannot use the older spiritual vocabulary, and has to say, incongruously, that we "fall prematurely out of the world, out of being."[84] Yet insofar as the "spiritual" self remains in the world, or insofar as we try to understand it in empirical terms, it appears as a modality of the super-ego: self-punishing and even sadomasochistic. It imposes the burden of a responsibility for others which not only exceeds my strength but which I cannot take up, since I am powerless and no longer exist as myself.[85]

Blanchot shows that it is not sufficient to replace an intentionalist or voluntarist terminology by one signaling the opposite. It might be alleged that he substitutes the ecstasy of patience for that of impatience; this, however, would be a simplification, a "jeu sémantique"[86] without a sufficiently transvaluative charge. For whatever one thinks of Blanchot's "transdescendental" analysis, it seems clear enough that he wants to evoke, by "une langue autre," a spirituality that cannot be confused with Christian triumphalism, Western imperialism, or the so-called "spiritual revolution" of fascism or fascistlike movements—of political exaltation in the name of the spirit.[87] Nor is he satisfied with scholarly disciplines—philosophy, history, sociology, art—which "produce" sense in the Hegelian manner, or "institute" meaning, wherever meaning or a positive and accruable knowledge is missing.

The negative labor of evocation—of having to transform rather than abandon spiritual words (including "spirit") tainted by the ecstasy of violence—makes *The Writing of the Disaster* at once a cryptic and a moving book in search of a post-Holocaust spirituality. Thus, by assigning "disaster" to the sphere of "non-savoir," making it fall out of experience (though a Hegelian and historicized idiom always draws it back in), and rejecting the uneasy satisfaction of living "after"—in the aftermath of a great event that still exerts its influence—Blanchot finds an equivalent to Heidegger's placement of words "under erasure." He sensitizes us to how desire, meaning, and expectation invest the most common words—"beginning," "end," "now," "come," "see"—with a pathos strong enough to provoke further disaster.[88]

The issue in Blanchot, then, is principally the seduction of style, or the relation of words to visibility, spirit, power. He does not evolve his theory of art and language by a meditation on the Holocaust, but he is able to join it to that meditation after gaining an understanding of the dynamics—the gravitational system, if you wish—of literary space through his analysis of modernist writing, starting (I simplify) with the quaternity of Hölderlin, Mallarmé, Rilke, and Kafka.[89] I suspect that the influence of Levinas adds itself gradually, as does an increasing awareness of the ideology of the written word in Judaism, and of the Holocaust as an imperative theme.

Imperative, because in the aftermath of the Shoah literary extraversion leads to an impasse. Narrative art, to summarize Sarah Kofman, "uses language as a tool to master the past; it thereby becomes both too reductive and too sovereign to do justice to the ultimate powerlessness of the victims and the void of disaster."[90] *There has to be a rebirth of language out of the spirit of powerless utterance, out of that which could not manifest itself in the camps.* Robert Antelme's note on *The Writing of the Disaster* characterizes Blanchot's style as a "parole désarmé" and adds: "Aurore de la 'faiblesse humaine,' souveraine" (Dawn of a "human weakness" that is sovereign).[91] The activism of the citizen-writer is one thing; the integrity of art—the integrity of literary space—is another, and often harder to bear in its marginality or extreme patience.[92] Both share a deep consistency, however, by way of Blanchot's concept of "refusal," which must safeguard itself, on the one hand, against the world, and, on the other, against any revolution that tries to abolish dissidence.[93]

The reorientation demanded by Blanchot's language, especially in *The Writing of the Disaster*, challenges settled assumptions about the will to power through words. Not everywhere in Blanchot, but certainly in this book, and in his lean if repetitive *anti-récits* (though *L'instant de ma mort* and *La Folie du jour* allow themselves a direct depiction of a "scène primitive"), he devises a post-traumatic style in which the disaster is not clinically or historically specifiable. One can object, of course, that such stylistic "asceticism" is merely another way to entice the reader. At least Blanchot does not "pour old words on new blood." The expression is Lawrence Langer's, and it returns us to Adorno's demand that no word intoned from on high—moral, spiritual, theological—should remain untransformed after the Holocaust.

I want to end with an example of such a transformation. Blanchot alludes at one point to Melville's Bartleby the scrivener, who one day simply gives up his bureaucratic task, and to every question "why?" obstinately repeats, "I prefer not to . . ." A non-consent of this kind, Blanchot writes, "belongs to the infiniteness of patience; no dialectical intervention can take hold of such passivity. We have fallen out of being, an outside where, immobile, proceeding with a slow and even step, destroyed men come and go."[94]

Blanchot in his younger days might have commended Bartleby for the sheer, spiritual strength of refusal. But the image that follows brings in and darkens Heidegger's concept of impassibility (*Gelassenheit*) by evoking the terrible lassitude of those in the concentration camps who had lost all hope, all desire to live, and were named *Muselmänner* ("Muslims"). There is no hint of sacrificial imagery here, no attempt to transform victims into martyrs, no suggestion of a meaningful, death-devoted act. Blanchot's turning away from the logos in its supersessionist pride means a new style that is neither mystical nor psychologistic, and above all without heroic pathos. "Talk," Sarah Kofman writes in *Paroles suffoquées*, thinking of her father murdered in the Holocaust, "Talk one must—without power: without a too powerful, sovereign language mastering the most aporetic situation."[95] "Little by little," Jabès tells us, "I discovered that, however one might disguise it, writing is never a victory over emptiness, but, on the contrary, its exploration through the voiced word."[96] Or: "D'un mot à un mot / vide possible (From one word to the next / Imminent vacuum)."[97]

CHAPTER THREE

Responding to the Infinity between Us

Blanchot Reading Levinas in *L'entretien infini*

Jill Robbins

Between Maurice Blanchot and Emmanuel Levinas, what is there? Friendship and conversation since their meeting at university in the twenties,[1] intertextual links, readable in the late forties, in their "communication" (always also with an absent third) around the conceptual figure of the *il y a*,[2] Levinas's welcoming reception of Blanchot's 1955 *The Space of Literature* and his suggestion that at issue in Blanchot's description of the literary work of art is a kind of speaking that is not ethical but is nonetheless distinct from the totality.[3] Arguably the most decisive "encounter" between the two occurs with Blanchot's *The Infinite Conversation* (*L'entretien infini*), a work which unforgettably registers the reading of Levinas's 1961 *Totality and Infinity*. Published in 1969, *The Infinite Conversation* responds to Levinas's mature philosophy in much the same way as the 1975 "Exercises de la Patience," the kernel of what will become *The Writing of the Disaster*, can be said to respond to Levinas's later philosophy, the 1974 *Otherwise than Being*.

This response is *essentially* response, attentive, waiting. "Responding does not consist in formulating an answer," Blanchot remarks.[4] It is response—even before I hear the call—to the other. Response—or responsibility—to the other that consists in speaking. Of this speech, he says: "It is a matter of holding to it and keeping it going" (*il s'agit de tenir et d'entretenir*) (*IC* 30). Responsibility to words as well, responsibility "to hold to words" (*tenir parole*), in the terms of the title of one of *The Infinite Conversation*'s texts on Levinas. Also, no doubt, responsibility to keep one's word, more like a promise than a constative statement. The question arises: Does one in fact *hold* a conversation, or rather, is one not *held* by it? This question might be reformulated in the terms that Jean-François Lyotard proposes in *The Differend*, namely as a question of obligation. He writes: "The question is to know whether, when one hears something that may resemble a call, if one is held to be held [*si . . . on est tenu d'être tenu*]."[5] One of the merits of this formulation is that it draws attention to the transcendental or quasi-transcendental motif in Levinas's ethical discourse. On a level more originary than the empirical, this discourse is concerned not with *an* ethics, or any particular moral precepts; it is, in Jacques Derrida's phrase, "an Ethics *of* ethics."[6] (Lyotard's formulation is also apt in that it alludes to the enigmatic nonphenomenality of the call, as well as to the constitutive misunderstanding it engenders.)

For the Levinas of *Totality and Infinity*, conversation introduces a rupture in a world in which most relations come back in the end to the self-same. In conversation, "the Same, gathered up in its ipseity [or selfhood] as an 'I,' leaves itself" (*le Même, ramassé dans son ipseité de je, sort de soi*).[7] Part of the challenge of responding to the Levinasian view of conversation lies in its concomitant demand to respect alterity, or otherness, a demand which Blanchot's reading of Levinas registers. In this essay I begin by attending in some detail to Levinas's descriptions in *Totality and Infinity*, marking the places where Blanchot's reading of Levinas takes off, and referring to the decisive readings of Levinas by Derrida and Lyotard as well. I go on to characterize Blanchot's singular inflection of Levinas's ethical thought. In considering the conversation between Blanchot and Levinas, conversation on the possibility of conversation, I hope ultimately to allow another infinite conversation to emerge, concerning the relation between speech and infinity.

According to Levinas, because the self's tendency is invariably assimilative, the habitual economy of the self represses and reduces alterity. This habitual economy involves a *concrete* system of exchanges between a self and a world (this is why it is not something that one would simply want to do away with). Levinas's examples of this concrete economy include the I in *identification, dwelling,* and existing *chez soi.* The I in identification absorbs all alterity into its identity as thinker or possessor, relates to all alterity as if it were finite. In the mode of dwelling, it finds in the world a site (*un lieu*) and a home (*une maison*). For an I which is always autochthonous—indigenous—dwelling is yet another reversion of the alterity of the world to the self-Same. "The *chez soi* [the being at home with oneself] is not a container," Levinas specifies, "but a space in which I can [*je peux*]" (*TI* 37). In being at home with oneself or in sojourning, the I affirms its seemingly limitless grasp: "In a sense everything is in the site, everything is, in the last analysis, at my disposal. . . . Everything is here, everything belongs to me, everything is caught up in advance with the primordial occupying of a site, everything is comprehended [*tout à l'avance est pris . . . , tout est com-pris*]" (*TI* 37). "In the world in which I sojourn, alterity falls under my powers" (*TI* 38).

Identification, dwelling, and existing *chez soi* are, then, the specific "moments" within the habitual economy that the encounter with the other interrupts. The other (whom Levinas also calls the Stranger) "disturbs the being at home with oneself. . . . Over him I have no power [*je ne peux pouvoir*]" (*TI* 39). This phrase could and should also be translated, "Over the other, I have no capacity, ability." This cessation of power and capacity is precisely ethical in Levinas's sense, the putting into question of the self by the presence of the other (*TI* 43). The putting into question of the self here is radical—consciousness put into question, as opposed to a consciousness *of* being put into question, in the words of Levinas's 1963 "Trace of the Other." For such a subject-less self, responsibility is not an ability to respond; it is nothing that the I initiates. It arises precisely from a ruined ability, from an *in*ability.[8] In Levinas's descriptions, the other is said to challenge not just my *pouvoir,* but my *pouvoir de pouvoir* (*TI* 198). Note that this challenge is not in the form of a greater power opposing a lesser one. The face of the other puts me into question at the very level where any particular power could originate.

The face looms up, in Levinas's descriptions, as that which breaks with the horizons of my world. The face (*le visage*) is neither a thing seen, a *visum*, nor a *visée*, an object of intentional consciousness. It is a nakedness, a misery, and an abandonment. (In describing the face, Levinas plays between the words *nu*, "naked"—for the face is without clothing or mask—and *denuée*, "destitute," to which he also gives the technical sense of signifying without attributes or qualities. The face signifies neither with reference to a context nor within the network of referrals that characterize sign systems; it signifies *kath 'auto*, "according to itself"; it signifies—in the terms he uses subsequent to *Totality and Infinity*—as trace.)

To encounter a face is to encounter a mortality, a being exposed to death and alone in its being-unto-death. Exposed to death, the face is exposed to murder as well: it is "face forward [*un être-de-face*] precisely as if it were exposed to some threat at point blank range."[9] The face is defenselessness itself. Yet, somewhat paradoxically within Levinas's account, the face commands me *in* its defenselessness. It orders, "thou shalt not kill" (*TI* 199). In this encounter with the other *by way of an interdiction* my—ultimately murderous—freedom is put into question. This is accomplished as shame, a structure which Levinas likens to an intentionality in reverse (*TI* 84). In the singular possibility of encountering another through an interdiction lies the *im*possibility of killing him or her.

Levinas claims that language, along with generosity, with which it is co-originary, is exceptional within the economy of the Same. Language maintains the radical separation and distance that characterizes the relation to the other, in Levinas's words, "without this distance destroying this relation and without this relation destroying this distance, as would happen with relations within the Same" (*TI* 41). This strange relation is, to use the distinctive Blanchotian syntax that Derrida has identified, relation *without* relation.[10] Relation comprised of an *infinite,* impassable distance, distance *as* approach. Relation to a face whose mode of revelation is *infinitizing*. In *Totality and Infinity* Levinas first introduces the face precisely as what he calls the "deformalization" of the Cartesian idea of infinity. The face is a concrete figure of a thought that thinks more than it can think. Levinas prefers the term "revelation" to the term "disclosure" because revelation implies something that does not come from me.

For Levinas, the language relation to the other does not totalize. It "at the same time spans and does not span the distance [*à la fois, franchit et ne franchit pas la distance*], does not form a totality with the 'other shore'" (*TI* 64). The conversation (*entre-tien*) with the other is, for Levinas, a "conversation that proposes the world. This proposition is held between [*se tient entre*] two points which do not constitute a totality, a system" (*TI* 96). (These are the sentences that Blanchot, as it were, translates. In fact, Levinas uses the term *entretien* much less frequently, preferring *discours* or *langage*.) Language preserves what Levinas calls metaphysical asymmetry, namely, "the radical impossibility of seeing oneself from the outside and in speaking in the same sense of oneself and of the others" (*TI* 53). Because of metaphysical asymmetry, any synoptic or panoramic view of the *entretien* is impossible. Like the encounter with the other, one can only speak of it from *within* the relation. "Language can be spoken," asserts Levinas, "only if the interlocutor is the commencement of his discourse, if, consequently, he remains beyond the system, if he is not *on the same plane as myself*" (*TI* 101). In other words, there is nonreversibility in the relation between myself and the other and there is *in*equality, an inequality more originary than the sense of us as equals.

Like language, generosity suspends the economy of possession and power that is the very way of the Same: "It is in generosity that the world possessed by me, the world open to enjoyment, is apperceived from a point of view independent of the egoist position" (*TI* 75). Speech, the discourse that "gives" thematization, is itself a kind of gift for Levinas: "The world in discourse is no longer what it is in the *chez soi*, where everything is given to me; it is what I give" (*TI* 76). The gift, in the analyses of both Levinas and Derrida, is aneconomic. Because it is outside of any balanced economy of exchange, the gift preserves the inequality and the asymmetry between me and the other. Levinas even writes that the generosity which goes out to the other without return *must* be received in ingratitude (*TI* 349). How to receive such a gift and to affirm it *as* a gift? How to receive it in a way that escapes not only the circle of restitution and recognition, warm thanks and gratitude, but also the bad ingratitude belonging to the economic sphere of the Same?[11]

At the time of the writing of *Totality and Infinity*, the sole phrase in the primordial lexicon is the other's command, "thou shalt not kill." (In essays from the preceding decade, a shortened form of this utterance is sometimes found. The face says "no."[12]) There are several registers of the impossibility of murder that Levinas lets resonate. There is the plain sense that murder is morally abhorrent. Even this plain sense is not so plain. In an interview Levinas glosses "thou shalt not kill" as "thou shalt do *everything* that the other may live."[13] In other words, despite its apparently negative form, there is a positivity in the prohibition. In its enlarged sense, the commandment "thou shalt not kill" refers to the *omission* of any act that could alleviate the other's distress. Similarly, the apparently negative terms with which ethics has been described have a positive sense. For example, in the arrest of the habitual economy, my freedom is converted to service, as Theodore de Boer puts it.[14] The cessation of the gaze in the face of the face has its positive production,

Levinas emphasizes, in generosity and conversation. This emphasis is found in *Totality and Infinity*'s first epiphany of face.

The face which is exposed to my gaze is wholly weakness: "From beneath the countenance it gives itself, all its weakness pierces through and at the same time its mortality, to such an extent that I may wish to liquidate it completely."[15] Note that the temptation of murder is here said to arise not just in the face's manifestation, but in the face's exceeding its own manifestation. Moreover, the face's resistance to murder—its "no"—arises out of weakness, not strength. It is the resistance of what has no resistance. Herein lies the *im*possibility of murder in yet another sense. The face's infinite resistance is one that, as Derrida puts it, "no finite power can restrict."[16] This is why murder is doomed in advance to a certain failure. Murder aims at a face, but it can only kill a being. It thereby misses the other, it misses that which in the other is beyond being.

The conversation with the other, in Levinas's descriptions, is largely empty of content (or prior to content). Because it is primordial, i.e., originary, this language is necessarily prior to language conceived of as a system of signs, and prior to figure as well. That is why, as a paradigm of ethical language, "thou shalt not kill" has something misleading about it. Lyotard notes that "Thou shalt not kill" is not necessarily a categorical prescription. It is more like what he terms "a prescription that there be prescriptions."[17] There is, in other words, something very general and empty about the face's speaking command. Levinas does say that ethical language is interlocutionary; it is invocation, address. It never speaks *about* the other but only *to* him or her. He asserts: "In language the essential is the interpellation, the vocative" (*TI* 69). Interpellation, he writes, is "the imperative of language, as it were" (*TI* 52). One might remark, following Roman Jakobson's functional description of the communication situation, that ethical language is conative, i.e., oriented toward the addressee. This function of language is exemplified by the vocative and the imperative. Both are cases, Jakobson remarks, of which one cannot ask the question, is it true or not?[18] Hence, to put this in grammatical terms, even though these terms (as well as Jakobson's description) would ultimately be incommensurable with the more originary speech that Levinas describes: my relation to the other is always in the vocative, in the imperative, or in the dative (case of the gift).

The very few additional examples of ethical language that Levinas supplies in his later work: "Here I am" (*hineni*); "Après vous, monsieur"; "Bonjour"—

are also very general. They are empty bits of everyday speech in which Levinas glimpses transcendence. The function of these utterances is neither referential nor denotative: they are either conative (oriented toward the addressee), or phatic, that is, contact serving to ascertain that contact is taking place. There is also a resemblance—albeit very general—between what Levinas calls ethical language and the performative dimension of language. Ethical language is not constative or descriptive; it gets something done with respect to the other. For example, "Here I am" (*hineni*) is a quasi-contractual announcement of readiness for service. "Après vous, monsieur," the simple courtesy of ceding one's place to the other, brings into view what Levinas calls "ontological courtesy," a being-for-the-other, a relinquishing of my place in the sun. Finally, the greeting—"bonjour"—is not of the order of knowledge. Think of it as not killing the other. In sum, within this opening conversation, the *fact* of speaking is more important than any content of the conversation.

The texts that Blanchot devotes to Levinas are an elaboration of Levinas's contention that the relation to the other consists in speaking. This seems remarkable in itself, given that Levinas seems intent on not filling his account in. More than an elaboration of this contention, Blanchot's texts are also its exemplification, insofar as he puts his reading of Levinas in the form of three "conversations." This is no doubt a response, and a responsibility, to Levinas's own emphasis that the relation to the other is interlocutionary. One might say, then, that Blanchot does not merely constate the ethical in *The Infinite Conversation;* he performs it. He does this despite the always possible misunderstanding and ingratitude that haunt such an asymmetrical performative.[19]

What Levinas leaves empty in the *entretien,* Blanchot guards as an experience of emptiness. He radicalizes the distinctive features of the already radical Levinasian *entretien:* the non-identity (or "without identity") of the interlocutors, the abyssal distance between them, and the precarious ontological status of the *entretien* as ethical event. In *Totality and Infinity* Levinas had asserted that "language accomplishes a relation such that the terms are not limitrophe within this relation" (*TI* 39). He suggested that in language the terms absolve (or "loosen") themselves from the relation (*TI* 64), thus playing on the etymological sense of *absolvere.* For Blanchot, this is "an absolute relation in the sense that the distance separating us will not be diminished but produced and maintained absolutely in this relation" (*IC* 51). Blanchot demonstrates further how misleading it is even to speak about the two interlocutors as two parties or two fixed poles. Joseph Libertson recalls that as Blanchot himself had put it a decade earlier in *The Space of Literature*, this image of two fixed poles responds "to the crude scheme of two powers."[20] There Blanchot had called it (with reference to thinking of the literary work of art as a suspension between the two poles of reading and writing) a "faulty image." In the case of the Blanchotian *entretien*, such an image would be faulty because it implies two already constituted poles of attraction "between" which speech appears. One should say rather that this originary *entretien* is what constitutes the interlocutors as such.

The *entretien*, as Blanchot elaborates it, does not bridge the gap between interlocutors; it deepens it. "True speech affirms the abyss between myself and the other," he writes (*IC* 63). Because of metaphysical asymmetry there is neither reversibility nor reciprocity in the relation between us. Nor can there be any common ground, recognition, or comprehension. "There is language because there is nothing in common between [them]" (*IC* 55). To the extent that the two interlocutors do arrive at an understanding, it is what Blanchot terms "an accord without accord" (*IC* 215).

The model of conversation here is at a distance from religious and hermeneutic philosophies of dialogue. Indeed, "plural speech" (*parole plurielle*), an important conceptual figure throughout *The Infinite Conversation* (and the title of its first part, in which the Levinas essays are found), is in fact explicitly posed in contradistinction to dialogue: "Rather than dialogue, we shall call it plural speech," which he defines as "the seeking of an affirmation that, though escaping all negation, neither unifies nor allows itself to be unified" (*IC* 215). "Dialogue," he writes, "is founded on the reciprocity of words and the equality of speakers; only two 'I's can establish a relation of dialogue" (*IC* 81). But the Blanchotian *entretien* does not take place between two subjects or selves.

The French verb *entretenir*, Libertson notes, has an intransitive reference. Without the sense of the activity and exchange that is implied in the word "conversation," it suggests for Libertson "the impersonality of a subsistence between, a pure abiding."[21] In Blanchot's unidiomatic usage, *entretenir*, suspended somewhere between *entretenir quelque chose*, "to communicate something," and *s'entretenir*, "to converse, to have a conversation," is without a subject (it is not reflexive) and without an object. It suggests something that stands and holds (itself) between.[22] This is, Blanchot writes, "what there would be between [us] if there were nothing but the word *between*, a pure interval, an empty space all the more empty as it cannot be confused with nothingness" (*IC* 68). The speech of the *entretien* is not present and cannot be understood in terms of presence. Blanchot writes: "What is present in this presence of speech, as soon as it affirms itself, is precisely what never lets itself be seen or attained: something is there that is beyond reach [of the one who says it as much of the one who hears it]. It is between us [*entre nous*], it holds itself between [*cela se tient entre*], and the *entretien* is the approach on the basis of this between [*l'abord à partir de cet entre-deux*], an irreducible distance" (*IC* 212). A certain nonpresence, then, of a speech never quite attained, an encounter with the other that is without meeting, this is an impossible approach. This impossible approach to the other is nothing other than approach *on the basis of* separation: "Attention is the sign of this between-two which brings near while separating [*cet entre-deux qui rapproche en separant*]" (*IC* 213). He also names it "relation of the third kind" and "interruption." At the limit, neither the *entretien* nor the ethical event can be said to take place. Nor do they take *a* place, having always already departed from all place. The conversation—but less than ever can we take for granted that we know what a conversation is—happens *without* happening. It happens "between us"—but we can no longer take for granted this "between." It is what Blanchot calls "the infinity between us" (*IC* 77)—but who is "us"?

"Plural speech" in Blanchot responds to an exigency to which Levinas had also responded in the late forties. In *Time and the Other*, Levinas had sought "a pluralism that does not merge into a unity" (*TO*, 42). He had sought thereby to break with Parmenides, i.e., a thought which thinks together Being and the One. Subsequently in *Totality and Infinity*, Levinas emphasized that plurality is not numerical: "The other and I do not form a number. The collectivity in which I say 'you' or 'we' is not a plural of the I. I, you—these are not individuals of a common concept. Neither possession nor the unity of number nor the unity of concepts link me to the Stranger" (*TI* 39). Blanchot also thinks plural speech as a break from Parmenides, a thinking of the multiple in which "the One is not the ultimate horizon . . . any more than is Being" (*IC* 67). To some extent, what was in Levinas originary pluralism becomes in Blanchot "plural speech."

When Blanchot first broaches "plural speech" in the opening pages of *The Infinite Conversation*, it is as a question and a search:

> How to speak so that speech is essentially plural? How can the search for plural speech be affirmed, a search no longer founded upon equality and inequality, nor upon predominance and subordination, nor upon mutual reciprocity, but

upon disymmetry and irreversibility, in such a manner that, between two instances of speech [*entre deux paroles*], a relation of infinity would always be
involved as the movement of signification itself? Or again how to write in such a
way that the continuity of the movement of writing might let interruption as
meaning, and rupture as form, intervene fundamentally? (*IC* 8)

The wording of Blanchot's questions suggests an urgency, even an obligation,
in the name of ethical asymmetry. But the quasi-rhetorical questions also
acknowledge that plural speech is not necessarily something that can be accomplished. More of a task than a given, it may require the invention of
another language altogether. Here Blanchot is close to the later Levinas, who,
in the 1974 *Otherwise than Being*, will seek to pass over discursively to what is
other than being, all the while acknowledging that his effort always risks falling
into a being otherwise, i.e., into a modality of being.

What differentiates Blanchot from Levinas is the literary specificity of "plural speech." Blanchot's third question ("How to write . . . ?"), rendered in
appositive syntax to the first ("How to speak . . . ?"), draws attention to the fact
that "plural speech" is closer to writing than speech. Similarly, at the close of
part 1, he contrasts the speech of totality and unity (speech of dialogue, speech
of the universe) to "the speech of writing," which "bears a relation of infinity
and strangeness" (*IC* 78). "Dialogue is plane geometry"; "plural speech" is
Riemannian, i.e., nonlinear (*IC* 81). "A change such that to speak (to write) is
to cease thinking solely with a view to unity" (*IC* 77). The relation of the third
kind is nothing other than "the experience of language, writing" (*IC* 73).

These conceptual developments are inseparable from *The Infinite Conversation*'s formal gestures. Part 1 ("Plural Speech") contains the three texts on
Levinas, texts written in dialogue form: "Knowledge of the Unknown," "Keeping to Words" (*Tenir parole*), "The Relation of the Third Kind." A fourth text,
entitled "Interruption," not in dialogue form, and where Levinas is not explicitly at issue, deepens a critical questioning of Levinas's ethical thought that
commences in the second text. (Note that many of the texts in *The Infinite
Conversation* were originally published during the decade 1959–1969 in *La
Nouvelle Revue Française*. Blanchot made significant revisions and added new
material when he published the book in 1969.)

Part 1 is framed by an untitled "dialogue" (initially published in 1966 in *La
Nouvelle Revue Française* under the title "Entretien infini"). Like many pieces
in the 1962 *L'attente oubli*, this is a theoretical text in the form of a dialogue, a

fragmentary text which juxtaposes narration and dialogue. The conversation occurs between two unnamed interlocutors, men, aging. One is robust looking, both are weary, although "the weariness common to both of them does not bring them together" (*IC* xiii). Nonetheless, fatigue is the condition of their *entretien*: "if I took the liberty of calling you, it was because of this weariness. . . . it keeps us speaking" (*IC* xiv–xv).

> ± ± "If you were not there, I believe I could not bear the weariness."—"And yet I also contribute to it."—"That is true, you weary me very much, but precisely very much within human limits. Nonetheless, the danger is not averted: when you are there, I still hold on. . . ."
>   . . . He can no longer distinguish between thought and weariness. . . .
>   Thinking weary. (*IC* xix)

While the dialogue portions of the text are separated by dashes and quotation marks, the fragments themselves are separated by the double plus or minus sign ± ±. This binomial, which according to Mike Holland announces the fragmentation of both author and book, marks "a repeated coming full circle, which is nothing other then the author-subject turning back upon himself, separating himself from himself, treating himself as another."[23] Because of its fragmentary character, we cannot even be sure if Blanchot's book *is* a book. It is, rather, in the terms of the title of part 3, "The Absence of the Book." In an introductory note to *The Infinite Conversation*, Blanchot explains that a book always indicates "an order that submits to unity" (*IC* xii).[24]

Thus plural speaking frames plural speaking in *The Infinite Conversation*. But the framing is inexact. The third conversation on Levinas also introduces an I who listens in on the two voices: "I listen in turn to these two voices, being neither close to the one, nor close to the other; being, nevertheless, one of them and being the other only insofar as I am not myself—and thus, from the one to the other, interrupting myself" (*IC* 72). Here, the frame around part 1 closes within part 1, bisecting it.[25] This is the place in *The Infinite Conversation* at which the critical questioning of Levinas gains considerable momentum. Blanchot will refer, in "Interruption," to "an alterity which holds in the name of the neutral" (*alterité qui se tient sous la nomination du neutre*) (*IC* 77). The ensuing polyphony of Blanchot's text—in which all the parts of the work converse with each other—contribute to an equivocality in isolating any of its argumentative threads. "Who speaks?" would be the operative question here.[26] Suffice it to say that with "plural speech" Blanchot brings Levinas's language relation to the other into literature and literary theory. This is a considerable achievement in that literary criticism would ordinarily be derivative upon Levinas's more originary questioning, part of a regional ontology. Blanchot translates Levinas, in that sense.

A distinctive feature of Blanchot's reading of Levinas is his emphasis on *im*possibility as that which renders alterity legible. In "How to Discover the Obscure?" (the place in *The Infinite Conversation* at which Blanchot first secures access to the Levinasian problematic of *Autrui*) Blanchot writes: "The impossible is not there to make thought capitulate but in order to allow it to announce itself according to a measure other than that of power. What would that other measure be? Precisely the measure *of* the other" (*IC* 43). The thought of the impossible for Blanchot is not just a *thought* of the impossible, a thought that would try to master the impossible and would find it impossible to think. It is the thought *of* the impossible, proper to it, "a kind of reserve in thought itself, a thought not allowing itself to be thought in the mode of appropriative comprehension" (*IC* 43). The conceptual figure of impossibility, already central to Blanchot since *The Space of Literature*, with regard to my relation to my own death, would seem to take on, in *The Infinite Conversation,* an ethical resonance.

Impossibility in Blanchot may be understood precisely as a way of getting beyond possibility, of getting beyond what Heidegger in section 31 of *Being and Time* calls *Dasein*'s *Seinkönnen,* being-possible. Such a critical contestation of Heidegger was also apparent in Levinas's account when he argued that in the face of the face I no longer can (*je ne peux pouvoir*). In "How to Discover the Obscure?" Blanchot asks if there is not in Heidegger's account an always possible slippage between possibility as capacity (*pouvoir*) and possibility as force or power (*puissance*) (*IC* 42). The (rhetorical) question is answered in the affirmative, even though such a question would be problematic in Heideggerian terms. "Power is latent in possibility," Blanchot asserts (*IC* 42).[27]

For this reason, any conversation with the other which would maintain the other's alterity must begin where possibility leaves off, and where power turns into impossibility. It must dispense with understanding, an essential mode of possibility in Heidegger's account (discussed in the subsequent section 32, as the hermeneutic circle). Thus for Blanchot the following exigency announces itself: to speak without power, what he calls *parler sans pouvoir.* This phrase also means to speak without the power, to speak without ability (to speak). The exigency is to speak without possibility, to speak out of *im*possibility and,

and in so doing to speak an impossible speech.[28] Ultimately, in Blanchot, responding *to* the impossible is nothing other than ethics.

In Blanchot's reading, the other, who speaks "at the level of weakness and destitution" (*IC* 63), speaks infinity: "When he speaks to me, he speaks to me by way of the infinite distance he is from me, his speech announces precisely this infinite" (*IC* 56). In the original sequence of texts published in *La Nouvelle Revue Française*, the 1962 essay on Robert Antelme, "The Indestructible," is in the place of "Relation of the Third Kind." The previous sequence made it seem as if Antelme's survivor narrative, which Blanchot calls "the reserved speech of *Autrui*," "a truly infinite speech" (*IC* 135), *were* the (contentless) speech of the infinite. Mike Holland suggests that to revert these fragmentary texts to their previous publication venues may be an exacting response to fragmentation in Blanchot."[29] In any case, such a procedure shows the way in which Blanchot's text may be said to differ from itself.

The relation between primordial speech and infinity also comes into view when the temptation of murder becomes the impossibility of murder. Speech occurs precisely on the level where killing is avoided. Lest we mistake such a speech as either irenic or hermeneutical, Blanchot underscores that this founding conversation is not simply nonviolent: "In this situation, either to speak or to kill, speech does not consist in speaking but first of all in maintaining the movement of this either/or. It is what founds the alternative. To speak is always to speak from out of this interval *between* speech and violence" (*IC* 62). In facing the other, the I, in Blanchot's reading, "comes under the command—speech or death" (*IC* 61).

Are Blanchot and Levinas conversing? Blanchot does indeed "translate" what Levinas calls the *entretien,* and in the course of this translation, he makes it very much his own: "Now it is to this hiatus and to this strangeness, to the infinity between us, that the interruption in language responds, the interruption that introduces waiting" (*IC* 73). Blanchot sets in motion a conversation that is unclosed-off and interminable, infinite in that sense. But in Blanchot's singular translation, in the formal polyphony of plural voices, something that was crucial in Levinas's account drops out: the *concrete* welcome of the other's face. The mobility of face, as expression and approach, seems frozen. The opaqueness of the encounter is emphasized at the expense of the way in which it obligates. Because of the absence of the violent imposition of a commandment, the positivity of the "thou shalt not kill" as it was posed in Levinas seems also absent.

Of course, if I say that a conversation between the two is not in the end possible, and does not take place, am I not just confirming what I have said about impossibility and the ethical? If ultimately Blanchot's response to Levinas's gift amounts to an ingratitude—inasmuch as he asserts that the relation with the other is a "neutral" relation (*IC* 73) or that "*autrui* is a name that is essentially neutral" (*IC* 72)—does this not confirm the asymmetry that obtains between giver and receiver? Is not the impossibility of receiving Levinas's gift something that every response to Levinas (including those by Derrida and Lyotard) must negotiate? In other words, does not Blanchot succeed in translating the *entretien* insofar as he fails? Perhaps. But were Blanchot not so much his own other (in Levinasian terms), another infinite conversation between the two might have emerged. Levinas writes in *Totality and Infinity:* "The alterity of the I that takes itself for another may strike the imagination of the poet precisely because it is but the play of the Same" (*TI,* 37). In *The Infinite Conversation* Blanchot is as it were the poet who thinks poetry can do the job of the ethical in responding to the impossible. (Such is the explicit extended argument of "How to Discover the Obscure?") Levinas simply does not think so. Whatever be the limitations of Levinas's rejection of poetry and despite the literary dimensions of his own ethical discourse—dimensions that Blanchot precisely helps to bring out—Blanchot's conversation may be nontotalizing, but it is still not yet ethical in Levinasian terms.

CHAPTER FOUR

Two Sirens Singing

Literature as Contestation in Maurice Blanchot
and Theodor W. Adorno

Vivian Liska

How deeply can literature involve itself in the world, in history, politics, and culture, before it loses its own voice, its space and specificity? How far can it retreat within itself before it turns into acquiescence with things as they are? The space Maurice Blanchot assigns to literature can be situated at an equal distance from an affirmation of the world and its established powers on the one hand, and from a Sartrian understanding of *littérature engagée* on the other. Theodor W. Adorno, while usually associated with an opposing school of thought, locates literature in a similar topography. Like Blanchot, he rejects the idea of literature as an embellishment of reality as well as Sartre's injunction for an explicitly political literary practice. But how far are Adorno's and Blanchot's views of literature from each other?

Extreme Contemporaries

Blanchot and Adorno were, both individually and in relation to each other, "extreme contemporaries."[1] They witnessed the major historical catastrophes of the mid–twentieth century in an almost complementary constellation of proximity and distance. While the French author of poetic prose and former

publicist of right-wing feuilletons retreated from the political arena and remained a silent bystander in Nazi-occupied France, the Jewish refugee and
Marxist sociologist fled into American exile and registered from afar the moral
bankruptcy and self-destruction of European civilization. In spite of their
different backgrounds, intellectual traditions, and ideological positions, they
were, at crucial moments, affected by the same events and developed their
theoretical work around a similar canon of authors.[2] Although they articulated
divergent views on the origin and role of art in modernity and became key
figures in the elaboration of theoretical paradigms often considered to be
incompatible, their reflections on literature and its relation to the world and
the larger domain of culture converge on many points. They wrote in very
different, yet equally complex styles against the use of language as a tool of
mastery and shared an understanding of literature that focuses on its power
to question the monopoly of reality as a measure for human possibilities.
Blanchot's opposition against modes of thinking and writing that limit the
deployment of the imaginary, and Adorno's disillusionment with the consequences of the Enlightenment meet in a similar rejection of the tyranny of
instrumental reason, exclusionary logic, and homogenizing abstraction. Both
turned from comparable perspectives against unifying and totalizing modes of
representation and insisted that it is only as an autonomous realm that literature can contest "that which is."[3] The importance accorded in the last decades
to the inherent proximity of literature to the nonidentical, the incomplete, and
the negative, as well as the theoretical construction of a modernist poetics of
fragmentation, interruption, and discontinuity, owe much to both Blanchot
and Adorno. Yet their names are rarely to be found on the same page and it is
only recently, in the specific context of reflections on the literary implications
of historical disaster, that they are occasionally considered in relation to each
other.[4] The critical works of both Blanchot and Adorno reveal continuities and
differences between their more general views of the relationship between literature and reality, and their statements about literature "after Auschwitz."
In tracing and juxtaposing these constellations in the work of both writers
through the lens of their respective readings of a single episode in Homer's
Odyssey one can devise an imaginary dialogue, a potential *entretien infini*.

What the Sirens Know

The Homeric episode of Odysseus's encounter with the Sirens assumes a
crucial role in Blanchot's *Le Livre à venir*,[5] his first major collection of literary

essays in the postwar years, as well as in Adorno's *Dialektik der Aufklärung,*[6] written with Max Horkheimer in the last years of the war. Blanchot wrote what would become the opening chapter of *Le Livre à venir* in the early fifties,[7] at a time when he had long withdrawn from the political arena into creative solitude and had begun to give shape to the "space of literature," which would become his most influential achievement. Adorno compared the conditions in which he and Horkheimer wrote *Dialectic of Enlightenment* to those of isolated, stranded navigators sending out a bottle-message addressed to an imaginary witness who would keep their melancholic missive from drowning (*DA* 273). For both Adorno and Blanchot the song of the Sirens figures as a call from an other shore, a deadly and enticing *promesse de bonheur* arising from another time, from another place.

The titles of the two texts are a first indication of the divergence between their respective concerns. The heading of Blanchot's chapter "The Song of the Sirens,"[8] which emphasizes the voices of seduction, initiates a poetic speculation about the genesis and ontology of literature. The title of Adorno's first excursus of *Dialectic of Enlightenment,* "Odysseus or Myth and Enlightenment,"[9] focuses instead on Homer's hero and introduces the book's central thesis, a cultural critique of modernity embedded in an all-encompassing philosophy of history. At a first glance, the two readings of the Homeric episode seem incommensurable. While Blanchot focuses entirely on the literary experience, Adorno reflects on the evolution and role of literature in a wider analysis of the developments of Western culture leading up to the rise of fascism and the catastrophe of World War II. These two highly idiosyncratic readings of Homer's canonical scene capture the essence of Blanchot's and Adorno's respective approaches to literature in those years and reveal in the most compact form the proximity of their positions as well as the challenge that they present to each other.

What inspired both authors to project their reflections about literature onto the narrative of Odysseus' sailing past the Sirens lies in the episode's self-reflexive dimension, which foreshadows many aspects of a modernist concept of literature. The situation in which a cunning, worldly hero is exposed to voices coming from elsewhere stages literature as an encounter with an alterity that potentially disrupts the modern understanding of identity, temporality, and language. Adorno and Blanchot read the challenge of the Sirens' song as a threat to Odysseus, the powerful, autonomous male who masters what stands in his way, who integrates that which is disparate into a unity, and who subjects everything to his will. For both, the enticing voices of the Sirens belong to a realm outside of the linear, progressive, and homogeneous time of history and introduce an alternative, mythical temporality into the epic continuity of the *Odyssey*. Above all, for both, the immediacy of the Sirens' song undermines the representational function of words and gives voice to a language beyond use and communication that simultaneously evokes the purposelessness of literature and the dangerous transformative power of its seduction.

The mighty Odysseus, who has triumphed over many obstacles and has survived many dangers, risks being lured by the beauty of the Sirens' song into a realm that would dissolve his selfhood, his position of strength and mastery. In tying himself to the mast, he undoes the Sirens' irresistibility, but the price he pays for his survival and the continuation of his journey homewards is the limitation of the power exerted by the song of the Sirens. When the Sirens, in the Twelfth Book of the *Odyssey*, sing to Odysseus: "Come this way," they initiate a primal scene of literature and possibly the first *mise en abîme* in its tradition. It has often been noticed that the content of the Sirens' song is nothing but the promise of a song, and that what they promise to sing is the *Odyssey* itself. We learn from the Sirens that the one who hears their song will "be pleased and know more than ever he did. For we know everything that the Argives and Trojans did and suffered in wide Troy through the gods' despite. Over all the generous earth we know everything that happens."[10] Hidden in the description of the Sirens' song one can read the poet's praise of the power of his own verses. Taking the Sirens at their word, we learn that the attraction of their song lies not only in the beauty of their voices but in the knowledge they impart. Like the invitation offered by literature and by the *Odyssey* itself, their song promises to join and confront the hero's own experiences with "everything that happens." It thereby both singles out and relativizes the perspective of the individual, and embeds it in a larger web of worldly connections. The Sirens' "double" knowledge refers to the oldest functions attributed to literature: In promising that Odysseus will "be *pleased* and *know* more than ever he did" the Sirens evoke the age-old claim of literature to combine *docere* and *delectare*. In bringing together the individual and the world in two distinct, paratactical expressions, they describe a knowledge that both joins and keeps apart the particular and the universal, establishing the space in which literature traditionally moves. But we are warned that the Sirens are not to be trusted; the deadly threat hidden in their voices could belie this tranquil promise. Their very song undermines that which they sing about, and thus the episode invites the projection of a more specifically modern understanding of literature.

The complex structure implied in the song's promise of a coming narration of past events embedded in the very narration of these events evokes a disrupted, nonlinear temporality.[11] Blanchot and Adorno hear in the Sirens' song a call that interrupts the hero's journey home, the path to stability and selfhood, through the encounter with a sublime Other. They read the hero's resistance against it as the self-imposed limitation on the subject's openness to hear this foreign voice and be touched and transformed by it. For both, the *Odyssey* is itself the result of the disempowered magic of the mythical Sirens' song, which, following Odysseus's resistance, loses its unmediated lure and turns into an epic narrative. This narrative no longer carries the seductive force of immediacy inherent in the original song, but it contains traces of that song in the form of reminiscences of a force that exerts a seductive and threatening power to transform anyone who is caught in its magnetic attraction. The encounter with the Sirens entices and instructs, but the one who truly exposes himself to their song is no longer the same as before the experience, just as the song itself does not remain unchanged. This double metamorphic power of the encounter attracts both Blanchot and Adorno to the Sirens' song and turns their readings, which radically reshape the Homeric original, into powerfully seductive episodes in the history of modern thought.

Contesting Odysseus

Adorno and Blanchot read Odysseus's encounter with the Sirens as a primal battle between a powerful, worldly instance of mastery, identity, and unity, on the one hand, and a disruptive, foreign, and ineffable force on the other. Blanchot speaks of "a metaphysical drama" or "struggle" (*LV* 15) between Odysseus and the Sirens, in which the former will "remain unbeatable as long as he keeps the limit and the interval between the real and the imaginary, which the Sirens precisely invite him to bridge" (*LV* 16). In a similar vein, Adorno's reading targets the coercion exerted by Odysseus as he resists the Sirens' lure and keeps their respective realms apart: "The separation of the two domains leaves both impaired" (*DA* 42). Both Blanchot and Adorno project their understanding of literature as a contestation of this division, which Odysseus's cunning self-protection against the allurement of the Sirens affirms and consolidates. But, while Adorno devises literature as an alternative way of escaping and therefore of overcoming their mythical song, Blanchot rescues its power and turns it into the secret source and magnet of the literary experience.

Unlike Blanchot's poetic reading of the episode, Adorno's interpretation is set in an explicitly conceptual framework. The central claim in his reading of the Sirens' episode states that the Homeric epic already knows "the right theory,"[12] the dialectic of enlightenment, according to which "myth is already enlightenment and enlightenment reverts to myth" (*DA* 6). That "the fully enlightened earth radiates disaster triumphant" (*DA* 9) is the dark and global diagnosis of *Dialectic of Enlightenment*. Far from bringing freedom, sovereignty, and emancipation, modernity and progress have turned out to be a myth, and are themselves exerting the repressive power of mythical forces. Adorno sees in Odysseus's encounter with the Sirens an allegorical origin and an illustration of this dialectic. The Homeric hero is, for Adorno, an early embodiment of modern man, the first bourgeois, who enacts the crucial movement of the dialectic of enlightenment, the transformation of progressive, rational disenchantment into oppressive and barbaric myth. In the process of overcoming the natural and supernatural forces, he has become "hard and strong" (*DA* 54) and has turned into the self-identical, unified subject that will be the central target of Adorno's critique. Odysseus's act of tying himself to the mast, his resistance against the Sirens, only seemingly disempowers the dark forces of myth. Instead of freeing himself from their lure, his self-limitation dialectically reinstates and confirms their fatal power. Odysseus is, for Adorno, the master and the ultimate "oppressor" (*DA* 41) who prefigures a civilization of terror and dominion. His trick, which allows him to enjoy the Sirens' song while resisting its seduction, embodies the cowardly self-protection of the bourgeois in his encounters with the "nonidentical." Tied to the mast, he hears the song, but "what he hears remains, for him, without consequence" (*DA* 40). Just like his other adventures, his triumph over the Sirens only leads to a further hardening and strengthening of his shielded self and to the tyranny of a world dominated by the tools that led to his victory.

For Blanchot, too, Odysseus is his own prisoner, who wants to experience the pleasure of the Sirens' song without risk. Like Adorno, Blanchot views Odysseus as a man of mediocrity who knows nothing but the light and order of the day and who tries to master or exclude that which threatens this world of sameness, stasis, and control. In his critique of Odysseus's cunning, Blanchot goes even further than Adorno: He speaks of the obstinacy, cowardice, and wiliness of the Homeric hero, of the "perfidious path he took" (*LV* 11), and calls him a "decadent Greek" who "took no risks but admired the Sirens with unemotional, calculated satisfaction" (ibid.). He condemns Odysseus's "rational stubbornness" (ibid.) with which he seemingly limits his own powers. But the strength of his self-disciplining will results in the coldness and calculation of a strategy that generates an even more total "universal empire" (*LV* 16) of which he is the unmoved and unshakable master. Blanchot calls Odysseus a man "who is deaf because he hears" (*LV* 11), because all he hears in the Sirens' song is that which links it to the world, because he doesn't hear the murmuring silence that lies at the source of the song's enchantment and resonates within it without expression or meaning. It is this deaf hearing, which, in Blanchot's reading, actually disenchants the Sirens. By making their song present, by turning the Sirens into "real girls" (ibid.), into creatures of the world, he divests them of their power.

Both Blanchot and Adorno see in the means by which Odysseus protects himself and his men from the Sirens' song a foreboding of the dominion of technology[13] and its fateful subjugation of the imaginary, the disparate and the nonidentical. Adorno calls Odysseus the "technically enlightened man" (*DA* 66), who, in tying himself to the mast, participates in the perpetuation of the ruling powers and impoverishes his capacities to devise alternatives. Blanchot condemns Odysseus's reliance on the technical tools of his protection in similar terms when he deplores his triumph over the Sirens as a victory of the "power of technology which always presumes to play without peril with the powers of the imaginary" (*LV* 11).[14] Although Adorno is concerned with the harmful effects of technology on the *world* while Blanchot explicitly situates them in the realm of the *imaginary,* Adorno too considers the "technical easing of life" as a repressive limitation that causes "the *imagination* to wither" (*DA* 42, my emphasis). Both Blanchot and Adorno invoke the threat that the modern reliance on technology presents to the powers of devising "that which is not," but their statements also reveal a crucial difference: While for Adorno, the imagination actually fades under the dominion of technology, Blanchot suggests that the technological triumph over the powers of the imaginary is only a *presumption,* an illusion of mastery. He thereby concedes to the imaginary, and with it to the space of literature, a greater resilience than Adorno, but it seems that the price he is ready to pay for this resilience is the world itself.

Singing the Sirens

While Blanchot and Adorno see Odysseus in a very similar light, they assign a different origin, power, and effectiveness to the Sirens. For Blanchot, they give voice to the imaginary, which cannot be subjected to the purposes of worldly concerns; for Adorno they embody the return of a repressed, natural, and manifold "nonidentical" other. In spite of these differences, the threat that they present to Odysseus is comparable. For Adorno as well as for Blanchot, the Sirens' song is the ultimate challenge to the obstinacy and aspired unity of the dominated and dominating subject embodied by Odysseus. In Adorno's reading the Sirens stand for everything the Western individual had to exclude and repress, "until the self, the identical, purposeful, male character was created" (*DA* 40). The Sirens' allurement originates in the "multitudinous," in "digression and dissolution" (*DA* 54),[15] in a plurality that Odysseus fatefully resists and leaves behind him as he sails beyond the reach of their song.[16] The seduction of this song derives its power from the reminiscences of a distant past that it awakens. Its beauty and knowledge belong to an ominous and enticing bygone age: The Sirens' "allurement is that of losing oneself in the past" (*DA* 39).[17] Luring the listener back in time, their song simultaneously carries within it the expectation of a future happiness, in which the self and that which it overcame and forgot will be reconciled. What lies in between the repressed past and this utopian future is the disaster of modernity inaugurated by Odysseus's failed encounter with the Sirens. The attraction Adorno's own song has exerted for decades is based on this simultaneity of one of the darkest diagnoses of human history to date and the messianic promise of a total and universal happiness. Between the primeval past and messianic redemption stands Odysseus, who, tied to the mast, subjugates his own drives and the forces of nature to his will, at once perpetrator and victim of the civilization that would ultimately lead to the catastrophe that Adorno witnessed as he was writing these pages.

Paradoxically, Adorno describes the linear, progressive temporal schema underlying his own description of the becoming of the modern self as a necessary, but nevertheless questionable achievement of the man of reason embodied by Odysseus. For Adorno, Odysseus projects a controlling human order onto a mythical, directionless time. The radical division that Odysseus thereby introduces between his present and his "former" self causes the repressive denial of the nonidentical. The threefold temporal schema is intended to free the present moment from the power of the past by "referring that power behind the absolute barrier of the unrepeatable and by putting it into the service of the present as disposable knowledge" (ibid.). This move allows Odysseus to separate himself from a former mode of being, which he then excludes and represses in order to strengthen the unity and coherence of his present identity. Although Adorno is critical of this exclusion, his own alternative remains caught in a similar temporality, which allocates a fixed, "controllable" position to the Sirens. They belong to an onto-phylogenetic past that contains not only an "irresistible promise of pleasure" (ibid.) while their song is heard, but, beyond that, carries the premonition of a "complete, universal and undivided happiness" (*DA* 65) in the future, a utopian dream that Adorno blames Odysseus for renouncing for the sake of his survival. The entire here-and-now falls out of this parenthesis as a nexus of blindness and guilt (*Verblendungszusammenhang*) that is revealed and unsettled in the encounter with the Sirens. It remains to be seen what, in the prospect of such totalities, can be conceded to the Sirens, to "multiplicity, digression and dissolution" and to the actual power of their song.

For Blanchot, the Sirens have a comparably disruptive effect on the world embodied by Odysseus. However, their encounter doesn't point at a future reconciliation of the identical with the nonidentical: it is, for Blanchot, the experience of alterity itself. The difference between these two visions is particularly revealing. For Adorno the attraction of the Sirens' song consists of the traces of a past that the self had to leave behind in the course of becoming the enlightened self. In shedding this former, more "natural" being, man has alienated himself. This process is accompanied by an ever recurrent nostalgia for a state predating his alienation. What Odysseus should have gained from his encounter with the Sirens is the insight and knowledge (*Erkenntnis*) of his own *aliénation*. Blanchot, on the other hand, sees the encounter with the Sirens as the very experience of *étrangeté*, of the unfamiliar as such, of that which, by definition, cannot be an object of knowledge. Unlike *aliénation*, the notion of *étrangeté* remains open for the unexpected and undoes the *telos* devised by Adorno. It must be added that although the substitution of the notion of *étrangeté* for *aliénation* is central to Blanchot's thought, the difference between Adorno's and Blanchot's position is nevertheless, in this respect, smaller than it seems: While for Hegel or Marx alienation is, in Françoise Collin's terms, a "becoming other that postulates a self,"[18] Adorno insists, not unlike Blanchot, on the primacy of the nonidentical and considers modern man as alienated *into* rather than *from* identity and selfhood.

For Blanchot, the song of the Sirens is itself flawed and unsatisfactory, and even if, in line with Adorno's thinking, it might point to a future place from which "real happiness" springs, that place is not a utopian fulfillment, but a happiness that is the song itself as an invitation to an infinite journey in that direction. The power of the Sirens' song is this promise and the insatiable desire of the encounter itself. The fatal danger of the Sirens' allurement is precisely that it awakens "hope and desire for a sublime beyond which, in fact, is only a desert . . . where silence, like noise, burns . . . all access to the song" (*LV* 10). This elsewhere is itself a nowhere, a void; to arrive there means death, and the luring song of the Sirens is the call coming from this void. As with the place, the time revealing itself in the encounter with the Sirens is a non-time; it is neither, as for Adorno, the luring call of "losing oneself in the past" nor a better future that is yet to come, and it is definitely not a here-and-now. It is also neither eternity nor entirely outside of time—just as little as the other place is a beyond. It is, instead, a time without a fixed point and without direction, in constant motion, continuously starting anew and incessantly repeating itself, a "fascinating simultaneity" (*LV* 22) in the course of which reality glides into the imaginary, "gradually but also in no time" (ibid.), turning everything into language and ultimately disappearing in it. What Adorno would call the mythical prehistory that Odysseus tries to master through imposing a fixed order on time turns in Blanchot's reading into the "*other* time" (*LV* 16), the time of metamorphoses toward which literature moves. Blanchot enters the circular temporality of myth that embroils the time of a narrative into it, leaving nothing the way it was, and changing nothing either. In order to narrate the encounter with the Sirens, this encounter must have already taken place, because it is only in this encounter that the capacity to speak and narrate originates, yet the encounter takes place only in the narrated imaginary itself. In this entwinement, reality and the imaginary fold in upon each other, undoing their distinction as they head toward a *dehors* that knows neither an interior space nor one that would oppose it.

Blanchot has two explanations for the origin of the flaw in the Sirens' song. For some, their song was "at any rate foreign to man; almost inaudible, capable of granting him the utmost pleasure consisting in a fall which he cannot realize in normal, everyday life";[19] for others it was "a more mysterious charm, in that the Sirens' song reproduced the ordinary song of humans. There was something marvelous and hidden in this real song, this common, simple, quotidian song, and they must have suddenly recognized this when it was sung unnaturally by foreign and probably imaginary powers: the abysmal song which, once heard, opened up an abyss in every word and very much enticed one to disappear in it" (*LV* 9). In this second, more mysterious explanation, the Sirens are not, as in the first, something completely other, and their allurement does not fall out of normal, everyday life. The seduction of their song doesn't invite the listener to "fall," to momentarily lose control and mastery over himself and then stand up again, rejoining the order of the day. Instead, the encounter opens up "an abyss in every word," it destabilizes the very foundations of reality from within, and it exerts a magnetic attraction tempting one to disappear in it forever. The claim of this second explanation is much more radical, but, unlike the temptation of "falling," the abyss it opens up occurs not in *life*, but in the *word*, and that which disappears in it may very well be the world itself. But, one wonders in the prospect of such a void, what is it that remains of the Sirens' addressee, what is left to seduce, to challenge, to undo?

The Double Bind

Tied to the mast, Odysseus can enjoy the Sirens' song without falling prey to their fatal allurement: What for Odysseus, and for generations of readers of the *Odyssey*, seemed like a perfect solution for an otherwise unresolvable dilemma becomes for Adorno and Blanchot the closure of the cunning, instrumental mind. Adorno calls Odysseus's encounter "happy-unsuccessful" (*glücklich-missglückt*) (*DA* 67), but the reverse would be truer: Odysseus restrains his pleasure and wriggles in his ropes, but is "successful" in his effort to survive. There is certainly little happiness to be felt in Adorno's reading of the episode. For him, Odysseus is wrong, no matter what he does: By tying himself to the mast, he masters the "archaic superior power of the song" (*DA* 66), but instead of gaining freedom he thereby even affirms and perpetuates his own subjugation. It would, in Adorno's eyes, of course also be wrong if he had not done so, if he had followed the Sirens' call and let himself dissolve in the nonidentical.[20] In Irving Wohlfarth's words, it is "either sheer survival for the sake of the future homecoming or blissful abandonment to the seduction of the present moment, which is tantamount to regressive self-surrender."[21] In the face of this hopeless choice between constraining self-assertion and fatal self-loss, the question of an alternative arises.

At a theoretical level, Adorno's rather vague alternative consists of a "remembrance of nature in the subject" (*Eingedenken der Natur im Subjekt*), thanks to which survival would no longer have to be bought at the price of a fully lived life.[22] His attempt to conceive of such an alternative on the level of the Homeric plot is hardly satisfactory. What other possibilities does Adorno hold out as a prospect for the Homeric hero? "Odysseus," he writes, "does not try to take another route that would enable him to avoid sailing past the Sirens. And he does not try to trust the superiority of his knowledge and to listen freely to the temptresses, imagining that his freedom will be protection enough" (*DA* 66). Does Adorno really propose these ways out? To avoid the exposure to the song in the first place, and sail home, no matter by which route? This would take place, however, at the price of the *Odyssey.* Or does he think Odysseus should approach the Sirens, but armored with the self-confidence of freedom, an option which may be read as Adorno's idea of a finally "truly successful enlightenment"? In both cases, Odysseus would remain equally inaccessible to the effects of the Sirens' song. This can hardly be the "solution" Adorno has in mind. What is it then that remains in the face of the alternative between being tied to the mast and dying on the Sirens' islands? The "narrow third possibility" suggested by Adorno "is art."[23] It is an art, and an approach to art that, unlike Odysseus' bound and blissful listening, have consequences.

Blanchot, too, addresses the double bind at the heart of Odysseus's encounter with the Sirens, and the alternative he suggests is not altogether different from Adorno's. He contrasts Odysseus with Melville's Ahab, who experiences a similar magnetic encounter with the sublime but who, lured by the whale, gives in: "The outcome of the encounter, which for Odysseus is a kind of victory, for Ahab is dark disaster. It cannot be denied that Odysseus half-heard that which Ahab saw. But where he was able to resist what he heard, Ahab got lost in his vision" (*LV* 16).[24] While Odysseus "refused the fatal metamorphosis promised by the Sirens,"[25] Ahab "penetrated into it and vanished" (ibid.). For Blanchot, literature originates in the lure experienced by both Odysseus and Ahab. With Odysseus remaining the same as he was before, and with Ahab "disappearing," both encounters would leave no trace behind, were it not for the very narrations of their victory and disaster. Both tales, like all art for Blanchot, arise out of the absence of a "real" alternative, of an alternative between mastery and disappearance. In contradistinction to Adorno, who, like the Homeric hero measures his "third possibility" by its effects in the world and devises an art that provides a different escape for Odysseus, Blanchot prefers to imagine an art that follows the trails of vanishing Ahab, toward that "space without world into which the world incessantly risks sinking" (*LV* 16).

Allegory and Event

Adorno calls the Sirens' episode a "foreboding allegory of the dialectic of enlightenment" (*DA* 41). "This is not an allegory" (*LV* 12), Blanchot writes in his reading of the episode.[26] This opposition itself indicates the distance separating Adorno's and Blanchot's conception of literature. For Blanchot, the episode, like all true art, does not represent an idea or a theory as for Adorno, but invites a reading that is itself the encounter that takes place in it.

"The compulsion to rescue what is gone as something alive instead of using it as the material of progress is appeased only in art" (*DA* 39). This central assertion about the role of art in the *Dialectic of Enlightenment* points at the conditions of "the third possibility" between repressive mastery and fatal self-loss. Art, Adorno maintains, plays the game of the evil powers of a repressive society as long as it "declines to pass as cognition [*Erkenntnis*] and thus keeps away from *praxis.*" In this case, he continues, "social *praxis* tolerates art as it tolerates pleasure" (ibid.). True cognition is thus the "right" approach to art that is opposed to the "false" social *praxis.* The latter resembles the attitude of Odysseus, who, tied to the mast, listens to the Sirens' song "without consequences." Cognition, on the other hand, can be provided by art insofar as it aspires to turn the past into an insight for the present and recognizes in the Sirens' song a forgotten knowledge for the future. But in order to fulfill this function, the song must be deprived of its power to seduce for its own sake. Only as a "representative of utopia" (*Statthalter der Utopie*)[27] can art justify its existence in Adorno's empire of melancholy.

For Adorno, the encounter with the Sirens is not an invitation to the transformative experience of the work of art. Instead, art is the disempowered residue of a former fullness embodied by the Sirens' song. Odysseus's failed encounter with the Sirens stands for all that brought forth the disaster of civilization. Therefore, in a civilization that failed to fulfill its promises and became a source of oppression and alienation, "all songs have become sick" (*DA* 67). Adorno reproaches the bad *praxis* of social progress for its impoverished notion of art, which, like the disempowered Sirens' song, is now experienced only in the tame context of a bourgeois concert hall, but at the same time Adorno himself disempowers art by *using* it as a corrective of the practice he rejects. Even the autonomy and purposelessness of art is thereby processed dialectically and functionalized for the "right theory." In merely redirecting the path from a false homeland and indicating the direction of a true one, it merely readjusts the prescribed journey without leaving an open-ing for anything unexpected. What matters for Adorno is not the artistic or literary experience as such but the faint hope that it harbors—as memory and direction—for the world. Just as the Sirens' song does not, for Adorno, feature as an intrinsic event but as a reminder of the past and a lodestar for the future, so the episode too does not bring anything into existence and does not disturb anything either. The "right theory" stops its ears with wax in order not to listen to the song itself. In this manner, Adorno's interpretation of the episode sails past the Sirens' island and arrives at the predestined homeland of his theory, which itself remains unscathed.

As opposed to Adorno, who aims at a "right theory," Blanchot does not speak of a "happy-unsuccessful" encounter of Odysseus with the Sirens, but of a *"navigation heureuse malheureuse"* (*LV* 11), because, unlike a happy or un-happy journey, only something that has a preconceived destination, a fixed goal, can "succeed." For Blanchot, the negation of such a destination, of which Odysseus's encounter with the Sirens gives an account, is the precondition of literature, its entire despair and its *ravissement,* its enchantment of being both everything and nothing. Odysseus's encounter with the Sirens doesn't point at anything else; it is itself the event. It is an experience that repeats itself at any place and at any time in which literature occurs, turning that place into a movement toward the outside of any place and its time into a movement of an other time, toward a past that never was and an ever receding future. What takes place between Odysseus and the Sirens is, in Blanchot's view, the struggle between reality and the imaginary, in which both "seek to encompass every-thing, to be the whole world, so that their coexistence with the other world is impossible; and yet both worlds have no greater desire than to coexist with and encounter the other . . . and make the world arising from this union the most terrible and beautiful of all worlds. Alas, a book, only a book" (*LV* 15).

Adorno's utopia of a reconciliation between reality and its alternative is prefigured dialectically in Odysseus's self-limitation. In the negative reflection of the hero's self-denial Adorno recognizes an indication toward a future "society that no longer requires renunciation and mastery, a society that will master itself, not to inflict violence on itself and on others, but to achieve reconciliation" (*DA* 63). For Blanchot, on the other hand, the world that results from the impossible reunion of the two realms is as beautiful as it is terrible, and lives in the imaginary, between the covers of a book, in a *livre à venir.* For both writers literature is at once monumental and nothing: for

Adorno it plays a crucial role in a grand historico-philosophical construction, but doesn't count in and for itself; for Blanchot, literature is both the absolute and the impossible event. Both Adorno and Blanchot read Odysseus's encounter with the Sirens as a manifestation of the power of literature to contest "that which is," but where Adorno reduces its intrinsic power by enrolling it in a *praxis,* Blanchot risks dissolving that which is to be contested to the point where contestation itself may be lost in a void.

Genres of Contestation

For both Blanchot and Adorno, the *Odyssey* results from the encounter between Odysseus and the Sirens. At the beginning of the section entitled "When Odysseus Becomes Homer," Blanchot asks: "What if Odysseus and Homer . . . were one and the same person? If Homer's *récit* was nothing else but the movement accomplished by Odysseus in the space opened up by the song of the Sirens?" (*LV* 14). Somewhat similarly, Adorno speculates about the analogy between Homer and Odysseus, who has survived the seduction of the Sirens' song to become the narrator of the epic. In both readings, Odysseus becomes Homer, who transforms the mythical song into the narration of the *Odyssey.* In both, the encounter between Odysseus and the Sirens leaves its traces in the shape of an interruption—a halting, an arrest, or a disruption— which echoes the Sirens' invitation to Odysseus to interrupt his journey. Yet, Adorno's and Blanchot's description of the origin of this transformation and of the effect of this interruption differ greatly. These differences are revealed most succinctly in the kind—or, more specifically, in the *genre* of prose the Sirens' song becomes after its transformation in the two readings. For Adorno, Homer turns the song into an *epic,* which is, for him, already a *novel.* For Blanchot, the entire epic is, paradoxically, already contained in the *récit* of the encounter, which is itself an "ode" that became "episode" (*LV* 11). From Adorno's perspective, the interruption inherent in the narrative mode of the novel signifies an overcoming of the mythical song. From Blanchot's it is the *récit* that, in contrast to the worldly discourse of the novel, captures and transports the encounter with the Sirens into the epic—which has itself only emerged from the encounter—and in turn engulfs the epic as a whole.[28]

Adorno believes that the Homeric episode already knows the "right theory" because it enacts the "third possibility" beyond self-limitation and self-dissolution, beyond enlightenment and myth. Homer acts, for him, as a corrective of Odysseus's "false" escape from the Sirens: unlike Odysseus, who, in acknowledging the Sirens' seduction, fails in his attempt to undo the powers of myth, Homer truly escapes because he dialectically uses the strength of the enemy—the mythical immediacy of their song—and transforms it into mediated prose, into the novel-like narration of Odysseus's adventures. The transformation from song into prose replaces the ontological fullness of pure sound with the ruptured mediation of language.[29] This rupture has a threefold function: it is a reminder of an unredeemed world, it undoes the false semblance of freedom, and it retains the memory of past disaster.

In the first instance, the disruption of prose mimetically reflects an unfulfilled present. As with modernist music that is defined by its dissonances, literature too is, for Adorno, only legitimate on the basis of its caesuras, which account for the "sickness" that has befallen all songs. These caesuras occur in the discontinuity implicit in "exoteric" prose forms, which undo the hierarchic order of society (*DA* 50) and which Adorno sets up in contradistinction to the mythical plenitude of the primal song. The Sirens' attraction lures its listeners to regress to myth. Adorno associates this regression with the fascist myth of *Heimat* and distinguishes it from a legitimate human desire (undoubtedly dictated by his own situation in exile) to settle and reach a home. *Heimweh*, this genuine longing for (a) home, turns into myth only when it stems from a nostalgia directed backwards, when it is a "phantasm of a lost, archaic time" (*DA* 86). "True *Heimat*," on the other hand, "*ist Entronnensein*" (ibid.), it is the state of having escaped—and what it has escaped from is myth. For Adorno, Homer's achievement in the *Odyssey* is such an escape. In transforming the mythical song into prose, into an epic that already resembles a novel, Homer "sweeps myth into time, revealing the abyss that separates him from home and reconciliation" (*DA* 86).[30] The escape from myth takes place as it turns into the narrative form of the novel and its historical time, the time of a philosophy of history that measures the disastrous present in terms of its distance from a fulfilled time that is yet to come. The interruption of prosaic discourse reveals this distance as an abyss.

The harmony of song in a civilization of alienation and disaster would in itself only reaffirm the evil powers of myth and its correlative, the subjection of human life to the dictates of fate. But Adorno compounds the issue: the "interruption in the discourse" (*das Innehalten in der Rede*) (*DA* 86) is not only true to the dismal state of the present, but also "marks the *caesura* . . . by means of which the semblance of freedom lights up [*Schein der Freiheit auf-*

blitzt]" (ibid.). In the double meaning of the word "Schein"—both "shine" and "semblance"—the ruptures of prose also undo the illusion of freedom that "civilization has never fully extinguished," that it has neither fulfilled nor forgotten.

Adorno presents the final destination of the Homeric transformation from song into epic as the recollection of human suffering. Commenting on scenes of cruelty in the *Odyssey*, Adorno spells out the "law of the Homeric prose-epic": "Discourse itself, language in contradistinction to mythic song, the possibility of retaining in the memory the disaster that has occurred, is the law of the Homeric escape and the reason why the escaping hero is repeatedly introduced as narrator. It is only the cold distancing of narration . . . that reveals the full horror, which in song is solemnly confounded into fate" (*DA* 86). Odysseus is thus not only the bourgeois homecomer; where he is presented as a narrator in the epic, he becomes one with Homer, becomes the one who brings back the tales of what he has seen and experienced. If the epic can witness past disaster it does so, dialectically, thanks to the "impassibility and coldness" (ibid.) of its mode of narration, which alone can capture the full terror of the events. Yet, it is in arresting the "inner flow" of speech that Homer truly prevents us from forgetting the victims and, in the rupturing of discourse, gives a voice to their unutterable agony.[31] The caesura, which differentiates prose from song, imposes a moment of silence that opens up a space in which disaster can be recollected and in which the horror and suffering that has been witnessed can be given a place in human memory.

The presence of Adorno's key motifs in Blanchot's reading of the Sirens episode—abyss, silence, and the transformation of song into narrative—reveal a surprising proximity as well as a striking distance between their positions. The transformation from song into prose, which, in Adorno's interpretation, signifies the defeat of myth, is, for Blanchot, the Sirens' very triumph. For Adorno, Homer escapes the Sirens by narrating the *Odyssey*. For Blanchot, Homer takes revenge for the deceived Sirens and brings Odysseus back into their magnetic field: "They lured him back to the place he wanted to avoid and, hidden in the heart of the *Odyssey*, which had become their grave, they enticed him—and not only him but many others—to undertake that happy, unhappy journey which is that of the *récit* and is no longer unmediated song, but narrated and seemingly harmless song, no longer ode but episode" (*LV* 11). The *Odyssey*, which, for Adorno, consists entirely of world, of history, and discourse, becomes in Blanchot's reading the space in which this world is swallowed up by the *récit* that is contained in it. What vanishes along with the world of the epic is Homer himself, who, "becoming Odysseus, goes towards that place where the power to speak and to narrate is promised to him on the condition that he disappears into it" (*LV* 14).

For Adorno, the mythical song is overcome and superseded by the novel through Homer's narrative act. For Blanchot, too, the novel originates in Odysseus's encounter with the Sirens, but for him it is not in the novel, which contains "all the wealth and breadth of life in its wonderful and superficial diversity" (*LV* 12), that the true encounter, the event of literature occurs. It happens "where the novel does not go" (ibid.): in the *récit,* the narrative form that does not give an account of an event, but is the event itself.

For Adorno, the novel transforms mythical into historical time and reveals the abyss that separates the present from a time of fulfillment. For Blanchot the *récit,* the ode that turned into an episode, retains the song as absence and abyss. This abyss inhabits the epic in the guise of the *récit,* of the encounter from which the epic springs. The remnants of the song open up a void in "every word" and turn the epic inside out, transforming its worldly, historical time into the space where literature comes into being and toward which it moves. In his essay on Proust that follows his reading of the Sirens episode, Blanchot describes this space as the "moving density of time become sphere" (*la densité mouvante du temps sphérique*) (*LV* 36). A sphere? But what of the interruption, and what of the abyss?

"After Auschwitz": An Excursus

At this point, a look beyond the two readings of the Sirens' episode is in order. The only explicit cross-reference between Blanchot's and Adorno's work is to be found in Blanchot's "Après coup,"[32] a brief retrospective essay published in 1983 as an afterword to two stories he wrote in the mid-thirties. Blanchot introduces his well-known statement that "no matter when it is written, every *récit* from now on will be from before Auschwitz"[33] with an implicit reference to Adorno's famous dictum that "writing lyrical poetry after Auschwitz is barbaric,"[34] which he repeated and modified throughout the postwar decades: "That is why, in my opinion—and in a different way from the one that led Adorno to decide with absolute correctness—I will say that there can be no *récit-fiction* after Auschwitz."[35] Blanchot's allusion to the proximity *and* distance between his statement and Adorno's invites a comparison between their two perspectives on literature "after Auschwitz" in the light of their respective readings of the Homeric episode of Odysseus's encounter with the Sirens.

Both Adorno's and Blanchot's sentences about literature "after Auschwitz" are intended to mark this historical event as a definitive caesura, as the ultimate interruption. Yet, as Blanchot himself indicates, there are significant differences between their positions: in qualifying the act of writing poetry "after Auschwitz" as "barbaric," Adorno characterizes it as of an earlier moment in the history of civilization and thereby dialectically evokes a similar temporality to the one he introduced in *The Dialectic of Enlightenment*. Blanchot, on the other hand, discursively—and freely—disposes of chronological order. While Adorno insists on the time "after Auschwitz," Blanchot explicitly mentions only its "before." In using the indefinite and shifting *désormais,* "from now on," he avoids actually inscribing the fissure caused by the event *into* literature, transporting it instead "backwards," to the safe haven of the potentially "idyllic" time "before."[36] This difference between Adorno's and Blanchot's approach to literature after Auschwitz is summed up clearly by Geoffrey Hartman: "Adorno wants to shield the Holocaust from profanation, doubting art's capacity to present it without meretricious stylization; Blanchot is concerned rather with defending art."[37] While Adorno indicts with an implicit ethical judgment the *act* of writing what should no longer be written "after Auschwitz," Blanchot displaces the temporal location of a mode of writing without implicating an agent or a deed. Above all, while Adorno invokes lyrical poetry, Blanchot, though he later extends his displacement to "all narration, if not all poetry" (ibid.), is concerned primarily with the *récit*.[38]

These differences between Adorno and Blanchot aside, one wonders how much of a difference—and what kind of an interruption—Auschwitz really makes in their respective views of literature as we have come to know them from their readings of the Sirens' episode. Is it not true that, for Adorno, lyrical poetry—the genre that is closest to the disempowered mythical song—has been "sick" ever since Odysseus's failed encounter with the Sirens? In that case, the caesura of Auschwitz would consolidate rather than disrupt a continuity that Adorno establishes between Homer's time and his own. This continuity implies a concept of history that knows no freedom and contingency, no space for human agency. From such a perspective, historical time becomes quasi-indistinguishable from a mythical temporality of inescapable fate which Adorno praises Homer for having "swept into history." If Auschwitz was a *necessary* outcome of a history that started with Odysseus's encounter with the Sirens,[39] if history displays the same inescapable continuity as myth, isn't the circle restored, the interruption undone?[40]

And Blanchot? At a first glance "Auschwitz" does indeed mark an interruption: in the face of the disaster designated by this name, he "delegitimizes" and literally "takes back" in time that mode of writing which he most values in his reading of the Sirens' song. But didn't the *temps du récit* always already confuse and undo the linearity of historical time? Furthermore, a closer look at Blanchot's characterization of the *récit* in "Après coup" reveals significant differences from its earlier description in "The Sirens' Song." In both cases Blanchot speaks of the *loi du récit*. In "Après coup" this law, which, "from now on," causes every *récit* to be from "before Auschwitz" is described as follows: "There is, in the récit, a joy in the midst of misfortune which continuously risks turning into an attraction. This would be the law of the *récit*, its happiness, and because of that, its misfortune. . . . But, even before any distinction between content and form . . . there is the unqualifiable Saying [*le Dire*], the glory of the 'narrative voice' that makes itself be heard in all clarity, without ever being obscured by the opacity or the enigma or the terrible horror of that which it communicates."[41] But wasn't the *loi du récit*, in Blanchot's reading of the Homeric episode, precisely the law of a writing which resists referential clarity,[42] which doesn't communicate or "relate" but which unsettles reality and introduces an "abyss into every word"? Wouldn't that make of the *récit* the most appropriate of genres to mark the caesura of Auschwitz?

Adorno establishes a continuity precisely where he means to inscribe the ultimate disruption. Blanchot, who, like Adorno, intends to mark the caesura of disaster, changes the terms on both sides of the fissure. In taking this step, he seems to undo beforehand that which should be ruptured, preventing the interruption from taking place. Unwillingly, he ensures the continuity that is to be arrested.

Two Sirens

Adorno and Blanchot locate the power of contestation inherent in literature in its capacity to rupture, to disrupt, to interrupt. Both speak of this interruption as an abyss. For Adorno, the abyss marked by Homer as he "sweeps myth into time" is that which reveals the distance between the tormented present and a future redemption. Yet, although Adorno implicitly conceives of the link he makes between the *Odyssey* and his own times as a "secret appointment" between a specific past and the present, as a particular constellation meant to break apart the continuum of time, the temporality of his theory nonetheless leads to the construction of a closed dome under which the present dwells. Blanchot too evokes the abyss that arises from a true encounter with the Sirens as an unsettling of the stability and fixity of reality, as that disruption which Odysseus, in his mediocrity and cowardice, resists. Yet, the disruption he invokes ends up in a spherical time, the most closed and continuous of constructions—an abyss eternally circling around itself. Could one say of Blanchot's abyss what he says of Nietzsche's Eternal Return: that "through the evidence that radiates from it, one cannot resist falling under the spell of its attraction as soon as one falls into it"?[43] Henri Meschonnic, in a sweepingly critical essay, speaks of Blanchot's "idea of literature, all the relations between living and writing, life and death, the individual and the social" as engendering "a circularity that is the greatest of temptations."[44] Irving Wohlfarth ends his analysis of Adorno's reading of the Sirens' episode with the warning that "the reader of this circular text must watch out that he doesn't succumb to its swirling attraction."[45] Adorno and Blanchot, two Sirens singing? Singing their own equally seductive, circular, and ultimately deaf monologues about a foreign call and the possibility of an encounter with the Other? The last sentence of "Après coup," a quotation from Emmanuel Levinas, voices a more compelling vision, one that applies to this imaginary conversation. It is the vision of a space defined by proximity and separateness, in which the two interlocutors remain within the reach of each other's voices, causing an interruption that is not a sublime silence but an invitation to listen: "Une voix vient de l'autre rive. Une voix interrompt le dire du déja dit."[46]

CHAPTER FIVE

A Fragmentary Demand

Leslie Hill

> ✕ . . . Waiting is always a waiting for waiting, withdrawing the beginning, suspending the ending and, within this interval, opening the interval of another waiting. The night in which we wait for nothing [*dans laquelle il n'est rien attendu*] represents this movement of waiting.
>
> The impossibility of waiting is an essential part of waiting [*appartient essentiellement à l'attente*]. —MAURICE BLANCHOT, "L'attente"

In 1959, together with such long-standing admirers of Heidegger as Jean Beaufret and other more recent friends of the philosopher as René Char and Georges Braque, Maurice Blanchot was invited to contribute to a celebratory volume in honor of Heidegger's seventieth birthday.[1] The proposal fell at a significant time for Blanchot. It coincided, in particular, with a crucial historical or, more accurately, historial moment that, with all due precautions, Blanchot was soon to describe as a change of epoch: a period of interruption, displacement, and indecision. A certain history, he suggested, had reached an uncertain point of closure; something unprecedented and necessarily indeterminable was in the offing, both on and beyond the horizon. As Blanchot was at pains to point out, the long-term consequences of that turning—if such exists, he conceded—were necessarily incalculable.[2] The more immediate effects on his own intellectual project were, however, dramatic.

In at least three ways.

First, the relationship between Blanchot's own fictional texts and the institution of literature underwent a complex mutation. *Le Dernier homme*, first published in 1957, bore its title like an ironic promise, and was to be the last of

Blanchot's *récits* or shorter fictional narratives explicitly to designate or present itself as such. True enough, Blanchot's fiction had long maintained an uneasy relationship with the expectations of the literary. From *L'arrêt de mort* onwards, all the writer's shorter narratives offer themselves to reading as interrogative explorations whose exorbitant status is paradoxically confirmed by the modesty with which they fall short of narrative and exceed their own boundaries by withdrawing from them. If stories such as *L'arrêt de mort, Au Moment voulu,* and *Celui qui ne m'accompagnait pas* belong to the genre of narrative, then it is only insofar as they give voice to the impossibility of narrative itself, the non-occurrence of the event or events they struggle to narrate, and their own infinite futurity as a witnessing of the finite.

Le Dernier homme did this too, but went one step further. For it ends, not by bringing a residual narrative to a proper, or improper, close, but by a vertiginous act—or non-act—of fragmentary and abyssal self-citation. In finishing or, better, in suspending the very possibility of its finishing, Blanchot's *récit* detaches itself from itself in order to display a singular logic of duplicitous self-repetition—something which, twenty years later, the text went on to reaffirm, in an astonishing manifestation of simultaneous self-referral and self-displacement, when suddenly, without changing in any other respect, the book began redescribing itself, to incontrovertible but undecidable effect, as a new version of itself, as *Le Dernier homme, nouvelle version.* This most perfect of repetitions, then, was also the purest of variations, and this most spectral of returns the most decisive of innovations. In future, after *Le Dernier homme,* as *La Folie du jour* had already intimated, there would indeed be "no more *récits.*" Each of the fictional, parafictional, or semifictional texts that followed, including the reissue of *L'arrêt de mort* in 1972 and of *La Folie du jour* in 1973, not to mention the 1972 printing of *Le Dernier homme* itself, as well as all subsequent editions of these texts, was to be ironically voided of explicit generic categorization.[3] The dividing line between what was and was not narrative, what was and was not literature, already under threat in the *récits* themselves, was indefinitely suspended, consigned, so to speak, to perpetual undecidability.

Undecidability does not, however, preclude the necessity of decision. On the contrary, it is what makes decisions both possible and necessary in the first place. The paradox is one that finds ample confirmation in the second of the important shifts in Blanchot's work that occurred in the late 1950s. For it was at that moment, too, that Blanchot chose to leave Èze, that village "in the South" which features so mysteriously (and anonymously) in *Au Moment voulu,* and where he had spent the bulk of the preceding decade. Blanchot's return to Paris in the course of 1958 was far from uneventful, for it coincided with a resumption of the writer's active involvement in politics, admittedly no longer as a journalist involved in the day-to-day commentary on political events (which had been his main activity during the period up to July and August 1940), but as a proponent of what he first described in 1984 as the right to unexpected speech, "*le droit à la parole inattendue.*"[4] And as he renewed his passionate interest in politics, Blanchot did so not as a dissident member of the nationalist right, but on the side of the radical noncommunist left, notably in partnership with Dionys Mascolo, whom Blanchot joined in rejecting de Gaulle's return to government as a so-called man of providence, and in campaigning for an end to France's undeclared war in Algeria. As Mascolo recalled many years later, Blanchot's letter to him on receipt of the first issue of *Le 14 Juillet,* the broadsheet Mascolo had founded with Jean Schuster to coordinate protests against de Gaulle, was uncompromising in its bold commitment to the future: "I refuse the whole of the past," Blanchot wrote, "and accept nothing of the present."[5]

But it was not only literary narrative and politics that bore the brunt of Blanchot's sense of an imminent change of epoch. It had an important bearing too on the future possibility of literary criticism. In this respect, the publication of *Le Livre à venir* in 1959 represented another threshold for Blanchot. The book gathered together a selection of the writer's monthly essays from *La Nouvelle Revue Française* for the period between July 1953 and June 1958. One early article briskly sums up what was at stake: "Où va la littérature?" "Whither literature?," it asked. The reply was disconcertingly straightforward. "Literature," Blanchot wrote, "is heading towards itself, towards its essence which is disappearance [*la disparition*]."[6] The goal of literature, Blanchot explained, meaning by that both its purpose and destination, could no longer be identified with some external source of (cultural, human, natural) value. But neither could it be located within the work itself, as a function of its status as truthful or alethic disclosure or an effect of its aesthetic autonomy as a self-referring artifact. Literature's end, as Blanchot put it, was inseparable from its ending as such, its erasure or effacement.

Blanchot went on to recall Hegel's celebrated remark from the first of the *Lectures on Aesthetics* of 1820–21 that "from the point of view of its highest determination, art is and remains, for us, a thing of the past [*ein Vergangenes*]."[7] Hegel's position, advanced, paradoxically enough, as Blanchot emphasizes, at a time of intense cultural activity in Germany, was that art in the modern age had forfeited its "authentic truth and vitality [*die echte Wahrheit und Lebendigkeit*]." It had lost, so to speak, its teleological mission. Art had parted company with history, truth, reality. Worldly action, science, and philosophy had taken over. For the first time in its existence, according to Hegel, art was now merely an object of aesthetic, literary critical contemplation—which is also to say that for the first time it was now properly constituted *as* itself, *as* art. The end of art, then, was also its beginning, and its demise the promise of its rebirth. In *Le Livre à venir,* Blanchot seems in the first instance largely to endorse Hegel's verdict—which is also the verdict of philosophy; but while he concurs that writing and truth have henceforth consummated their divorce, he disagrees forcibly as to the implications of this development. For Blanchot, the fall of art is not proof of its historical submission to philosophical truth; it is the sign of a more essential lapsing into the necessary possibility of its own perpetual self-questioning. And art that continually questions itself, Blanchot argued, which *as* art is inseparable from the essential necessity of its own self-questioning, cannot, paradoxically, exist *as* art, but only as a withdrawal or retreat from art, as the fleeting trace of its own self-erasure. No sooner does literature appear to itself as possibility, then, than it disappears as impossibility; no sooner is the work of art constituted as such than it gives way to the worklessness that is the irremediable trace of its necessary incompletion.

But if the artwork is that which, paradoxically, cannot by definition coincide with itself, what of the literary criticism that derives its reason for being from the prior existence of an object called literature? Here too the situation is complex. On the one hand, it is the non-coincidence of literature with itself that makes literary criticism possible in the first place. Without literature's absence from itself, criticism would have nothing to say. But belonging as it does to another order of discourse, it is clear too that criticism cannot remedy or overcome the essential incompletion of the work it seeks to address. The only course available to it, so to speak, is to repeat in its own words the question the artwork already asks of itself. In that process, criticism is brought to the uncomfortable realization not only that it is necessarily parasitical on the art work, but also that it cannot impose itself on the work with any finality as a statement of what is true. However, if this were not the case, literary criticism would have no alternative but to fall silent entirely. Paradoxically, it is the essential failure of literary criticism to deliver what is expected of it that turns out to be the best guarantee of its survival; its very future, so to speak, is a function of its ultimate impotence.[8] If literature is disappearance, it seems criticism for its part has no option but to accompany literature into the emptiness that endures within it as a dual condition of finitude and infinity. Literature and criticism, then, share a similar fate. As a result, in Blanchot, as in the work of many other contemporary writers, the border between literature and criticism, *récit* and essay, without ever being erased, becomes increasingly difficult to maintain. The hierarchical relationship by which the one aims to subject the other to the truth of its decisions proves unsustainable; what remains instead is a shifting network of fragmentary forms where the only law that obtains is the counter-law of singularity itself.

Admittedly, this was not the first time that, inverting the Hegelian schema, the completion of philosophy might be said to give way to the incompletion of art. Nor was it the first time that the boundaries between literature, philosophy, and literary criticism had been boldly redrawn, and the writing of the fragment affirmed as the essential embodiment of art's self-questioning. The effort to integrate the finite and the infinite, the complete and the incomplete was a central concern of those contemporaries of Hegel with whom the philosopher himself soon showed his displeasure: the Jena Romantics—notably Friedrich Schlegel and Novalis—who in the brief period between 1797 and 1800 had been the first to explore the compositional dynamics of the literary fragment and the implications of fragmentary writing for thought itself. It has often been remarked that there are many aspects of the *Frühromantik* that find an echo in Blanchot's own work.[9] These might be thought to include, for instance, the conviction that "where philosophy stops, so literature [*Poesie*] must begin," as Friedrich Schlegel puts it in fragment 45 of the *Ideen* of 1800, which, as we have seen, Blanchot reworks in his own distinctive way. Another aspect is the recasting of the critical essay as semifictional dialogue, already apparent in Schlegel's "Gespräch über Poesie" ("Conversation on Literature") of 1800 and explored, too, by Blanchot, albeit in markedly different fashion, in various texts from the late 1950s and early 1960s subsequently collected in *L'entretien infini*. A third commonality is the recourse to authorial anonymity, which was a feature not only of the fragments published in the *Athenäum* but also of much of Blanchot's own later political writing. Also the appeal to friendship—with both the familiar and the unknown—as enacting the plural space of literature itself; moreover the very notion that history itself might be subject to an upheaval whose character far exceeded what it was possible to think under the rubric of the political. And not to be forgotten is that ironic self-reflexivity, without which the critical thinking of the *Frühromantik* would not have been what it was, and which, in its own way, is a central, albeit problematic trait of Blanchot's *récits*. But this last point serves as a reminder that to gather together these different traits is also to ignore the essential dispersion that inhabits them, as it does all fragmentary writing as such. For there is also a crucial and irreducible distance between the thinking of the *Athenäum* and that of Blanchot, which Philippe Lacoue-Labarthe and Jean-Luc Nancy, for their part, for instance, describe as the difference between incompletion (*inachèvement*) and worklessness (*désœuvrement*), the difference, that is, between an art of the fragment that is nostalgic for unity and totality and one that exceeds such yearning—without it necessarily being the case that any such difference is itself ultimately decidable (as Blanchot underlines in *L'écriture du désastre*).[10]

What these convergences between Blanchot's work and the *Athenäum* serve to emphasize most of all is the extent to which the mutation traversing Blanchot's fiction and his critical and political thinking was more than simply a response to the anxieties of the postwar world, for it was fundamentally related to the very constitution of (modern) art itself. As Blanchot was quick to realize, literature's future as disappearance necessarily returned it, together with the literary criticism that was its shadow, to the very place where both had always already begun, which is to say, in philosophy itself. Yet as literature and criticism rediscovered this common origin, they did so with the enduring sense that there was something in literature—and therefore in philosophy too—that remained inassimilable to the philosophical. Hegel's own founding words, according to Blanchot, already implied as much. While philosophy had indeed supplied literature with a birth certificate, it had handed it a death warrant too. It had launched literature into the world as an autonomous possibility, subject to its own effectivity, freedom, and finality; but by the very same gesture it had dismissed it as that which was servile, ineffectual, constrained, and interminable, which survived itself indeterminately, therefore, as worklessness, ineluctable demand, and boundless error. Which was why the ending of literature, for Blanchot, was anything but an end; it affirmed instead the future—as that which is still, and forever, yet to come.

By the end of the 1950s Blanchot's critical thinking had entered into a new and more radical phase. From *Le Livre à venir* onward, it was less committed to defending an implicit canon of modern or modernist literary texts and took on a more explicitly philosophical turn. This is not to say Blanchot in later texts does not return to the works prominent in his earlier writing; Hölderlin, Mallarmé, Kafka, and Char, for instance, remain persistent points of reference. But Blanchot's treatment changes, becoming more oblique and digressive, more varied and more responsive to the semifictional or the fragmentary. It also becomes more reticent, more suspicious of itself. In 1961, for instance, in a piece about Beckett's *Comment c'est*, a voice in one of Blanchot's critical dialogues asks whether it is reasonable still to be speaking "about" books at all, and in particular whether there is any sense in praising a novel traversed with such uncompromising power of contestation as that of Beckett.[11] Two years later Blanchot began an essay on Louis-René Des Forêts in much the same vein, by assuring readers that his intention was precisely *not* to write as a critic, since to do so would amount to little more than a refusal to read and serve merely to demonstrate criticism's congenital inability to assume the "almost infinite nihilism" of a *récit* such as *Le Bavard*.[12] It was no longer possible, Blanchot concluded, to read literary texts by referring them to those ideological, political, moral, ethical, philosophical, even aesthetic values that had hitherto mobilized critical thinking and which, perversely, had themselves sought in literature the endorsement needed to confirm their authority. Something had changed. The challenge now, Blanchot wrote in 1959, was altogether more urgent: it was to confront "the task of both preserving and releasing thought from the notion of value, and consequently opening history up to that which, within history, is already moving beyond all forms of value and is preparing for a wholly different—and still unpredictable—kind of affirmation."[13]

It was later the same year that the Festschrift for Heidegger's seventieth birthday was due to appear. That Blanchot agreed to contribute to the book was no doubt a function of various factors. First, it was an opportunity to pay tribute. Heidegger, for Blanchot, was the preeminent contemporary thinker whose work, from the beginning, had accompanied him more closely than that of any other, with the possible exception of Emmanuel Levinas. This is not to say Blanchot's reading of Heidegger had ever been slavish. On the contrary, already in 1946, for instance, in an essay on the poems of Hölderlin published in *Critique*, Blanchot had written admiringly, but with discriminating severity, about Heidegger's appropriation of the poet.[14] But throughout the 1950s the strength of Blanchot's interest remained constant, and it is readily apparent that he continued to read Heidegger (which he did in the original German) and to engage in detail with a succession of important works, notably *Holz-wege* (1950), *Was heisst Denken?* (1954), *Vorträge und Aufsätze* (1954), *Zur Seinsfrage* (1956), and *Identität und Differenz* (1957).[15]

The relationship between Blanchot and Heidegger became complex for other reasons, too. In 1950, when it fell to Heidegger to express his admiration for an article on Hölderlin that had appeared in *Critique* (bizarrely, was Heidegger referring to the 1946 essay mentioned above?), he did so by inadvertently attributing it not to Blanchot, but to Blanchot's friend Georges Bataille, not realizing that Bataille's role had simply been to commission it—or, more accurately, suggest it to Blanchot—in his capacity as editor of the journal.[16] But whatever the reason for this embarrassing lapse of memory on Heidegger's part and the subsequent misunderstanding, this flattering, if wayward response to the writer Heidegger declared (albeit by proxy!) to be "the best mind in France [*la meilleure tête pensante française*]" evidently deserved a considered reply, and this was surely a further reason for Blanchot's decision to contribute, for it gave him the chance of responding directly—which is to say, in the circumstances: indirectly—to Heidegger in his own—improper—name.

Blanchot's contribution to the Festschrift was therefore understandably oblique, both in manner and in content. It consisted of a short, five-page text entitled "L'attente."[17] It shared its title, with a similar yet separate text, with which it is sometimes confused and with which admittedly it has material in common, which came out in the journal *Botteghe Oscure* the previous summer.[18] Like its companion piece, Blanchot's Festschrift contribution belonged to the generically undecidable work in progress—half narrative, half essayistic meditation—that three years later was to be published as *L'attente l'oubli*. As it happens, most of "L'attente" is in fact contained in *L'attente l'oubli*, in that the vast majority (but not all) of the passages given in "L'attente" reappear in the later volume. They do so, however, in a number of unpredictable ways, in a different sequence and in different combinations with other elements of text. And as they travel from one place to the other, few of the passages in the text remain unchanged. "L'attente," then, is not a torso, nor is it simply a taster for what was to follow; it is a separate (and separated) text that traverses and is traversed by the larger text that it announces, but in spectral, nonidentical manner.

Heidegger's Festschrift, for its part, was divided into five sections: Philosophy; Theology; Art and Literary Criticism; Medicine and Physics; Poetry, Sculpture, and Painting, with Blanchot's text appearing in the third of these subdivisions. But whatever the Festschrift's editors may have thought, Blanchot's homage to Heidegger was transparently not literary criticism. But neither was it straightforwardly readable as philosophical commentary or even as literary narrative, since (like Melville's scrivener) Blanchot evidently preferred *not to* respect the conventions of either, but to explore the interstices of both as an implicit challenge to all future readers.

Blanchot's choice of motif, or theme, for his contribution was not an arbitrary one. In attending to the question of waiting, he was responding to one of the abiding concerns of Heidegger's thinking. (Much the same may be said of the motif of forgetting, in "L'attente" and elsewhere; to read Blanchot on forgetting as already a forgetting of forgetting is inevitably to be reminded, so to speak, of Heidegger's own discussion of truth [*aletheia*] as unforgetting or unconcealment.[19]) The question of waiting, in Heidegger, is not an isolated one. It touches on a host of further issues about the relationship between past and future, between the task of thinking and the question of the unthought, between the closure of metaphysics and its overcoming. These were issues Heidegger in the 1950s had made his own. Faced with the challenge of the future, Heidegger wrote in 1952, the only valid response was to wait. Waiting, he explained, did not mean the deferral of thinking. It meant "to be on the look-out [*Ausschau halten*] within the already thought [*des schon Gedachten*] for the unthought [*dem Ungedachten*], which still lies concealed in the already thought [*das sich im schon Gedachten noch verbirgt*]. Through such waiting we are already engaged in thinking on a path towards that which is to be thought [*das zu-Denkende*]."[20] "At issue here," he argued elsewhere, addressing the threat of modern technology, "is whether as keepers [*Wärter*] and guardians [*Wächter*] we may ensure the silence of the demand in the speaking of Being [*die Stille des Zuspruches im Wort vom Sein*] prevails over the claim of the principle of sufficient reason [*principium rationis*] to be the basis of all representational thought."[21]

Waiting, then, is not passive temporization. It points to a relationship with time irreducible to the representational structures of Western metaphysical thinking for which futurity, as Heidegger and Blanchot both agree, is first and foremost a thing to be grasped, a deferred present measured according to an economic calculus of investment and return, prediction and control. This had been Heidegger's lesson to Blanchot from the outset, and it is what had enabled him in his early writing on literature, responding to Heidegger, to question the metaphysical understanding of the artwork as an aesthetic object posited at a distance and contemplated as such by an experiencing subject, and therefore, often in response to Mallarmé, to begin thinking of the poem—and poetic language in general—as playing a primary, foundational role, rather than a secondary, mimetic one. These were key Heideggerian themes to which Blanchot, then, plays ample and generous homage.

But there was more. "L'attente" was one of the first of Blanchot's texts to have extensive recourse to paronomasia as a style of thinking or argumentation. This, too, was strongly reminiscent of Heidegger; indeed, to retrace the intricate verbal construction of "L'attente" as it explores and exploits the semantic resources of such near-homophones or etymologically cognate terms as *attente, attention, attendre,* or *atteindre,* is at times not unlike reading Heidegger when he muses on the etymologies of various idiomatic German words. And there are indeed perhaps moments, as Timothy Clark has suggested, when "L'attente" even reads like a translation into French of passages from Heidegger.[22]

Blanchot's text, in other words, was a worthy, personal tribute to the thought of Heidegger. It gathered together some of the central philosophical motifs which by the late 1950s had come to bear the unmistakable imprint of Heidegger's thought.

But Blanchot's offering to Heidegger was also in the form of a series of fragments.

Thirty-five, to be precise, of radically differing extents, the shortest consisting merely of a few words, while the longest covered nearly a page, as though to mark discreetly—and discretely—that the measure of any life, even one lived to the biblical limit of three score and ten, was immeasurable as such, to the necessary degree, as Heidegger had long maintained, that Dasein was inseparable from the inherent possibility of an incalculable, unforeseeable future. Thirty-five fragments, then, might seem to invoke only half a life. But what is half a life, if not necessarily and in principle already the possibility of the whole of a life? And what is the possibility of the whole of a life, if not the necessary prospect of its imminent ending?

Birthdays, then, are by implication always death days, and vice versa; and it is not without significance perhaps that Heidegger's own birthday, September 26, fell only four days after Blanchot's own, and that the philosopher's seventieth birthday coincided almost exactly with the second anniversary of the death of Blanchot's mother.[23] In such circumstances, what more appropriate birthday present might Blanchot send to Heidegger than a meditation on time, death, and the future?

Which is not to say Blanchot's gift does not need to be carefully unwrapped. For it is soon apparent that Blanchot's tribute to Heidegger was also in the form of a challenge. To some this may seem ungracious; but, as every birthday boy or girl will know, the best presents of all are those that are unexpected and, rather than encouraging complacency, stimulate the recipient to think anew of the impending future. Such, I want to argue, is the strange calculation—calculation without calculation—embodied in Blanchot's present to Heidegger.

First, to the extent that it incorporates a thinking about time and was offered as such to the philosopher at a significant moment in his life's course, there is little doubt that "L'attente" constituted a reader's response to *Sein und Zeit*, which Blanchot had first encountered in the company of Emmanuel Levinas in 1927 or 1928. Sixty years later he was still able to recall vividly the powerful impact of that first exposure.[24] In giving the title "Waiting" to his Festschrift offering, it seems clear that what Blanchot was recording, then, was first of all his long-standing debt to *Sein und Zeit,* and in particular to Heidegger's remarks on death in division 2, chapter 1 of the book, for it is there, in §53 of Heidegger's text, toward the close of the discussion of Being-towards-death (*Sein zum Tode*), that the account of dying is linked to an analysis of waiting, in the form of a description of expectation, or waiting for . . . (*Erwarten*).[25]

Heidegger's purpose in that chapter will be familiar enough. It is to gain an ontological understanding of Dasein in respect to its relationship with the end (*Ende*) and with its own totality or wholeness (*Ganzheit*). Death, Heidegger famously argues, "is the possibility of the absolute impossibility of Dasein [*die Möglichkeit der schlechthinnigen Daseinsunmöglichkeit*]." "Death, as the end of Dasein," he adds, "is Dasein's ownmost possibility—non-relational, certain and as such indefinite, not to be outstripped [*die eigenste, unbezügliche, gewisse und also solche unbestimmte, unüberholbare Möglichkeit des Daseins*]."[26] But there is, we discover, more than one way to face the imminent prospect of dying, more than one way to respond to the impossible. It is a persistent feature of anonymous everyday life, says Heidegger, that death—this most proper of possibilities—is experienced primarily as a banal event affecting only others. The standard response to death, he says, is for Dasein to take refuge in idle chatter (*Gerede*). Nobody, it seems, really dies; dying is done by a nameless, impersonal neuter: "*man* stirbt," "*on* meurt," "*one* dies." For Heidegger, this lapse into anonymity is a temptation, resulting from Dasein's need to avoid the possibility of death by treating it as an occurrence that has already taken place. The everyday experience of death is "evasive concealment [*ver-deckende Ausweichen*]," a "constant fleeing [*ständige Flucht*]" before death's imminence, all of which serves to confirm, in Heidegger's analysis, the degree to which Dasein is a hapless victim of the inauthenticity (*Uneigentlichkeit*) that is the characteristic signature of the fallenness or falling [*Verfallenheit*] of Being.

Such failures are not contingent ones. They are a necessary consequence of the forgetting and withdrawal of Being, according to Heidegger. As such, however, they underline the extent to which nevertheless, in spite of all, there is an authentic, properly proper relationship to the possibility of impossibility which is death. Such a relationship (with that which suffers no relationship) cannot be in the form of an expecting (*Erwarten*) of death, since to expect is precisely to seek to establish a transitive relationship with death and thus to substitute for the possibility of impossibility the predictable and impersonal possibility of realization. It is nevertheless possible, says Heidegger, with very different implications, to anticipate (*vorlaufen*) the possibility of death. Indeed, without such anticipation it would not be possible to conceive of death as possibility at all. "Being-towards-death, as anticipation of possibility [*als Vorlaufen in die Möglichkeit*]," Heidegger argues, "is what first *makes* this possibility *possible* [*ermöglicht allererst diese Möglichkeit*] and sets it free as possibility."[27] This distinction, then, between the transitivity of expecting (*Erwarten*) and the intransitivity of anticipation (*Vorlaufen*) is paramount, and it is no surprise to find again, in division 2, chapter 4 of *Sein und Zeit,* that Heidegger has similar recourse to the contrast between (on the one hand) awaiting, waiting for . . . , or expecting (*erwarten, warten auf . . .* , or *gewärtigen*) and (on the other) anticipation (*vorlaufen*) in order to secure the crucial difference between proper and improper, authentic and inauthentic. "The inauthentic future [*Die uneigentliche Zukunft*]," one reads in §68, "has the character of awaiting [*des Gewärtigens*]," whereas "there lies in anticipation [*im Vorlaufen*] a more primordial Being-towards-death [*ein ursprünglicheres Sein zum Tode*] than in the concernful expecting of it [*im besorgten Erwarten seiner*]."[28]

Anticipation of death's proper possibility, then, is what separates an inauthentic future from an authentic one. But what if the opposition between expectation and anticipation, between waiting *for* something and just waiting, between transitive and intransitive, with all that it is calculated to support in Heidegger's analysis, were somehow more fragile than Heidegger's language gives us to understand? What if it were not to be possible to separate the future from itself according to that distinction? What if it were not possible to make the death that is necessarily mine the site of a decision, a deciding, or dividing, between proper and improper, authentic and inauthentic, *eigentlich* and *un-eigentlich*? What if what announced itself as the horizon of death's possibility were after all the *im*possibility of dying, in which case I—or one—would have to conclude that it is the inevitable fate of the horizon itself to be interrupted, effaced, or fragmented? What if, as Blanchot contends in *L'espace littéraire*, the anonymity of death, and my anonymity in the face of death, were the only possible—i.e., in these circumstances, *im*possible—response to the imminence or futurity of death? And what if the indecision of this relationship (without relationship) with the necessary impossibility of death—this *comédie*, as Bataille terms it in his famous essay "Hegel, Death, and Sacrifice"—were the place without place where literature—neither true nor false, authentic nor inauthentic, complete nor fragmented—became unavoidable?

The question: "What if . . . ?," Blanchot suggests, is one that "literature," in its constitutive indirection, perpetually asks of philosophy.

Blanchot agrees that there is a crucial and necessary distinction to be made between the waiting that is an expecting and that which is pure anticipation. It is in those terms that the tribute to Heidegger begins: "Waiting [*l'attente*] begins," Blanchot writes, "when there is nothing left to wait for [*attendre*], not even the end of waiting [*cette attente*]." But in writing these words Blanchot was perhaps mindful that, some ten years or so earlier, Samuel Beckett (who once wrote to Blanchot to express his own affinity with the writer of *L'attente l'oubli*) had at one stage hesitated whether to call his celebrated 1953 play *En attendant Godot* or simply *En attendant.*[29] Beckett's indecision is telling. It reveals a fundamental uncertainty about the syntax of the word *attendre,* which Blanchot exploits to vertiginous effect in "L'attente." *Attendre* (meaning both "to wait" in the absolute and "to wait for . . ." in determinate manner), together with the noun *l'attente* (meaning, according to context, any one or more of: "waiting," "waiting for . . . ," or "expecting") is indifferently both transitive and intransitive; as a word, it hesitates between such possibles according to an irreducible undecidability or neutrality. As all translators from the French will know, a perpetual ambiguity attaches to the word, which context is not always sufficient to resolve. Is the primary meaning of *attendre* "to expect," or "to wait"? The answer, if such exists, is in the last resort of little consequence. For wherever the word *attendre* is used, the ghostly aura of one meaning will always be present alongside the other; indeed, what manifests itself par excellence in waiting (but often precisely by *not* manifesting itself) is precisely this indecision. "Whatever the importance of the object of waiting [*l'attente*], it is always infinitely exceeded [*infiniment dépassé*] by the movement of waiting." What is at stake here, in Blanchot, is not the meaning of a word as a retrieval of the origin or a remembering of the true, but the plural hesitation of syntax. In sentences like these, it is as if the distinction between expectation and anticipation is maintained, but also suspended, inscribed yet also effaced, with the result that the term *attente* in Blanchot (where it is precisely not a term) is affected with a kind of self-referring and self-deferring neutrality. The logic it obeys is a logic of supplementarity: "Waiting occurs [*C'est l'attente*]," writes Blanchot, "when time is always superfluous [*de trop*] and yet when time lacks time [*le temps manque au temps*]."

Whatever its necessity, then, Heidegger's distinction between expectation and anticipation is no sooner displaced from its native German idiom and transposed into French, than it trembles. Its repeatability is traversed by an indecision it can neither avoid nor control. Indeed, all that is required for Heidegger's distinction to be problematized, even in its own idiom, is for waiting to become affected by an internal, abyssal fold. What happens when we wait for waiting? Do we tend expectantly toward the future, or are we suspended in an indeterminate present? To wait for waiting is not a movement external to waiting itself, a secondary distortion of its originary identity. It is, writes Blanchot (and Beckett agrees), an essential part of waiting as such. Such internal doubling is not unique to waiting; it is a trait, Blanchot argues, that is always liable to affect (among others) such limit experiences as forgetting, suffering, illness, or fatigue, which have in common the singular circumstance that what is being experienced, by its very nature, compromises the separation of subject and object on which the possibility of experience itself depends. A waiting that has an object that is not an object is only a waiting to the extent that is not a waiting; its possibility is forever inseparable from its impossibility, without either term having priority over the other with respect to the future. In such moments, the reflexive self-relating of experience staged by Blanchot does not operate (as it did for the Romantics) to the benefit of absolute subjectivity. On the contrary, subjectivity is posed only to be deposed; what remains in its place, as a form of radical contestation, is the singularity of an exposure to the outside. In the movement of waiting for waiting, no sooner is the act of waiting folded back upon itself than it loses its object, forfeits its self-identity, and is denied the possibility with which it began; excluded from all projective temporality, waiting becomes an exposure to an absence of foundation that may be approached only as perpetual contestation, as an endless question which cannot even be formulated as such. "He says he is searching, he is not searching and, if he asks a question, this is perhaps already to be unfaithful to waiting, that neither affirms, nor questions, but waits." "Waiting," Blanchot adds, "bears a question which can never be posed [*qui ne se pose pas*]. Common to both the one and the other is the infinity [*l'infini*] which is in the merest question [*la moindre question*] and the most purposeless waiting [*la plus faible attente*]. As soon as there is questioning, no answer comes that might exhaust the question."[30]

Blanchot's purpose here is not to propose a phenomenology of waiting. It is, beyond all prescriptive reference to the proper or improper, the authentic or inauthentic, to respond in writing to the demand of the future which speaks in the indecision and ungraspable impossibility of dying "as such." The future, as Blanchot's account of waiting shows, cannot be approached except as interrupted, fragmented, or effaced. Which is no doubt why what arrives in Blanchot's writing in the late 1950s for the first time (which is *not* a first time), in response to the promise (or threat) of historial change, is the demand of the fragment.[31] To the extent that fragmentary writing is necessarily marked by interminability and incompletion, any fragment is always already both an expecting and a waiting. But what speaks in fragmentary writing for Blanchot is not only the anticipation of the future and thus of what Heidegger calls the still-to-be-thought, which for the resident of Todtnauberg was synonymous with the question of Being; what exerts its demand over Blanchot in the form of the fragment goes further than this, for it is the impossible infinity of the unthinkable as such. Blanchot explains "the thought of waiting" in one of the Festschrift fragments: "The thought that is the waiting for that which does not allow itself to be thought [*ce qui ne se laisse pas penser*], the thought that is borne by waiting and adjourned in that waiting."

What "L'attente" says here about waiting, articulated as it is in fragmentary form, necessarily also says something about the fragment. Like waiting, the fragment appeals to a future that cannot be made present. But what future is it that resists presentation?

Here, too, Blanchot debates with Heidegger. In allusive manner. For in "L'attente," this birthday offering to Heidegger, Blanchot signals the detached, fragmentary status of the text's component elements by attaching to them a cross: ×. Elsewhere, as readers may know, diverse other typographical symbols are used to similar effect, including such devices as: ❖ (*L'attente l'oubli*), ±± (*L'entretien infini*), ◊ (*L'amitié* and *Le Pas au-delà*), ◊ (*L'écriture du désastre*). Oddly enough, these various icons rarely recur from one text to the next and are for the most part specific to the place in which they occur. While they gather together verbal material to form a series of textual fragments, identifying them as such, they also mark the singular placement of those fragments, which therefore remains irreducibly dispersed. And this double movement of gathering together and scattering apart is reflected in the given typographical devices, which function as a series of discrete syntactic markers implying crossing (and crossing out), astral (i.e., dis-astral or dis-astrous) dispersion, neutrality, and violent inscription or incision.

In "L'attente," the × motif has at least two functions. First, it is a citation. Written into the margins of a homage to Heidegger on his seventieth birthday, it remembers perhaps a passage from Heidegger's 1951 lecture "Bauen Wohnen Denken" ("Building Dwelling Thinking"), where the place of the thing in Western metaphysics is identified by the thinker as being like "an unknown X [*ein unbekanntes X*] to which perceptible properties are attached."[32] Heidegger's response is to go on to think the thing, in more originary fashion, according to the figure of the fourfold (*das Geviert*). The fourfold crosses heaven and earth, mortals and immortals. At its center, its literal crux, stands death. Death, Heidegger reminds us, means "having the capacity for death as death [*den Tod als Tod vermögen*]."[33] In thinking the fourfold, Heidegger privileges in overwhelming fashion the figure of *Versammlung* (usually translated as gathering, or assembling), which refers to the act of calling or drawing together, the gathering that then ensues, as well as the united collectivity or community that is summoned together as a result. The motif of *Versammlung*, as readers will know, permeates much, if not indeed all of Heidegger's later thinking, and in particular his treatment of such questions as that of space or place, thinking, remembering, language, *logos*, even (but this is no surprise) Being itself.[34]

Blanchot knows this, but his writing remains skeptical. For Blanchot's citation of Heidegger's lecture is also necessarily an erasure; if it gathers up a fragment of Heidegger's abiding thoughts on the rootedness of Being, it thereby also disperses it to the four corners of the Babelian library.[35] This is the second function of the × that attaches itself, thirty-five times over, to Blanchot's gift, like a necessary memento of the eternal imminence of the impossibility of dying. (Readers of *L'arrêt de mort* will remember here the doctor's prognosis regarding the narrator: " 'X.? My dear sir, you can cross *him* off [*il faut faire une croix dessus*].' ")[36] But if Blanchot's citation of Heidegger is an erasure, this is no doubt because that erasure is itself also a citation. It will be remembered how in "Zur Seinsfrage" (*The Question of Being*), first published, under a different title, in 1955 as a sixtieth birthday homage to Ernst Jünger, Heidegger himself adopts the motif of the St. Andrew's cross as a kind of emblematic erasure.[37] Its use is restricted, however, to the word *Sein* ("Being"), which it serves to preserve and protect against metaphysical reduction or misappropriation. As such, it marks the possibility of that strategic stepping back (*Schritt zurück*) from metaphysical thinking by which Heidegger aimed to uncover a more originary and truthful relationship to Being.[38] That the word (for) Being was forced to appeal to an erasure to protect it from another form of erasure, or that the linguistic device of a St. Andrew's cross was charged with guarding against the deleterious effects of language itself—none of this seems to have given Heidegger pause for thought. At any event his commitment to the originary gathering of Being was undiminished. Blanchot, though, was not so sure. From Blanchot's perspective, it was precisely the possibility of erasure as a thinking of infinite fragmentation that forced him to suspect the privilege conferred on Being in Heidegger's writing. Blanchot's step beyond, in other words, is anything but a step back. It does not aim to restore thinking to a regathering of the origin, but bears witness, in its own bifurcating neutrality as a step (*pas*) that is not (*pas*) a step (*pas*), to a thinking of effacement and reinscription that is irreducible to Being. "Writing," Blanchot's own text tells him, "as the question of writing, the question that bears the writing that bears the question, denies you this relationship with being—understood primarily as tradition, order, certainty, truth, any form of rootedness—that you once received from the past history of the world."[39]

For Blanchot there is no gathering without simultaneous dispersion. Indeed, more than this, it is plain that for Blanchot all gathering is already a dispersing, all dispersing already a gathering. Here, then, whatever Blanchot's admiration for Heidegger, or Heidegger's admiration for Blanchot, their paths divide: irreconcilably. They belong, so to speak, to different turnings, as is readily apparent from their respective readings of such other literary, philosophical figures of the turn as Hölderlin and Nietzsche.

I want to conclude at this stage, however, by drawing attention to two divergent, perhaps even opposing deliberations on the question of the fragment. The arena of this polemic, appropriately enough, so to speak, is Heraclitus.

Heraclitus, it will be remembered, was the subject of one of the last official lecture series given by Heidegger, in the summer of 1943 and 1944, when the fate of more than one historical (historial?) community—or *Versammlung*—hung in the balance. Ten or so years later, Heidegger extracted from those lectures the material for a presentation published in 1954 under the solemn, even portentous title "Aletheia." In the course of his exposition Heidegger subjects one particular Heraclitean fragment, fragment B 72, to his own idiosyncratic form of philological and philosophical scrutiny. He ends by proposing the following translation (as rendered into English by Frank Capuzzi): "From that to which for the most part they are bound and by which they are thoroughly sustained, the λόγος, from that they separate themselves; and it becomes manifest: whatever they daily encounter remains foreign (in its presencing) to them [*Denn sie am meisten, von ihm durchgängig getragen, zugekehrt sind, dem* λόγος, *mit dem bringen sie sich auseinander; und so zeigt sich denn: das, worauf sie täglich treffen, dies bleibt ihnen (in seinem Anwesen) fremd*]". And Heidegger comments: "Mortals are irrevocably bound to the revealing-concealing gathering [*dem entbergend-bergenden Versammeln zugekehrt*] which lights everything present in its presencing [*das alles Anwesende in sein Anwesen lichtet*]. But they turn from the lighting [*von der Lichtung*], and turn only towards what is present [*an das Anwesende*], which is what immediately concerns them in their everyday dealings [*im alltäglichen Verkehr*] with each other."[40] As the reading develops, it becomes quickly apparent that, in interpreting Heraclitus, Heidegger is unfolding, yet again, as though for the first time, the thought of ontico-ontological difference. Heidegger had begun the lecture by announcing that Heraclitus the Obscure (*der Dunkle*), as he was traditionally known, ought more properly be known as Heraclitus the Lucid (*der Lichte*). Indeed, if Heraclitus was the Obscure—and this is Heidegger's closing verdict—it is only "because he thinks questioning into the lighting [*weil er fragend in die Lichtung denkt*]."

Attending to the selfsame fragment in January 1960, Blanchot remains recalcitrant. The author of *Thomas l'obscur* (*Thomas the Obscure*)—a novel (or *roman*), then a shorter narrative (or *récit*), that owed at least half of its given name to Heraclitus—diverges. True, Blanchot has recourse to a slightly different translation: "*Le logos,*" he quotes, following Clémence Ramnoux, "*avec lequel ils vivent dans le commerce le plus constant, ils s'en écartent; et les choses qu'ils rencontrent tous les jours, elles leur semblent étrangères.*"[41] What is crucial here, he contends, is not the turning aside from Being and the fall into the oblivion of the everyday, but the mobility of Difference itself, embodied in the rhythmic motion of Heraclitus's own written fragments, which is that of writing itself as a double movement of proximity and distance, gathering and dispersion.[42] Admittedly, Blanchot was no philologist, even if in his early years, as Christophe Bident records, he was expected at mealtimes to address his father in Latin.[43] Nevertheless, in his account of Heraclitus, Blanchot displays an acute sensitivity to the language of the surviving fragments. Moreover, in approaching the fragmentary writings of Heraclitus, he was also mindful of the fragmentary poems of René Char, who, though now a friend to Heidegger and one of the three other French contributors to the 1959 Festschrift, was also—perhaps more importantly—a crucial reference for Blanchot's own thinking about literature, fragmentary writing, and the future.[44]

Blanchot's Heraclitus was very different to the thinker portrayed by Heidegger. Where for instance in fragment B 72 Heidegger had found originary confirmation of the hierarchical twofold of ontico-ontological difference, Blanchot for his part found radical horizontality, movement, and disjunction. Disjunction, for Blanchot, as for Heidegger, was also injunction. But the demands to which the two thinkers sought to respond were markedly different ones. What was crucial for Blanchot was the exacting legacy of fragmentary writing: the silent confirmation of a thinking that had long ago parted company with the privilege of the visible and which accorded—or dis-corded—itself instead with the unthinkable impossibility of the future. For as Blanchot deploys them, waiting and forgetting, though their meaning may depend on the existence of a past and a future, do not allow either to be grasped as horizons of pure possibility. Waiting and forgetting are the two conditions for the future, since to respond to the future it is necessary to forget (the past) and to wait (for the future); but these two conditions of possibility are also conditions of impossibility. For if we wait for the future (as we must), the future will not occur except as (a continuation of) the present; and if we forget the past, we are unlikely to recognize the future when it arrives, as indeed it must. The future, it seems, is unthinkable, but we are nevertheless required to affirm it. "Act in such a way that I may speak to you [*Fais en sorte que je puisse te parler*]," "Act in such a way that I may speak to you [*Faites en sorte que je puisse vous parler*]," says one voice to the other, now with one personal pronoun, now with another, in *L'attente l'oubli*.[45] Such words are self-contradictory, self-defeating, circular, and aporetic. It is as if the future has become literally inconceivable. Except that, living in time, it is precisely the future that we are forever bound to conceive—the future for which we are forever required to be responsible, even when the future is precisely what falls beyond all responsibility. As Blanchot reminds us, in the words of "L'attente," "the waiting that gathers, also disperses; the forgetting that disperses, also gathers."

In contributing to Heidegger's seventieth birthday celebrations, what did Blanchot expect? Of Heidegger? Of philosophy? Of literature? Or, more simply, more urgently: of the future? The answer to the question, if such exists, is, I think, disconcertingly simple. What Blanchot expected was—nothing. But in the nothing of that expectation, traversing it like a thought of impossibility, was hope. Not the hope of any determinate thing, but something more urgent, burdensome, terrible, inexorable even—the hope of hope, that is, no doubt, but also—hope without hope.[46]

Blanchot says of the fragment that its contestation knows no bounds. But this is not because literature, if such exists, is endowed with power or authority, but simply because it has neither, and because the writing of the fragment, as it gathers together totality, philosophy, literature itself, thereby disperses them, responding as it does so to that strange impossibility which is the call of the future itself.

CHAPTER SIX

Anarchic Temporality

Writing, Friendship, and the Ontology of
the Work of Art in Maurice Blanchot's Poetics

Gerald L. Bruns

Does Literature exist?   —MALLARMÉ, "La musique et les lettres"

The poem is the truth of the poet, the poet is the possibility of the poem;
and yet the poem stays unjustified; even realized, it remains impossible.
                                        —BLANCHOT, "René Char"

Poetry as Unhappy Consciousness

It is well known that in Maurice Blanchot's early criticism writing appears
to be less a productive activity than a self-reflexive movement. For example, at
the outset of "Littérature et la droit à la mort" (1947–48) he remarks that
literature begins when it becomes a question for itself.[1] What sort of question,
exactly? Evidently not Jean-Paul Sartre's sort of question, "What is literature?,"
which like all "what-is" questions carries a demand for justification. Inquiring
after the nature of a thing is a way of asking why there is such a thing at all, on
Leibniz's principle that nothing is without reason (for essences are reasons,
and everything is something). Or, again, it is a way of asking literature to
identify itself by locating itself in a scheme of things. For example, how does
poetry stand in relation to prose?—where prose, on Sartre's description, is
basically a prosthetic attachment to subjectivity. The writer, Sartre says, "is
invested with words. They are prolongations of his meanings, his pincers, his
antennae, his eyeglasses. He maneuvers them from within; he feels them as if
they were his body; he is surrounded by a verbal body which he is hardly aware
of and which extends his action upon the world."[2] As Hegel said, "an individual cannot know what he is until he has made himself a reality through

action."[3] Prose is a mode of action. Sartre says: "The word is a certain particular moment of action and has no meaning outside it." Prose is (as it certainly was for Sartre) an alternative to group action. Prose is the way the free individual grasps the world and shapes it into something for others.[4] Prose knows itself in knowing what it can do: it is a project of world-making in which the writer first of all makes himself real (if "himself" is the word) by becoming immanent in his effects. Poetry meanwhile does not use words; it contemplates them from the outside as if they were things—but to what purpose? There is a good chance that poetry does not know what it is, much less what it is for. It is (anarchically) on the hither side of principles and reasons. It is very likely a condition of what Hegel called "unhappy consciousness":[5] it exists in the form of a question, inaccessible to theory or redemption, divided against itself (without identity), opaque, gratuitous, and *unwirklich*. Whoever enters into this condition enters into an absolutely singular mode of existence, one that cannot be separated into a before and after or subsumed into contexts, categories, or totalities of any kind. So who can call it real?

The Impossibility of Writing

In what follows I want to try to clarify this state of affairs and to extract from it something like Blanchot's conception of the ontology (or perhaps the ontological peculiarity) of the work of art. My thought is that anything that shares this ontology—no matter how trivial or commonplace the thing or however it was materially produced—can claim the status of a work of art. The difficulty is that this excludes very little, almost nothing, not even people. So at the very least we are up against the old modernist's question of what counts as art. Blanchot speaks of "the challenge brought against art by the most illustrious works of art in the last thirty years" (*PF*294/ *WF*301). Is *Un coup de dés* a poem or *Finnegans Wake* a novel? Is a Cubist collage a painting or Duchamp's *Fountain* a sculpture? By what criteria? Modernist works notoriously define themselves by the negation of criteria (and so frequently they are just "works" or "things" that do not fall under any generic description). Blanchot cites "surrealism as a powerful negative movement" that rejects all definitions of what counts as art. This is not just nihilism, however, "because if literature coincides with nothing just for an instant, it is immediately everything, and this everything begins to exist" (*PF*294/ *WF*301–2). This is perhaps all that modernism means: all criteria are negated and everything is possible; nothing is to be excluded—there is nothing that cannot count as a work of art. Modernism is aesthetic anarchy, a moment of pure negative freedom in which anything goes. However, under these anarchic conditions in which there are no conditions—no stipulations, no rules or principles, no models or genres, in short no logical conditions of possibility—how is literature possible?

This is the question that occupies much of Blanchot's early critical writings, starting with *Comment la littérature est-elle possible?* (1941).[6] From Mallarmé Blanchot inherited the idea that poetic writing is not a mode of lyricism but an exercise of language, where language is not an instrument under my control (not, *pace* Sartre, a prosthetic device). As the Surrealists became aware, "words have their own spontaneity. For a long time language laid claim to a type of particular existence: it refused simple transparency, it was not just a gaze, an empty means of seeing; it existed, it was a concrete thing and even a colored thing. Surrealists understand . . . that language is not an inert thing; it has a life of its own, and a latent power that escapes us" (*PF*93/ *WF*89). So writing is not a pure possibility but limited or finite; it is always in some sense or to some extent impossible. The idea here is that language limits my power in the very moment that I try to extend it, and this is what happens in literature: "literature consists in trying to speak when speaking becomes most difficult" (*PF*25/ *WF*17).[7]

It is possible to think of poetry as an experience of the *resistance* of language to the designs that we place upon it. This was Heidegger's topic in "Das Wesen der Sprache" (1957): what he calls an "experience *with* language" occurs not when we speak but when words fail us. "In experiences which we undergo *with* language, language itself brings itself to language. One would think this happens anyway, any time anyone speaks. Yet at whatever time and in whatever way we speak a language, language itself never has the floor." It is only when language ceases to be a form of mediation that an experience with language is possible: "language speaks itself as language . . . when we cannot find the right word for something that concerns us, carries us away, or oppresses us. Then we leave unspoken what we have in mind and, without rightly giving it thought, undergo moments in which language itself has distantly and fleetingly touched us with its essential being." Moreover, having such an experience is what makes the poet. The poet, Heidegger says, "is someone compelled in his own way—poetically—to put into the language the experience he undergoes with language."[8] But if the failure of language is a condition of such experience, how is poetry possible? Or is it that, as Sartre complained, "Poetry is a case of the loser winning"?[9]

Writing is never a possibility that can be experienced.[10] This does not mean that my intentions cannot be realized because they exceed my capacity—it is not that they are too grandiose. It does not even mean that I cannot write something. It is rather that in writing I always discover that I cannot be fully myself: my subjectivity is, in a certain sense, not a plenitude; there is something lacking, a weakness where there should be strength, a destitution where there should be power. Sartre will say that it is precisely language that enables me to take up the slack of subjectivity and to make something of it. But Blanchot would answer that in this event when I speak I can no longer say "I" without a bad conscience, since it is not just "I" who speaks but also that part of my subjectivity that belongs to language (and who knows to what more besides?). In writing I experience that part of my subjectivity which does not belong to me; I experience, in other words, the *malheur* of a divided consciousness (I am myself and also another), a state in which, as Hegel showed, I fall short of being in the world.[11] For Blanchot the locus classicus of this state is to be found in Kafka's *Diaries,* where being in the world and writing are incommensurable forms of life—two different orders of existence, two different spatial and temporal registers in which I am nevertheless compelled, simultaneously, to comport myself. We might want to say that to write requires a transition from the one order of being to the other; but this is a movement that no longer belongs to the time of actions that I might undertake (the crossover time of possibility where one thing follows another for a reason). Rather it is a movement in which the "I" is turned inside out and is no longer in the position of agency. Blanchot says—a statement he repeats again and again in his early criticism— "Kafka grasped the fecundity of literature . . . from the moment that he felt literature was the passage from *Ich* to *Er,* from I to He" (*PF*28–29/*WF*21). However, to enter into this passage is not at all to travel from one point to another. It is rather to enter into a zone in which nothing happens. The writer is outside the time of possibility. Passages now are more like rooms than corridors, and rooms are no longer places of habitation ("Poor room, have you ever been lived in?" [*AO*13/*AwO*4]).

Outside the Subject

It is in Kafka's *Diaries* that Blanchot uncovers the internal link between writing and dying. Both are movements in which I lose the power to say "I"— lose self-possession, mastery, disappear into the event itself. "I am dying" has the grammar of "It is raining" and the mode of being of the *il y a*. In any case I am turned out of my house. It is never given to me to say "I am dead" or "I am finished."[12] Both writing and existence are interminable—this was, Blanchot says, Kafka's experience: "Existence is interminable, it is nothing but an indeterminacy; we do not know if we are excluded from it (which is why we search vainly in it for something solid to hold on to) or whether we are forever imprisoned in it (and so we turn desperately toward the outside). This existence is an exile in the fullest sense: we are not there, we are elsewhere, and we will never stop being there" (*PF*17/*WF*9). Interminability is one of the faces of anarchy, where anarchy is to be understood in its etymological sense as that which is on the hither side of beginning, the *an-archē* whence things begin only to begin again, and then again, without possibility of coming to a point. Mallarmé had asked: "Is there a reason for writing?" (*Très avant, au moins, quant au point, je le formule:—A savoir s'il y a lieu d'écrire*).[13] Likewise Blanchot: "What we want to understand is, why write?" (*PF*25/*WF*17). But the truth is that writing is without why; it is more event than action—as much an interruption of discourse as a species of it, which is why the fragment (which is not a form) becomes for Blanchot the instance or event of writing par excellence.

In "The Paradox of Aytré" (1946) Blanchot asks: "Where does literature begin?" (*PF*73/*WF*68), and to answer he cites Jean Paulhan's story of a sergeant named Aytré who is asked to keep the logbook of a colonial expedition as it proceeds across Madagascar. "There is nothing extraordinary in this log: we arrive, we leave; chickens cost seven sous; we stock up on medicine; our wives receive magazines, etc." (*PF*73/*WF*68). But then "the writing changes": "The explanations rendered become longer. Aytré begins to go into his ideas on colonialization; he describes the women's hairstyles, their locks joined together on each side of their ears like a snail; he speaks of strange landscapes; he goes on to the character of the Malagaches; and so on. In short, the log is useless. What has happened?" (*PF*73/*WF*68). Suddenly writing has become gratuitous, a nonproductive expenditure, an excess of the limits of genre (genre is always purposeful and just; it is writing that is susceptible to formal description and differentiation from an ensemble of alternative possibilities). Writing is at all events no longer under Aytré's control; it now appears of itself, without reason and without end (in principle Aytré could be writing still, like Beckett's Unnamable, of whom Aytré is certainly a prototype). It seems worth remarking that, however gratuitous, Aytré's writing never ceases to be descriptive; it is made of predicates. There is no sign of a schizophrenic's word-salad. One has to say that his writing never ceases to be true of the world. It is only that categories like true and false that define the world's discourse no longer have a coherent application. What categories should one apply to Aytré's writing? It is in fact perfectly ordinary writing, but it no longer belongs to the world that it describes with such unexceptionable precision. The writing is absolutely singular, refractory to all categories: outside all possible worlds.

Anarchic Temporality

What threshold did Aytré cross? One answer is that he has entered what Blanchot calls "the essential solitude," which is an obscure zone of existence that turns subjectivity inside out—reverses polarities, so to speak, so that the writer who holds the pen is suddenly "gripped" by it, which is why Aytré cannot stop writing:

> The writer seems to be the master of his pen; he can become capable of great mastery over words and over what he wants to make them express. But his mastery only succeeds in putting him, keeping him in contact with the fundamental passivity where the word, no longer anything but its appearance—the shadow of a word—never can be mastered or even grasped. It remains the ungraspable which is also unreleasable; the indecisive moment of fascination.
>
> The writer's mastery is not in the hand that writes, the "sick" hand that never lets the pencil go—that can't let it go because what it holds it doesn't really hold; what it holds belongs to the realm of shadows, and it is itself a shade. Mastery always characterizes the other hand, the one that doesn't write and is capable of intervening at the right moment to seize the pencil and put it aside. Thus mastery consists in the power to stop writing, to interrupt what is being written, thereby restoring to the present instant its rights, its decisive trenchancy. (*EL*19/*SL*25)

Mastery: the ability to stop writing! Here certainly is what Sartre is reacting against, namely writing that turns upside down the world of freedom and the exigency of tasks. As Blanchot says in one of his texts on Kafka, "it is not a matter of devoting time to the task, of passing one's time writing, but of passing into another time where there is no longer any task; it is a matter of approaching that point where time is lost, where one enters into the fascination and solitude of time's absence" (*EL*67/*SL*60). What is this other time—this time outside of time? Blanchot explains: "Time's absence is not a purely negative mode. It is the time when nothing begins, when initiative is not possible. . . . Rather than a purely negative mode, it is, on the contrary, a time without negation, without decision, when here is nowhere as well, and each thing withdraws into its image while the 'I' that we are recognizes itself by sinking into the neutrality of a featureless third person. The time of time's absence has no present, no presence" (*EL*26/*SL*30). A Sartrean would have us imagine a hole in existence through which time drains away instead of progressing toward the future in its usual fashion. Or perhaps time is now passive; it does not cease or come to an end but merely pauses, more or less indefinitely, as in the time of waiting. Time in this event is no longer productive of a future. The trick is to understand that this is not altogether a bad thing.

Let me try to elucidate this temporality with a series of glosses:

1. It may have been Mallarmé who discovered this hiatus in which time ceases to pass (without alluding to any eternity). Recall *Igitur; ou, La folie d'Elbehon*, in which a young man is required (at midnight) to descend into the crypt of his ancestors in order to perform a ritual throw of the dice. But the descent takes him across a threshold into a different order of things. Igitur says: "I have always lived with my soul fixed upon the clock"; "The clock has often done me a great deal of good."[14] But midnight on this occasion does not belong to the schedule of clocks. Midnight is "a room of time," not a passage of it (*OC* 438/*SPP* 92). As Igitur descends the stairs he enters another temporality, a moment of "pure time or *ennui*," a vigil in which, in the end, nothing was to have taken place. Midnight is a pure present. It disappears into itself, evacuates itself, instead of moving on (the figure is of midnight passing through a mirror). So there is no transition of the future into the past, nor any *Aufhebung* of the past into the future (*OC* 440). There is a similar moment in Mallarmé's "Mimique" in which a mime's performance occurs in an absent present, an absolute caesura between any before or after: "This—'The scene illustrates but the idea, not any actual action, in a hymen (out of which flows Dream), tainted with vice yet sacred, between desire and fulfillment, perpetration and remembrance: here anticipating, there recalling, in the future, in the past, *under the false appearance of a present.* That is how the Mime operates, whose act is confined to a perpetual illusion without breaking the ice or the mirror: he thus sets up a medium, a pure medium, of fiction' " (*OC* 310/*SPP* 69). The scene is an interruption of mimesis as a project of bringing something back or anyhow

into the present: it is a mimesis without intentionality (it is not *of* something). More exactly, it is a pure performance in which the mime mimes miming: the imitation itself is the thing being imitated. (We'll come back to this.)

2. In a text dating from 1927, evidently the unfinished second part of *Sein und Zeit,* Heidegger takes up Aristotle's conception of time, with its focus on the paradoxical temporality of the "now"—paradoxical because the "now" is both foundational for clock-time and uncontainable within it. "The now," says Heidegger, "has a peculiar double visage. . . . Time is held together within itself by the now; time's specific continuity is rooted in the now. But conjointly, with respect to the now, time is divided, articulated into the no-longer now, the earlier, and the not-yet-now, the later." In other words, the now is nothing in itself. It is a fold in time: "the now that we count in following a motion is *in each instance a different now.*" That is, "the now is always another, an advance from one place to another. In each now the now is a different one, but still each different now is, as now, always now. The ever different nows are, *as different,* nevertheless always exactly *the same,* namely, now." But this sameness is always a difference in itself: "nowness, being-now, is always *otherness, being-other.*"[15] One can imagine that the "now" is the time of unhappy consciousness.

3. Emmanuel Levinas, in "Realité et son ombre" (1948), remarks that in conventional phenomenology the image is understood as a form of mediation on the model of the sign, the symbol, or the concept. We suppose it to be a transparent looking-glass onto the world of things. But Levinas proposes that the image is simply an event of resemblance, where resemblance is not merely a relation between an image and its original; it is an *event*—"the very movement that engenders the image": "Being is not only itself, it escapes itself. . . . Here is a familiar everyday thing, perfectly adapted to the hand which is accustomed to it, but its qualities, color, form, and position at the same time remain as it were behind its being, like the 'old garments' of a soul which had withdrawn from that thing, like a 'still life.' And yet all this is . . . the thing. There is then a duality in . . . this thing, a duality in its being. It is what it is and it is a stranger to itself, and there is a relationship between these two moments. We will say the thing is itself and its image. And that this relationship between the thing and its image is resemblance."[16] A thing is what it is and also how it appears. It has a kind of double ontology: it is "that which is, that which reveals itself in its truth, and, at the same time, it resembles itself, is its own image. The original gives itself as though it were at a distance from itself, as though it were withdrawing from itself." A good example of an image in this sense would be

the cadaver. An image is, so to speak, a materialization of being: it is an event in which the essence of the thing withdraws from it, leaving behind a remainder that no longer belongs to the order of things but which, of course, is not just nothing. The cadaver is a being that has, one might say, lost its reason for being. Its existence is gratuitous. Its time has stopped: its past no longer continues into the future because it no longer has a future. But it is not nothing.

What Levinas wants to know is: What is the "ontological significance" of the materiality of the image, this being without essence, this "mere" resemblance, this stoppage of time? A statue appears to belong to this order of things: namely, to a peculiar temporality: "A statue realizes the paradox of an instant that endures without a future. Its duration is not really an instant. It does not give itself out here as an infinitesimal element of duration, the instant of a flash; it has in its own way a quasi-eternal duration. . . . An eternally suspended future floats around the congealed position of a statue like a future forever to come. The imminence of the future lasts before an instant stripped of the essential characteristic of the present, its evanescence. It will never have completed its task as a present, as though reality withdrew from its own reality and left it powerless."[17] The temporality of the statue is like the temporality of dying: "In dying, the horizon of the future is given, but the future as a promise of a new present is refused; one is in the interval, forever an interval." In this temporality, the being of things has been interrupted. It is not that nothing exists; but what exists falls short of being—remains in some fashion on the hither side of being in a between-world that is neither one thing nor the other, in a temporality of the pure *now* that is at once no longer and not yet. Levinas calls this the "meanwhile" (*entre-temps*): "never finished, still enduring—something inhuman and monstrous." This interval in being is what art brings about: the mode of existence of the work of art is this between-time or *now* that the movement of time is unable to traverse.[18] The meanwhile is the time of vigilance, waiting, dying—and art.

4. The movement of time (that is, clock-time) cannot traverse the interval of being because, as Blanchot says, time in this event is no longer dialectical. It is a "time without negation." This means (among other things) that it is outside the order of conceptual determination in which a merely natural thing is transformed into something essential—an object of consciousness, a thing of the spirit, an identity or universal: an object in the full sense of objectivity (*pour soi*). However, whereas Levinas sees the interval of dying as something

"inhuman and monstrous," Blanchot sees it as something affirmative or, more exactly, as an affirmation outside the dialectical alternatives of positive and negative, namely an interruption of the "death" in which we make sense of things by objectifying them as this or that theme of predication. In "Littérature et la droit à la mort" Blanchot cites Hegel's line: "'Adam's first act, which made him master of the animals, was to give them names, that is, he annihilated them in their existence (as existing creatures)'" (*PF*312/ *WF*323). Mediation is a kind of murder: "When I speak, death speaks in me. My speech is a warning that at this very moment death is loose in the world, that it has suddenly appeared between me, as I speak, and the being I address: it is there between us as the distance that separates us, but this distance is also what prevents us from being separated, because it contains the condition for all understanding. Death alone allows me to grasp what I want to attain; it exists in words as the only way they can have meaning. Without death, everything would sink into absurdity and nothingness" (*PF*313/ *WF*324). To speak—that is, to predicate this of that, to bring things under the rule of identity—is to destroy their singularity or alterity as existing things by integrating them into the order of the same.

However, literature, which is to say writing, is not structured on the model of "I speak." The passage from *I* to *he* that makes writing possible is not a dialectical movement: "It is no longer this inspiration at work, this negation asserting itself, this idea inscribed in the world as though it were the absolute perspective of the world in its totality. It is not beyond the world, but neither is it the world itself: it is the presence of things *before* the world exists, their perseverance after the world has disappeared, the stubbornness of what remains when everything vanishes and the dumbfoundedness of what appears when nothing exists" (*PF*317/ *WF*328). Literature is (this is Blanchot's thesis) the refuge of what is singular and irreducible. It "is a concern for the reality of things, for their unknown, free, and silent existence; literature is their innocence and their forbidden presence" (*PF*319/ *WF*330). This is a presence, however, which now belongs to the interval between past and future: it is the time of the nonidentical, the now, which, as Heidegger says, "is *always otherness, being other*," irreducible to the traversal of this-as-that.

5. Literature belongs to the temporality of *difference in itself*, that is, the dimension of singularity outside the logic of differentiation that distributes things along the plane of identity and difference. In *Logique du sens* (1969) Gilles Deleuze calls this the temporality of the *Aion*, which in contrast to the chronological progress of "interlocking presents" is an event that breaks *ad*

infinitum into "elongated pasts and futures," that is, dimensions that move apart rather together into any sort of unity, continuum, or totality. Deleuze writes (and notice that he cites Mallarmé's "Mimique" as an example of what he has in mind):

> The Aion endlessly divides the event and pushes away past as well as future, without ever rendering them less urgent. The event is that no one ever dies, but has always just died or is always going to die, in the empty present of the Aion, that is, in eternity. As he was describing a murder such that it had to be mimed— a pure ideality—Mallarmé said: "Here advancing, there remembering, to the future, to the past, under the false appearance of a present—in such a manner the Mime proceeds, whose game is limited to a perpetual illusion, without breaking the mirror." Each event is the smallest time, smaller than the minimum of continuous thinkable time, because it is divided into proximate past and imminent future. But it is also the longest time, because it is endlessly subdivided by the Aion which renders it equal to its own unlimited line.[19]

The Aion is the pure event, irreducible to a segment in a chain. It is the time of the absolutely singular—what Deleuze and Guattari elsewhere refer to as a *haecceity,* which is never an instance of anything but itself: for example, five o'clock this afternoon, but one's whole life would do as well so long as one does not imagine such a thing, Aristotle-like, as a totality with a plot. It is rather an absolutely random and contingent event. It is historicity itself. "We are all five o'clock in the evening, or another hour, or rather two hours simultaneously, the optimal and the pessimal, noon-midnight, but distributed in a variable fashion. . . . A *haecceity* has neither beginning nor end, origin nor destination; it is always in the middle. It is not made of points, only of lines. It is a rhizome."[20] (Rhizome means: structured more like crabgrass than like a tree.) So a *haecceity* is always a fragment—not a part broken off from a whole, but something uncontainable within any totality or structure, a testimony to an ontology without integration in which the aleatory—the happening outside of any sequence (or anarchy, for short)—gives the definition of reality, or in any event a definition of the only reality that human beings are ever likely to inhabit (the reality of complex systems).

6. In "La Double séance" (1970), Derrida reads Mallarmé's "Mimique" against some passages from Plato's "Philebus" in order to distinguish two orders of *mimesis:* (1) the order in which *mimesis* is always linked to truth in the sense that *mimesis* is always about "what is." It is important to stress that

everything (truth, reason, the order of things) depends on the "discernibility" *between* "what is" and its imitation, where the one comes first in the order of the things and the other second, and where the one is simple and the other is double (multiplies or supervenes upon the one).[21] (2) "Mimique" gives us a second order, which we might call "*mimesis* in itself," because (as Derrida reads it) Mallarmé's mime simply mimes: "There is no imitation. The Mime imitates nothing. And to begin with, he doesn't imitate. There is nothing prior to the writing of his gestures. Nothing is prescribed for him. No present has preceded or supervised the tracing of his writing. His movements form a figure that no speech anticipates or accompanies. They are not linked with *logos* in any order of consequence."[22] To be sure, it is not that the mime is actually *doing* something, although of course he is not *not* doing anything, either. Derrida tries to sort out the difficulty as follows: "*There is* mimicry," he says. It is just that in this case "we are faced . . . with mimicry imitating nothing; faced, so to speak, with a double that doubles no simple, a double that nothing anticipates, nothing at least that is not itself already double. There is no simple reference. . . . This speculum reflects no reality; it produces 'reality-effects'" (206). So what have we got? "In this speculum with no reality, in this mirror of a mirror, a difference or dyad does exist, since there are mimes and phantoms. But it is a difference without a reference [that is, a difference indifferent to any identity, or difference in itself], or rather a reference without a referent, without any first or last unit, a ghost that is the phantom of no flesh, wandering about without a past, without any death, birth, or presence" (206).

What the mime discloses is a pure *between,* a caesura in being that interrupts the logic of identity and difference, real thing and image, single and double, same and other. Derrida notices that "the word 'between' has no full meaning of its own."[23] One thinks of Blanchot's favorite words ("common words," he calls them)—"perhaps," "almost," "maybe," "unless," "meanwhile."[24] Derrida tries to locate this *between* with words like *différance, tympan, hymen, pli* or "fold"—spatial metaphors for what Blanchot figures temporally when he locates writing in the interval between *archē* and *telos,* design and completion, past and future: the *entre-temps* of dying, suffering, waiting, Igitur's "midnight," and so on. This interval is outside the order of reasons in which productions can be justified—outside the order of *this* as *that* (or *this* for *that,* or *this* about *that*): outside any subsumptive order that places one thing in the service, branch, or business of another. The singular belongs to this *between* or caesura that disengages the relation of universal and particular. The singular is difference in itself, the one thing that is unlike anything: the nonidentical, unrepresentable, absolute alterity outside all relations of the one and the two, the same and the other, this and that.

Ontology of the Snow Shovel

Consider in this context Marcel Duchamp's snow shovel, which he buys at a hardware store and then exhibits in his studio under the title, "In Advance of a Broken Arm." What is the relation between the snow shovel in the hardware store and the shovel in the studio? The shovel has changed neither formally nor materially, but it *has* changed. The trick is to say how. Elsewhere we thought in terms of change-of-place.[25] Now we have the resources to think in terms of temporal change (or change of temporality) as well. Notice that the logical or universal language of identity and difference doesn't reach this change. To be sure, the shovel is still, empirically, a snow shovel; in fact it is *that* very snow shovel, the same as it ever was, except it is now different without ceasing to be the same. At some point (what should we say?) it has come to occupy the world differently, as if having been inserted into things differently—perhaps it is now more image than thing without ceasing to be the thing it is, rather the way Levinas was trying to get at when he said that, in art, each thing is its own image, both itself and a stranger to itself, always lagging behind itself a little, or perhaps standing a little in front of itself, but never quite coinciding. As if in Duchamp's hands *that* particular shovel were *materializing* differently from the way it did in the hardware store, not in the sense that it is now made of different matter or is formed differently (how could it be?), but that it now occupies reality the way Heidegger's hammer does when someone discovers that it is broken. It has thickened sufficiently to interrupt our relation to it; we are now "with" the thing differently, suddenly at odds with the temporality of tasks. It has ceased its prosthetic mode of existence in the way the words of a poet do. What Duchamp's snow shovel does *not* do is concretize a universal; on the contrary, it is particularized to the point where it no longer has a share in the category to which it logically (and functionally) belongs. It is to all appearances your typical shovel, but not quite, or maybe it is a little too much of one: a shovel in excess of its function. If, when Heidegger's hammer breaks, it falls out of the world in which hammers have a place, so does the shovel fall out of the snow-covered-sidewalk world when it enters Duchamp's studio. It enters not only a different space but also a different temporality, one that (like

Aytré's writing) cannot be exhausted by the accomplishment of clearing the driveway. You could break into Duchamp's studio and steal his shovel (which in any case vanished without a trace, or rather with only the trace of a photograph, which in any event may not be a reproduction of the original shovel but only a replica of what the real thing, when it was a work of art, looked like: in other words, the trace of a trace)—you could steal Duchamp's shovel and return it to the temporality of shoveling, but it might very well retain the aura of its history. Of course, the question arises: for whom would it retain this aura? One answer is: possibly no one. The thing would look for all the world like any other shovel. But it would be *metaphysically* different in virtue of its history; its history does not depend on anyone observing it or reconstructing its itinerary. It is rather that one has to inhabit this history in order to experience the shovel's difference. And of course if one enters *this* zone, *everything* is different.

I mean that, for one who encounters Duchamp's provocation, *no snow shovel is any longer just a snow shovel:* objects become just things again. Having had, let us say, a Duchamp experience, one can no longer experience snow shovels in their (as Heidegger would say) merely "equipmental" being. The snow shovel, all snow shovels, and perhaps all sorts of equipment, have been translated into the temporality of the work of art, without (and this seems crucial) leaving the temporality of production in which implements help things like walks to get shoveled. Duchamp's provocation simply opens up or onto another temporality adjacent to the one we inhabit in our workaday shoveling form of life, which means that it is possible for every mundane object, however trivial in itself, to lead a double life as both instrument and artifact. Anthropology is another way of encountering this double temporality.

It is possible that only as artifacts can everyday objects have a history at all, and then only as objects in natural or art history (or perhaps the history of science and technology) of the kind memorialized in museums. In his essay "La Parole quotidienne" Blanchot makes the argument that the everyday as such falls beneath the threshold of history (or, like Ponge's things, beneath the threshold of description). The everyday is "existence in its very spontaneity and as it is lived—at the moment when, lived, it escapes every speculative formulation, perhaps all coherence and regularity." Of course, Blanchot, existentialist that he is, is thinking of the everyday subject, that is, one of us—one of Heidegger's "they" (*das Man*): the one who is no longer a subject (no longer says "I," is no longer even a "who"). "The everyday escapes. Why does it escape? Because it is without a subject. When I live the everyday, it is any man, anyone at all who does so; and this anyone, properly speaking, is neither me nor, properly, the other; he is neither the one nor the other and, in their interchangeable presence, their annulled irreciprocity, both one and the other—yet without there being an 'I' or an 'alter ego' able to give rise to a *dialectical recognition*" (*EI*364/ *IC*244). But this only means that at the level of the everyday the subject "does not belong to the objective realm. To live it as what might be lived through a series of technical acts (represented by the vacuum cleaner, the washing machine, the refrigerator, the radio, the car) is to substitute a number of compartmentalized actions for this indefinite presence, this connected movement (which is, however, not a whole) by which we are *continually,* though in the mode of discontinuity, in relation with the *indeterminate* set of possibilities" (*EI*364/ *IC*244). The point would be that Duchamp's shovel likewise escapes the "objective realm" when it shows up in his studio. Heidegger would say that it now has the density of the thing rather than the transparency of an object. It is now "a shovel," where the quotation marks map the *between* to which the thing now belongs. But then of course there is the question of whether it is any longer properly a shovel: the quotation marks map out the region or temporality of the "not quite" or "no longer"—the region of the "irreal" that, for Blanchot, constitutes the space between something and nothing that he calls *l'espace littéraire.*

When Aytré's writing begins to exceed the limits of the practice he was assigned to perform, his language undergoes the invisible transport of the snow shovel. "To write is . . . to withdraw language from the world, to detach it from what makes it a power according to which, when I speak, it is the world that declares itself, the clear light of day that develops through tasks undertaken, through action and time" (*EL*21/ *SL*16). Language itself does not change, does not cease to be language—does not cease to be made of words we know how to use, does not cease to mean—but it is now *materialized:* language and also the image of language.

L'amitié

But how is it, not just with words and things, but with other people? Here we come upon the boundary that Blanchot shares with Emmanuel Levinas. Can people materialize in the way that the words of writing do? And, if so, how does this happen? As we have seen, they can become cadaverous. Less drastically, or perhaps more, to materialize is to cease to be a thing of the spirit or affair of consciousness; it is to be reinserted into the world as a porous and vulnerable subject rather than as a philosophical subject who, anyhow, only exists on paper. Levinas clarifies this state of affairs by way of sensibility, the caress, and the nudity of the other who approaches me outside of every context that I have for appropriating the world; in the same stroke the other interrupts my self-relation, turns me inside out, exposes me to the world (to the third person and to the claims of justice). I am no longer a cognitive subject; I am my skin. Levinas calls this condition of exposure, of subjectivity outside the subject, ethics (or, more exactly, the ethical). Blanchot calls it, among other things, friendship—or, more exactly, the relation of "one for the other" that occurs in the *between* or *entre-temps* between friends (or, for all of that, between lovers).

The crucial thing is to understand that for Blanchot friendship is not an intersubjective relation. It is not a side-by-side relation of collaboration in which we act or exist as one, as if sharing things in common, whether a language, a world, or a sense of identity or purpose. Friendship for Blanchot entails foreignness or separation as one of its conditions. It is an ethical rather than fraternal relation, a face-to-face relation in which I am responsible to and for the other and not just for holding up my end or keeping my side of the bargain. So in contrast to Aristotle, Blanchot does not think of friendship on the model of logical integration in which the bond between me and my friend, my sense of oneness with him as if we were interchangeable, can become foundational for a more comprehensive order of things. In other words, friendship is not utopian—not an incipient or exemplary community (unless in Bataille's anarchic sense of "a community for those who have no community"). It is on the contrary a relation without terms, a relationship of dissymmetry and non-identity. One inhabits this relation not as a sovereign "I" but as a "who" or a "me"—a mode of being in the accusative rather than executive or declarative position.

For example, in "L'amitié" (1971), Blanchot says that the "I" of Georges Bataille's writings is

> very different from the ego that those who knew him in the happy and unhappy particularity of life would like to evoke in the light of a memory. Everything leads one to think that the personless presence at stake in such a movement introduces an enigmatic relation into the existence of him who indeed decided to speak of it but not to claim it as his own, still less to make it an event of his biography

(rather, a gap in which the biography disappears). And when we ask ourselves the question "Who was the subject of this experience?" this question is perhaps already an answer if, even to him who led it, the experience asserted itself in this interrogative form, by substituting the openness of a "Who?" without answer for the closed and singular "I"; not that this means that he had simply to ask himself "What is this I that I am?" but much more radically to recover himself without reprieve, no longer as "I" but as a "Who?," the unknown and slippery being of an indefinite "Who?"[26]

In this respect there is an internal coherence between friendship and writing (*l'écriture*). Like writing, friendship is less an executive performance than a space (or temporality) into which one is drawn that deprives one of all the various familiar possessions and initiatives (like the ability to begin or end). Friendship is what Blanchot calls a relation of the third kind, which is neither a relation of cognition nor an "I-Thou" relation of philosophical dialogue but rather "a relation without relation" (*EI*104/*IC*73)—one can think of it as a kind of ecstatic relation outside the alternatives of identity/difference, same/other, presence/absence, being/non-being, past/future. It is "a pure interval" (*EI*98/*IC*69), "an interruption of being" (*EI*109/*IC*77), that suspends us together in what Blanchot calls "the infinite conversation"—an example of which prefaces *L'entretien infini* and punctuates *Le Pas au-delà*. There we have two old men, or at any rate two people no longer young, who for who knows how many years have been talking together much the way Aytré writes:

> ±± "*I asked you to come . . .*" *He stops an instant:* "*Do you remember how things happened?*" *The interlocutor reflects in turn:* "*I remember it very well.*"—"*Ah, good. I was not very sure, finally, of having initiated the conversation myself.*"—"*But how could I have come otherwise?*"—"*Friendship would have sent you.*" *He reflects again:* "*I wrote to you, didn't I?*"—"*On several occasions.*"—"*But did I not also call you on the telephone?*"—"*Certainly, several times.*"—"*I see you want to be gentle with me. I am grateful. As a matter of fact it is nothing new; the weariness* [fatigue] *is not greater, only it has taken another turn.*"—"*It has several, I believe we know them all. It keeps us alive.*"—"*It keeps us speaking. I would like to state precisely when this happened, if only one of the characteristics of the thing did not make precision difficult. I can't help thinking of it.*"—"*Well, then we must think of it together. Is it something that happened to you?*"—"*Did I say that?*" *And he adds almost immediately, with a force of decision that might justly be termed moving, so much does it seem to exceed his resources of energy:* "*Nothing that has happened,*"

yet along with it this reservation: "Nothing that has happened to me."—"Then in
my eyes it is nothing serious.—"I didn't say that it was serious." He continues to
meditate on this, resuming: "No, it's not serious," as if he perceived at that instant
that what is not serious is much more so." (EI xiii/ IC xv)

Obviously this is not a philosophical dialogue of the kind Gadamer recommends—namely, two friends, more or less identical, engaged in a disinterested give-and-take that tries to elucidate a subject matter (*die Sache*). Like the dialogue between the lovers (if that is what they are) in *L'attente l'oubli*, Blanchot's "infinite conversation" does not have a logical structure, a *logos;* neither has it an *archē* or a *telos*. It cannot be made intelligible by comparison either with the logical proposition, which is why it does not appear to be about anything, or with the dialectic, since it doesn't go anywhere. It has the structure of waiting. Of the lovers in *L'attente l'oubli* it is said: "There is no real dialogue between them. Only waiting maintains between what they say a certain relation, words spoken to wait, a waiting of words" (*AO52/ AwO25*). Waiting is how one inhabits the anarchic temporality of friendship (or of writing, suffering, fatigue, dying . . .).

Blanchot emphasizes the opacity of the friend (or lover) who is a presence that cannot be comprehended, who is "radically out of my reach" (*EI98/ IC69*) and whose intimacy does not dissipate the strangeness between us. So I am not privy to my friend, about whom I must therefore remain discreet—"discretion" captures in one word the basic idea of Blanchotian ethics: "We must give up trying to know those to whom we are linked by something essential; by this I mean we must greet them in the relation with the unknown in which they greet us as well, in our estrangement. Friendship, this relationship without dependence, without episode, yet into which all of the simplicity of life enters, passes by way of the recognition of common strangeness that does not allow us to speak of our friends but only to speak to them" (*A300/ F291*). Hence the idea that friendship is an ethical relation on the hither side of or beyond being. It is also a relation that "exposes me to death or finitude";[27] that is, friendship belongs with writing to the temporality of dying, or to the interval of art in which my relation with the other is always shadowed, even constituted, by the imminence of his death (if "his" is the word). In *La communauté inavouable* Blanchot writes:

> Now, "the basis of communication" is not necessarily speech, or even the silence
> that is its foundation and punctuation, but the exposure to death, no longer my

own exposure, but someone else's, whose living and closest presence is already the eternal and unbearable absence, an absence that the deepest mourning does not diminish. And it is in life itself that that absence of someone else has to be met. It is with that absence—its uncanny presence, always under the prior threat of disappearance—that friendship is brought into play and lost at each moment, a relation without relation or without relation other than the incommensurable. (*CI*46/ *UC*25)

This is certainly strange, but it recalls Levinas's reworking of Heidegger's analysis of Dasein's self-awareness as Being-toward-death. For Heidegger this awareness is (says Levinas) "a supreme lucidity and hence a supreme virility"—Heidegger's notion of authenticity is shaped entirely by the ontology of the Greek hero (as the German romantics imagined him) who confronts his destiny in a history set apart from everyday life. "It [*Sein-zum-Tod*] is," says Levinas, "Dasein's assumption of the uttermost possibility of existence, which makes possible all other possibilities, and consequently makes possible the very feat of grasping a possibility—that is, it makes possible activity and freedom."[28] For Levinas by contrast my death, however much it hovers and looms, is the plain and simple limit of my virility precisely because it is always (like the friend!) outside my reach as a cognitive subject; like the Messiah it is an impossibility, an event in which "something absolutely unknowable appears" (71). My death, such as it is, is more Kafkaesque than Homeric: always premature, it will come too late for me to experience it. I am gone in the very instant it arrives. Think of Kafka's K. Everyone will be privy to my death but me. Death is the end of discretion.

It turns out that this is pretty much Levinas's point as well. Before everything else it is the death of the other that stares me in the face, weighs upon me and thus constitutes me as an ethical subject: "In its mortality, the face before me summons me, calls for me, begs for me, as if the invisible death that must be faced by the Other . . . were my business. It is as if that invisible death, ignored by the Other . . . were already 'regarding' me prior to confronting me, and becoming the death that stares me in the face. The other man's death calls me into question, as if, by my possible future indifference, I had become the accomplice of the death to which the other, who cannot see it, is exposed; and as if, even before vowing myself to him, I had to answer for this death of the other, and to accompany the Other in his mortal solitude."[29] Interestingly, it is a condition of roughly this sort that the narrator of Blanchot's *L'arrêt de mort*

(1948) inhabits: his love affairs are prolonged, cadaverous experiences of mortality; he himself meanwhile appears to embody the impossibility of dying: "What makes it happen that every time my grave opens, now, I rouse a thought there that is strong enough to bring me back to life? The very derisive laughter of my death."[30] As if exposure to death became a kind of interminable vigil.

In *L'instant de ma mort* Blanchot recalls, or imagines a Blanchot-like narrator recalling, "a young man—a man still young—prevented from dying by death itself."[31] During the Occupation he is hauled out of his château one evening and placed before a firing squad:

> I know—do I know it—that the one at whom the Germans were already aiming, awaiting but the final order, experienced then a feeling of extraordinary lightness, a sort of beatitude (nothing happy, however)—sovereign elation? The encounter of death with death?
>
> In his place, I will not try to analyze. He was perhaps suddenly invincible. Dead—immortal. Perhaps ecstasy. Rather the feeling of compassion for suffering humanity, the happiness of not being immortal or eternal. Henceforward he was bound to death by a surreptitious friendship. (5)

CHAPTER SEVEN

The Contestation of Death

Philippe Lacoue-Labarthe

Translation by Philip Anderson

L'instant de la mort is probably Maurice Blanchot's testamentary book.

This very brief story, if it is a "story," in which, as we know, Maurice Blanchot recounts how, on July 20, 1944, he had the "good fortune of almost being shot" (his own terms, reported by Jacques Derrida),[1] was considered such by many of us when it was published six years ago.

"Testamentary book" can be understood in various ways; the word, the concept of testament (attestation, testimony, etc.) are among the most difficult to think rigorously, and I think I am aware of the many analyses that have been devoted to them in recent times, even if, in some cases, their artful virtuosity seems to me to be precisely *contestable*. (I will come back, where appropriate, to what unites and divides "attest," "contest," "protest," "detest," "test," among other terms.) I take "testamentary book" to mean, in the simplest possible way here, "last book": the last book of Maurice Blanchot, the last words uttered or the last words written for publication, under the authority, if the term can be ventured, of the three instances which can be said to have governed (or disoriented), organized (or unworked) what one must resign oneself to calling his work, despite the impossibility of laying out its limits: Politics (or History), Experience of death and Literature. But "the last book" also means, at the same time, just that: *the last book,* the last words of the "last to speak," final words. The end of Literature.

"End," in turn, is yet another word that can be understood in several ways: culmination (term, stop), completion (finishing), goal (according to what is called the principle of finality). I would happily put the accent on a supplementary meaning, derived from the Aristotelian interpretation of the *telos* but entirely reworked by modern thought since Rousseau and Kant: here the end is thought as the very origin. This does not mean either the beginning or, still less, the cause, although Aristotle conceived of the *telos* in the framework of his theory of causality or, more precisely, his onto-aetiology. Nor does it even mean "essence," a word that Maurice Blanchot nevertheless used frequently about literature, in syntagms of this sort: the essence of literature is to go toward its own essence, which is its disappearance. Rather it means the *condition* of possibility: and I highlight the transcendental concept of "condition," which others will translate by "negativity" or "mediation" (Hegel, Hölderlin, for example), to designate precisely the register on which the logic of origin operates, which is indeed, despite the speculative *doxa,* the register of finitude.

In this way, provided that these premises are accepted, it should be clear that if *L'instant de ma mort* is the "last book" (by Maurice Blanchot), it only signifies the end of Literature inasmuch as it has as its only end the marking of its origin. The death of Literature would be its birth. This would be less a question of its essence than its very existence. Or, more bluntly put again, a question of its right to existence.

(I open here a brief parenthesis, in internal exclusion: an impossible place, then, as is that of existence *itself.* And thus also the place that *must be* occupied or *inhabited;* and the place in which, probably, *there are* together the three instances that I invoked just before: Politics, Experience of death, Literature.

Blanchot has been much accused, in recent times, of having been the victim, beyond doubtful political illusions [and, the reverse, of "narcissistic"[2] self-indulgence], of a historicist and teleological conception of literature, undoubtedly stemming from Mallarmé—but has Blanchot ever concealed his debt, and an immense difficulty?—and, beyond Mallarmé, sometimes from the romanticism of Jena, sometimes from Hegel, that is to say from Kojève-Bataille as well, when it is not from Heidegger. Some of the clearly and deliberately blunt propositions I have just formulated seem to be dialectic in style and could lead to thinking that I thereby confirm and approve that "line of descent"—as the argument goes. That is worthy of reflection. But not *here;* this is not the "place" for it.

What I would like to put forward, on the other hand, and this is therefore really my first hypothesis, is that there is no literature or, let us acknowledge it, no literary work that does not wish to be *definitive.* What literature has wanted or sought, since some such thing has existed, if it exists, is its end: the secret of its origin, the condition [rule, law, prohibition] it must undergo to be possible. What literature wants or seeks—we should all know and take account of this— is the impossible.

I close the parenthesis.)

And I put forward my second hypothesis.

The "lesson" of *L'instant de ma mort,* its testamentary legacy if you will, is to affirm that to write—to write "in its major sense," in the words of Roger Laporte, whose unique work *Une vie* happens to culminate, to come to completion and to end with a volume entitled *Moriendo*—is not to recount, whatever modality of time be chosen, how one lives or how others live, which is one and the same thing. But it is to say how one has died. And it is the very exercise of thought, which is not to find it surprising that "I am," or to marvel at it, but which is to sustain the fact that "I have no longer been," perhaps "I already am no longer" or "I never have been," and to be overwhelmed, devastated by it. Which strictly defines existence, as I hope to touch on further on.

The experience of death—that pure impossibility—could be the condition, the end and the origin, indeed the categorical imperative (the unconditioned "there must be") of literature and of thought.

I set aside for the moment the mention I have just made of thought and, thereby, of ethics—things which are indeed indissociable.

I will keep, or try to keep to literature alone.

From the standpoint of *L'instant de ma mort,* from the term or the end that this book represents today, that is to say provisionally (the said "end of Literature" is infinite, it is interminable in law), three things at least seem to me to be worthy of mention:

1. The recurrence of similar scenes, not only, as one might expect, in the work of Blanchot (*L'arrêt de la mort, La Folie du jour, L'écriture du désastre*), nor even only in that of Bataille, which is so close to it, in particular in the texts

written during the war (*L'expérience intérieure, La Pratique de la joie devant la mort*); but again in some monuments of literature contemporary with Blanchot, or that Blanchot judges to be contemporary with his own.

I take but a few examples, rapidly, and only from French literature. There is the obvious case of the same scene, or almost, in 1944, recounted by Malraux, but in "scatty" mode, as he would have put it, in the *Antimémoires* (a significant title, as Maurice Blanchot knew well, having talked about it). It matters little that it may have been suggested, "mythomania" playing its role too, by a famous letter by Dostoyevsky, or that it is treated with cocky humor: *Lazare* is also there, close at hand, with its far greater gravity, telling the same "experience without experience," "in-experienced" (these are Blanchot's terms) of death. There is, further, the story Artaud tells of his death while undergoing electric shock treatment, at Rodez—or, it comes to the same thing, on Golgotha two thousand years ago—in his famous "Conférence du Vieux-Colombier" (of which I have spoken elsewhere).[3] That this may have been suggested by the Nietzsche, notably, among others, of *Ecce homo* ("Inasmuch as I am my father, I am already dead; inasmuch as I am my mother, I am still alive and getting old.") matters little either, despite the enigma of the identification: with Christ, with Dionysus, with both of them at the same time. Behind these "cases," and I could quote others, we are well aware that there stands, in our literary tradition, Mallarmé—with Hegel, of course, undeniably: the "I am perfectly dead" in the letter to Cazalis, or "destruction was my Beatrice," and so many poems. And therefore Baudelaire's hell or Rimbaud's *Saison*, not to put too much emphasis, all the same, on Chateaubriand's *Mémoires d'outre-tombe*, a title which, to say the least, is eloquent.

It has been said recently that this paradox of the impossible possibility (of the experience) of death owes a lot to Poe. Baudelaire, Mallarmé *obligent*. A Poe period or century has even been suggested, overdetermined by English romanticism and the English fantastic. (But why not German romanticism, the German fantastic? Where does Poe come from, via Coleridge, if not from Schelling? And is not one of Blanchot's major references, outside the Jena circle, Kafka's "Gracchus the Hunter"?) Maurice Blanchot would be indebted to such a "Poe century"; and thereby "dated." Poe, in such a case, would be reduced to Monsieur de Valdemar's famous and evidently impossible declaration: "Can't you see I'm dead!"

Let us assume this nevertheless—for a moment. After all, in our Letters, as one says, no one is ignorant of the role played by Poe, his importance, to the point where he can be considered, in many ways, to be a "French author." And his standing in *Weltliteratur* cannot, of course, be underestimated.

But just as I pointed out the "Malraux case"—the case of an author *named* in *L'instant de la mort*—I was moved, during a dialogue with Jacques Derrida[4] at Cerisy, four years ago, on exactly that text, to mention two other cases, both from our so-called autobiographical tradition, and thus from our supposedly fictional literature. These two precedents of the "scene" of the in-experienced experience of death are both prior to the romantic age (and to the appearance of the *concept* of Literature): the story Montaigne tells of a fall from a horse, in chapter 6 of book 2 of the *Essais*: "De l'exercitation" ("On practice"); the second "Promenade" in Rousseau's *Rêveries,* which can justly be considered as a quotation of Montaigne, less because of the accident evoked (a hard fall, in both cases) than on another account, less often evoked, which is that Rousseau finds in Montaigne the precise formulation of the *paradox* that can lead him to grasp his "feeling of existence."

I quote, for the record:

> But practice cannot help us in the greatest task we have to perform: dying. . . .
>
> Yet it seems to me that there is a way of accustoming ourselves to it [death] and to some extent trying it. We can have experience of it [my emphasis], *if not whole and complete, at least such as not to be useless and to make us stronger and more steady. If we cannot come to grips with death we can approach it, we can reconnoiter it; and if we do not reach its stronghold at least we will see and explore the approaches to it.*[5]

It is true that Montaigne's words are inscribed, deliberately so moreover, in an immense tradition of ancient wisdom and meditation of death: the famous chapter 20 of book 1 alone, so often misunderstood: "To philosophize is to learn how to die", already shows as much. From remarks of this sort one could draw nothing but a schoolish and assiduously accumulated collection of *topoï.* Nevertheless, in the telling of an anecdote borrowed from Seneca, Montaigne does not refrain from radicalizing the paradox of the "experience" of death, since that is indeed the word he uses, speaking of "philosophizing not just unto death, but into death itself." Above all, he describes a real experience, in which the paradox of possible-impossible death is not simply resolved by way of the "semblance of" or the "as if" (and still less of the "quasi" or the "almost"), but, on the contrary, is maintained, takes firmer shape, or is fixed in the sudden and stupefying onset of the "feeling of existence" (of the *fact* of being), which is each time, in the three texts, identified with a "feeling of lightness," of detachment and inexplicable elation. As the last sentence of Blanchot's brief story summarizes it, "There remains only the feeling of lightness that is death itself or, to be more precise, the instant of my death still pending."[6] That perhaps, quite simply, is the feeling of *immortality,* from the very beginning at the foundation of what we call ethics. And I am not only thinking of Spinoza and of a particular proposition in the *Ethics,* affirming that we feel or experience ourselves to be immortal. I am also thinking about the *Phaedo,* to which I will return, which was so scandalously mistreated by the scholastic tradition of antiquity—and what followed it.

2. One could argue, and I would willingly do so, that literature as we still understand it (in its "modern" sense) is not born—if it is born at a given moment, somewhere—with the novel, which derives from the epic form, but with so-called *autobiography.*

But is easy to see the countless questions that come forth.

Where, for example, can this autobiography be seen to start from, and where can one situate its end to begin with and its origin? With the Modern Age, between Dante and Montaigne? With Christianity, the test of confession, Saint Augustine? Earlier, in Plato, for example the Plato of "Letter VII"? Or in the Platonic and Neo-Platonic tradition?

Does this genre—but is it a genre, as classical genre theory would understand it?—when it is established, as it must have been, suppose a change in the *autos,* in the *ego,* in the "I," the Self, in what we have called, in short, since the dawn of Modernity, the subject? Is that connected to the regime of enunciation? And if a profound change in the *autos,* etc. must be supposed, does that necessarily mean that this genre is enclosed in what Heidegger, with and against Hegel, set down as a "metaphysics of subjectity," from Descartes to Nietzsche and beyond? Or must one think on the contrary that there must already be a "genre" of autobiography for a book like the *Discourse on Method* to come to light or be possible?

Or again, behind this "subject," what understanding of the said "experience" is at stake? Is it "lived experience," *Erlebnis,* as Heidegger would be quick to say? But what would the relationship be between this "lived experience" and the *bios* which is found not by chance, both in the Greek, in the concept of *biography,* and (before that?) in syntagms or titles à la Plutarch: *Lives of Famous Men,* etc.? Or is it ex-perience, in the strict sense: being in and out of—

traversing (*ex-*)—peril (*periri*); in German: *Er-farhung* (*fahren, Gefahr,* etc.)? And what is the relationship between experience understood thus and, in Latin, what Latin gives French as *épreuve,* with its meanings relating to feelings, judicial proceedings, narrative, religion, science, etc. (and which "trial" in English, with its associated notions of being put or putting to the *proof,* partly covers)? How far does experience (or trial), in the lexicon of mysticism or philosophy suppose, as Bataille said, "bringing *life* itself into play"?

I obviously cannot answer all these questions, limited though they be in relation to those I could have asked.

What I would like to point out quite simply, based on the few examples I have evoked, is that if autobiography, in general, both in its end and its origin, supposes an *experience* in the strict sense, and if that experience is regularly one and the same as going through (or undergoing the trial of, being proved by) death, however infinitely paradoxical or impossible that may be, then one is at least constrained to modify that "generic" index and to talk—at the least— of *autothanatography.* This proposition or formulation is neither new nor original. Several people contributed to developing it, twenty years ago, around the work of Roger Laporte. But I think I can still lay claim to it, *at least* within certain limits.

It is quite plausible that, in the concept of ex-perience or the syntagm "going through death," there remain hidden or veiled the remains of very old initiatory and mytho-epic schemata. I have had occasion, on the subject of Artaud (but Nietzsche, for example, would lead one's thoughts in the same direction), to recall the ancient *nekuia:* the descent to Hell and meeting the dead that is the (exact) center of the *Odyssey,* the *Aeneid,* the *Pharsal* even; and which is repeated ceaselessly, from Dante to Poe and Rimbaud, right up to the present, as can be seen. That is, *at least* right up to Maurice Blanchot, and I am also thinking, as it happens, of the use he made of the myth of Orpheus, to indicate precisely the end of Literature as its beginning. The remanence of myths, or their somber and stormy redeployment, is perhaps what should not be consented to; or should be *contested.* However, we can but recognize it here.

3. A last remark, then: I very quickly evoked, just before, a possible change of regime of enunciation both at the end and at the origin of "autobiography." I was thinking on the one hand, as goes without saying, of the tripartite Platonic division of modes of enunciation: diegetic, mimetic, and mixed, which, via a few misunderstandings, is at the source of the tripartite division of genres

in classical theory: lyric, dramatic, epic. As the diegetic mode is the one reputed to be specific to the *autos* or the *ego* (of the "I"): "*I* here in person speak and say that . . . ," the conclusion ended up being that lyricism is a "subjective genre," and was very nearly fatal to it. Now neither in Platonic dithyramb nor in classical or modern lyricism nor even in the oratorical genre is there a place for the "subject" of autobiography. Unless one considers Montaigne to be a lyric poet, since such things are tried, in school text books, on Rousseau . . . The subject of autobiography, if there is one, has to be of a quite different substance. And if one calls this "genre" *autothanatography,* then there can, by right, be no further question of a *subject* (*subjectum,* indeed *substantia*). And if it is an "I" that speaks there, which remains to be shown, it probably no longer has the least *con-sistency;* and nothing guarantees that it remains, or even quite simply is itself or the same: *autos, ho autos.* What sort of subject could say: "I am dead"?

That is why, moreover, I thought this: there only exist, to my knowledge, two "autobiographical" texts by Maurice Blanchot: *L'instant de ma mort* and that short page, detached like a fragment in *L'écriture du désastre,* entitled "(Une scène primitive?)," of which moreover a first version is available, with a much less suspensive or more definitive title: "Une scène primitive."[7] (Other texts, "autobiographical" in appearance: *Après coup, Foucault tel que je l'ai connu, La Communauté inavouable,* indeed the [unpublished] "Memorandum," are rather of the order—I will not say of testimony—true or false, it matters little—but of *attestation:* an *other,* in fact [Dionys Mascolo, for example] or by right [the anonymous crowd of the revolutionaries or, as euphemism has it, of the "*contestataires*" of May 68], in fact *and* by right [the latter, and Bataille, who died in 1962, but Levinas too et al.] could put this attestation to the *proof,* which is *always* possible: prove it or invalidate it, whatever views are held on the matter by all those who twist Celan's words: "No-one bears witness for the witness." As soon as there is witness, or *attestation,* another, whoever that may be, is *always* implicated, that is to say *contested* (*cum-testari*) in the strict sense. Would that this had not to be recalled, even this elliptically.)

L'instant de ma mort, "(Une scène primitive?)," then. A childhood scene, the death scene. They really are "scenes." When one thinks it through, Maurice Blanchot may well have reduced "autobiography," more effectively than Nicolas de Cues, to its (almost) pure form.

Now the remarkable and difficult thing in these two texts is that Maurice Blanchot speaks of himself—or of "him"—in the third person. Even though the I as the (supposed) addresser of the text intervenes explicitly in *L'instant de ma mort* (for example: "In his place [in the place of "the still young man," who is the "character" of the "story"], I will not try to analyze this feeling of lightness"[8]—the verb, left as it was in the manuscript, is in the future tense, leaving the enigma unresolved); and it intervenes implicitly, through an act of direct address, in "(Une scène primitive)": "You who are living later on, near a heart that beats no more, suppose, suppose it: the child . . ."[9] That strange dissociation of the "subject" in question is not simply that which the general phenomenon of enunciation implies (it is at least re-marked upon); nor is it of the same order as that of classical narrative enunciation; and we know moreover that Blanchot explicitly, and even solemnly denied or dismissed narrative as such, notably in the final sentence of *La Folie du jour*. But one cannot but wonder, were it only because of the address itself, in its form and its "impossible" meaning—"You who are living later on . . ."—if Maurice Blanchot does not reveal, in a single stroke, the regime of all supposedly "autobiographical" enunciation, which is decidedly *autothanatographical,* since the "subject" clearly must be somehow *already dead* to be able to say itself and write itself *as an other:* to accept summoning "itself" or contesting "itself," thereby summoning or contesting death (or the deceased) in himself: producing together the witnesses of both parties.

In which case autothanatography is in fact always, to venture a slightly simpler term, *allobiography.*

There is no chance, in any case, of ecstasy occurring at the heart of the "story" in either of these texts. In *La Communauté inavouable,* thinking of Bataille, Blanchot says of ecstasy: "Its distinctive feature is that whoever experiences it is no longer there when he experiences it, is therefore no longer there to experience it."[10] Yet it nevertheless takes place: *there is* ecstasy. The structure here is rigorously the same as that of "the experience without experience," "inexperienced," of death: "I is another" *(Je est un autre),* in a much more radical sense, probably, than that which Rimbaud gave the expression he invented (despite the *Saison* and Rimbaud's being, in Mallarmé's terms, the "opéré vivant de la poésie" [the bearer of the open wound of poetry]). That is why death is *immemorial,* just like birth, and has always already dismissed the subject. It is put this way in *L'écriture du désastre:* "To die means: dead, *you* [my emphasis] already are so, in an immemorial past, having died a death that was not yours. . . . That uncertain death, always foregone, *attestation* [my emphasis again] of a past without present, is never individual."[11]

Autothanatography (allobiography)—and this is true for Montaigne, for Rousseau, for so many others—is the register (I dare not say genre or form) of the *desistance* of the subject, to use a word here which was Jacques Derrida's generous gift to me. The subject disappears therein, gives way, withdraws and fades away, has in reality already disappeared, retired from itself, taciturn (*infans*), absent (as is said of someone who is distracted), lost; and yet it remains or comes back to say, in another voice (exactly the same), what happened without it (with and in it), an impossible attestation, witness of which it is not the witness but which it persists in bearing, because "it" was (not) there and "it" was (not) it(self). Blanchot's relentless situating of the "birth" of Literature in the shift from the first person to the third person, from "I" to "it," indeed to the impersonal "it," is well known. It is perhaps that, finally, which is essentially in *question* in the "autobiographical" *process;* with or without argument, it matters not, just as the sincerity or the accuracy of the witness—veracity—is of no interest. What counts and counts alone is the *litigation* and the *contestation,* the old French "litiscontester" (*litem contestari*)—litigate—which meant "to bring proceedings, to go to trial."

It is in any case this position that leads me here and now to propose a last hypothesis, probably more "litigious" than those preceding, but which I feel I must submit to judgment.

Coming back to Montaigne, considered in this particular case to be the initiator of the "genre"—obviously a shortcut and a drastic one—two aspects seem to me to require emphasis.

The first of them has long since been noticed and I will only sketch it in: it is, in all the meditation on death, the predominance of the Socratic *exemplum* and the constant reference to Plato's *Phaedo.* Assuredly, beneath the care for wisdom and for care itself, for the *melete tou thanatou,* care about death and "accustoming ourselves to [it]," it is the entirety of ancient ethics, including the Roman *cura,* that is called up, from the preaching of the Stoics to the arguments of Epicurius and Lucretius. But Socrates remains the only example of a philosopher who dies philosophizing and who dies from practicing philosophy, the inaugural figure deciding that death is the condition of thought itself. There is no need to insist: it is so for the whole tradition, Nietzsche and Heidegger included.

The second of these aspects is less often noted. It is nonetheless clear. The episode of the fall from the horse recounted in the chapter "De l'exercitation" is in reality about an ambush and a military and political incident. Montaigne does not expressly say so. But he situates the scene "during our third period of disturbances or the second," and the expression indeed designates the Wars of Religion (which Montaigne calls moreover "civil," writing for example that he is "in the midst of all the trouble of the civil wars of France"); he designates as directly as possible the Protestants ("our neighbors"); he speaks of "arque-busades" (gunshots), which were numerous during the incident and, more-over, very probably caused his horse to bolt. He is no doubt not a target himself: it is not an attempt on his life, at most a kind of unforeseen chance skirmish, as happens in all "guerrilla warfare," when Montaigne thought he was "entirely safe and so close to [his] retreat" (the scene takes place near his château, on the boundary of the Périgord). But it must not be forgotten that the political role of Montaigne during that whole period was an important one, not only in Bordeaux but at the court and, above all, with Henri de Navarre, whose conversion to Catholicism he is said, plausibly, to have en-couraged so as to guarantee the succession of the French crown and restore "civil" order. Montaigne could thus be, with Bodin, one of the earliest political thinkers, at least in France, to envisage the reality of the developing nation state, which is less "willing servitude" as such—inherited all the same by La Boétie from Nicolas de Cues[12]—than it is subjection, via religion, to the po-litical world or the generalized "political"—which slowly becomes "life" as a whole.

I would not insist on that political aura which, in Montaigne, surrounds his "experience" of death, if it were not found in all the "stories" I have evoked concerning *L'instant de ma mort*: in Malraux's story, for example, it is obvious; but also in Artaud's story, subjected as he is, for want of being able to flee, to repression directed against the "avant-gardes" and "degenerate art" and to the unspeakable psychiatric policy of the Vichy regime. And if it were not also found, although less distinctly or clearly so, in Blanchot's own "story" and in that of Rousseau.

Like Montaigne's "story," like Malraux's moreover, Blanchot's "story" seems to belong to the genre—if it is a genre—of the "war story." It is enough to reread the opening to be convinced of this. Now if the episode is clearly situated at a given moment of the war, that of the counter-offensive launched by the German army and in particular by the "Das Reich" SS Division against the Allied forces after the D-Day landing, nothing indicates that Blanchot has a combatant role in it (at most he is an accomplice of or a sympathizer with the young peasant Resistance fighters of the hamlet in the Haute-Saône—the scene of the story—in which his family has a house. Everything is done, on the other hand, to suggest that there is in fact a *civil* (and social) *war* rumbling beneath the military operations taking place, however much they have a world-war scope and however particularly spectacular they may be: the presence of the SS officer who speaks French "disgracefully," the Russian soldiers from Vlassov's army, the final allusion to the taking back over, indeed to the purging of the *Nouvelle Revue Française* and the Gallimard publishing house compromised during the Collaboration period (what goes for meeting Malraux and Paulhan goes just as much for the suicide of Drieu la Rochelle). Several clues of this nature lead one to believe that the episode forms part of the long ideological and political struggle that has divided the French intelligentsia since the thirties, indeed the twenties—a struggle in which everyone knows Blanchot took part as a recognized representative of and spokesperson for the nationalist (Maurrassian) far Right, indeed of and for a "French Fascism" (an anti-Nazi and anti-Hitlerian version all the same), up to 1938 (the Munich Agreement) if not to 1942–43 (the time of his meeting Bataille). That is why, moreover, *L'instant de ma mort* can also be read as the "story" of a deliverance and a redemption—or a defense. Death is *contested* there, the "almost-deceased" in Blanchot, in other words the "always-already-deceased" in him (the other "he" is), is summon(s)ed as the witness of a conversion, or of a radical break. And suddenly, as if miraculously, freed of death and of the *mortiferous.* In the name of another politics, without injustice or anything unjustifiable, whose sole object will be to loosen the grip of the political and whose fleeting upsurge will be recognized by Blanchot in May 1968. In other words, in the name of a *survival* which is perhaps nothing other, nothing more in any case, than existence. (And it must not be forgotten that this text is written in July 1994, in other words at a time in our recent history in which certain intellectuals, "humanists" of recent date and at little cost, dissatisfied, it would appear, with intellectual purges, have stepped up their more or less vengeful insinuations about Blanchot's "fascist," "anti-Semitic" (and so on) past, visibly relieved to be able to relativize the difficulty, the exigency, and the intransigence of the man.)

But that is the case again, all things being equal, of the "Deuxième promenade" of Rousseau, who is perhaps the first of that line to dramatize the theme of injustice, wrong, and persecution. Remember how, once the incident is related (inasmuch as it is possible to tell the "story" of one's own absence to oneself), Rousseau's text seems to go astray or get incomprehensibly stuck in a long "paranoiac" digression (the episode takes place in the very year when Rousseau tried in vain to place the manuscript of the *Dialogues* (*Rousseau Judge* [my emphasis] *of Jean-Jacques*) on the high altar of Notre-Dame de Paris and distributed in the street his satire *To All Frenchmen Who Still Love* Justice [my emphasis again] *and Truth*: the following day all Paris knew about it, his enemies were delighted, he was attacked (by the police, by Madame d'Ormoy), an edition of writings to be falsely attributed to him was under way, a provincial newspaper announced his death, etc., etc. One might laugh or feel sympathy. But that is to be blind: the persecution was very real; from at least the publication of *Emile* and the *Social Contract*, books which were burnt and condemned, Rousseau had been censured, pursued, ridiculed, banned, and betrayed by the very people he might have thought to be his friends, humiliated, travestied, and jeered at, forced to keep moving from place to place. This was the period 1776-1777: intellectual and religious (politico-religious) civil war was raging, a real war, however much it may have been hidden beneath carefree appearances. An *event* is in preparation, or is announced by Rousseau himself.

If this review is in any way justified—and once again, for each of the names I have happened to quote in passing, I could carry out an analysis of the same sort—then a very simple truth is clear: the autothanatographic (allobiographic) situation is nothing other than the Socratic situation: an endemic state of civil war, of *political* war, in the true sense of the word (it is the *stasis* so feared by the Greeks); a thinker, who also plays an important part in political life and is, in many ways, a revolutionary, although Plato makes him out to be the most famous of reactionaries; a backlog of hatreds, calumny, accusations of all sorts, mostly based on religion (impiety . . .); a public trial and condemnation, and death—accepted, indeed invoked, as the very gesture of thought itself: of philosophizing.

I do not evoke Socrates here again, and the Socrates of the *Phaedo*, to infer that every "autobiographical" project might necessarily be marked by the Socratic *exemplum* and refer to it. I clearly do not evoke it either, even if I alluded to the feeling of "immortality," to bring into play the metaphysical operation that Plato—who was not witness to it—stitched together around Socrates's death. I evoke him rather because I think, and Blanchot reminds us of this point to which I am coming, that Literature itself is closely bound to that death.

Nietzsche said, in a note almost contemporary with *The Birth of Tragedy*, that Plato had, fundamentally, "invented the novel of antiquity." That is a very seductive remark but one which does not convince me. If he invented anything, it would rather be what we still call too hastily "autobiography": an absent addresser, but marked as such and self-referring: "That day, it is written, Plato was not present"; another, referred to and by name (him, Socrates), but who utters the very words attributed to him by the one then absent, as if he were not at all speaking "in person" but in a sort of absence to himself, and who thinks, as he dies, his own (?) thoughts, in a state of detachment, serenity, almost the lightness of consent to death; a feeling of immortality, which Plato hastens to translate and to fix in the language of proof (of *logos*), but which Plato him"self" could not not understand as a "Dead, you are already so"— otherwise, why would he have written instead (and at the incitement?) of he who did not write and would perhaps not, by "himself," leave any trace of his existence? Or a few platitudes reported by Xenophon and the doxographers? And I say nothing of the constant recalling of injustice, of unjustifiability, of a condemnation that is never anything but the exact consequence of political injustice in general. And all injustice is political.

It did not often happen that Maurice Blanchot quoted or recalled Socrates. The name comes up only twice in *L'écriture du désastre*. The second occurrence is on the page that immediately precedes the long fragment: "To die means: dead, you are already so . . ." I certainly have not made a commentary on those lines, but they have been constantly in my sight: "Certainly Socrates does not write, but, beneath the voice, it is through writing that nevertheless he gives himself to others as the subject both perpetual and perpetually destined to die. He does not speak, he questions. Questioning, he interrupts and interrupts himself ceaselessly, giving form ironically to the fragmentary and through his death devoting speech to the obsession of writing, just as he devotes the latter to testamentary writing alone (but without a signature)."[13]

I placed *L'instant de ma mort*, at the beginning, under the authority of three instances that govern the work of Maurice Blanchot right up to its last pages: Politics, Experience of death, Literature (I can now say: Writing), collected together as the exercise of thought itself. Now we find them again, at the end, and Blanchot himself consents to this, in the Plato's *Phaedo*, or in one of the inaugural texts of Western philosophy, which is, in short, offering itself as the impossible autobiography of Socrates, "the one who did not write," but the founding text of *contestation*—of death. I do not know if the *Phaedo* is the *birthplace* of literature, in other words of autothanatography (of allobiography). What I glimpse is that it has a status of *origin*, and therefore of *end*, and that no literature, in relation to that end as origin, can call itself quit or acquitted.

CHAPTER EIGHT

The Counter-spiritual Life

Kevin Hart

"The *spiritual life*": we have heard those three words many times, though it comes as a surprise to hear Georges Bataille saying them.[1] They cross his lips in 1942, in his apartment on the rue Saint-Honoré in Paris, when talking with a group of friends he hoped would help him form "the Socratic College," a community that would be dedicated to that very life. It is not the first time he has said those words. There have been preliminary discussions about how to figure this way of life, he informs his audience, and the most important of these have been with Maurice Blanchot, who "formulated propositions of a rather accomplished design" that Bataille took up "while writing a book" (11; 6:285). He is alluding to *L'expérience intérieure* (1943), where indeed we read that in conversation with Bataille the young Blanchot set out the foundation "for all 'spiritual' life."[2] The scare quotes and the italics, while not co-extensive, equally suggest what Bataille has already told us: that the expression I quoted at the outset is phrased "in problematic terms" (11; 286). Perhaps it should be cast as "*negative inner experience*" (11; 286). That would translate both "spiritual" and the quotation marks around it, he seems to think, although before we could grasp what was at issue we would need to know how the adjectives "negative" and "inner" qualify "experience," and what "experience" itself means for Bataille and Blanchot.

There is no better way of beginning to establish the values of those words than to ponder what Blanchot said to Bataille on that day in 1941 or 1942, with their own reflections on that exchange kept firmly in mind. He said that all "spiritual" life must,

— have its principle and its end in the absence of salvation, in the renunciation of all hope,
— affirm of inner experience that it is authority (but all authority expiates itself),
— be contestation of itself and non-knowledge [*non-savoir*].[3]

The experience is "negative" in that it has no aim to feature in an economy of redemption, and it is "inner" in the sense that it begins with a self. No one could be any more precise at this stage, since both "subject" and "object" are called into question by the experience. That process of self-interrogation could not occur with a thoroughly isolated individual, a "beautiful soul" who clings to his or her subjectivity. A solitary person can of course have inner experience, although "solitary" must be understood in Heideggerian terms as a deficient mode of being-with. It is the noun rather than either adjective that gives one most pause, however. "Experience," Bataille says, does not distinguish itself from "the contestation," and he readily includes in that judgment both its authority and its method (15; 6:289). Plainly, we are not to take "experience" in its calm Kantian or Husserlian senses; we might be better advised to look between the lives of the two philosophers and take our chances with Hegel: not that "experience" for Bataille or Blanchot is the same as the dialectic, or that the *Aufhebung* is grounded in *Erfahrung* (as Heidegger came to think), but that "experience" or "contestation" is best identified against the ground of the dialectic.[4]

In the late 1930s Bataille had been impressed by Alexandre Kojève's lectures on Hegel's philosophy of religion presented at the École des Hautes Études (1933–39), and agreed with him that history is already over, more or less: only the *dénouement*, world revolution, remains. Yet in the early 1940s Bataille was less concerned with the coming revolution and the withering away of the state than with his recent experiments in philosophizing and meditating. The "spiritual" life or negative inner experience should be, he thought, "the *incessant interrogation of existence by itself*" (15; 6:289). He said that with a glance to

Socrates advising us that the unexamined life is not worth living—hence the name "Socratic College"—and the Socrates that came into focus there is not the man who knows he knows nothing, the *faux naif,* the master of elenchus, but the sage conjured by Lev Chestov: the wise man of *Phaedo* 64a for whom philosophy is the study of death and dying.[5] It is this Socrates, the one who stands alongside Dostoyevsky and Nietzsche, who could tolerate or even encourage Bataille's experiments in meditation. If we examine life closely enough, as inner experience requires us to do, we will see that it affirms "the existence of a beyond" (15; 6:289). It is not an afterlife but contact with the unknown. In the lecture delivered at rue Saint-Honoré Bataille is discreet: he does not say anything about his own techniques of meditation. He had been using photographs of a Chinese man being tortured during the Boxer Rebellion in order to produce a state in which he found himself sliding from the familiar and the known to the unfamiliar and the unknown. Nor does he say anything about St. Ignatius Loyola's *Spiritual Exercises* or the discipline of yoga, both of which had laid claim on him in recent years.[6]

In 1937, several years before he lectured on the Socratic College, Bataille had posed a question to Kojève. It was this. Were history to end, what would happen to the negativity in human being that until now had been dedicated to creating history? He believed he could supply an answer: human being would become unemployed negativity. And he could answer confidently because he had already started to venture to the end of the possible in himself. The experiences he enjoyed or suffered on that path have not determined his "I" in an ever more concrete fashion, as is said to happen in the dialectic; rather, the sovereignty of the "I" has been called into question by them. His project has been to escape from the realm of project, and insofar as his experiences cannot be accorded a meaning or a truth he judges himself to be on the right path. Thinking of this project to escape all project, Blanchot says, with characteristic clarity: "We enter with a leap into a situation that is no longer defined by useful operations or by knowing [*savoir*]. . . but one that opens up onto a loss of knowledge [*connaissance*]."[7] This is indeed a jump away from the universe of Logic, Nature, and Spirit so forcefully imagined by Hegel. If we take the *Phänomenologie des Geistes* to be describing the experiences of *Geist*—the exile and return, as mediated, of what was once supposed to be immediate to consciousness—then Hegel is offering an account of the life of the Spirit. It is, to be sure, an intellectualist account of experience, for the objects that consciousness examines are present to it in their representations. No surprise, then, to find Bataille defining "negative inner experience" against or alongside the dialectic. Such experience opens onto uncharted territory, there is a *perte de connaissance,* and it is dedicated to non-knowledge, *non-savoir.* We might say that experience in this nonintellectualist sense of the word is counter-spirit. What Bataille calls *"spiritual life"* or " 'spiritual' life" is perhaps better understood as "counter-spiritual life."

I want to suggest that, from the early 1940s, Blanchot has never ceased to meditate on this counter-spiritual life, especially on its relation with the life of the Spirit. He calls that rapport a "relation without relation" in *L'entretien infini,* and it becomes one of his main concerns to keep it in play without suborning it to the understanding.[8] And I want to suggest also that, for all his single-minded intensity and the apparent seamlessness of his prose, he has emphasized quite different aspects of counter-spirituality over the years. More particularly, I wish to draw attention to its three main figures: inner experience as a quasi-mystical ecstasy; literature as the experience or non-experience of an event as image, an exposure to a "beyond"; and contestation as a mobile and plural way of being in relation. I do not think that these are wholly distinct moments in Blanchot's thought: one can find the first in his final *récit,* the piercing narrative *L'instant de ma mort* (1994), and in advancing the third, more overtly social and political, understanding of the counter-spiritual life he does not thereby deny the second.[9] Also, I do not think that these three formulations are interchangeable. They are proposed in different contexts, and are themselves consequences of the incessant self-questioning that is contestation.

The French word "spirituelle" and the English word "spiritual" do not quite coincide, yet they overlap significantly. In one context "spiritual" will indicate piety; in another, morality; and in still another, the intellect. So I should say right at the start that Blanchot writes as a convinced atheist: *counter* can mean "acting in opposition" (as in "counter-player"), and with regard to the positive religions he claims the friendship of the "No."[10] Not that Blanchot's atheism comes into focus as a simple opposition to theism: it draws inspiration from the neutral, not just from dialectics. Besides, being an atheist does not stop him from doing a little theology from time to time since, as he reminds us as late as 1980, "atheism . . . has always been a privileged way of talking about God."[11] He also draws deeply from scripture, both Jewish and Christian, and is not untouched by Gnosticism: *counter* can also denote "making an angle with" (as in "counter-bar"). It should be kept in mind that, before it fell out of use, "counter" could mean "encounter," and I would like to keep this sense in mind throughout. For Blanchot has concerned himself time and again with an en-counter with that which falls outside the dialectic which he speaks of by way of an "experience of non-experience."[12]

Years before Blanchot coined that expression, Bataille had associated his friend with "the new theology (which has only the unknown as object)."[13] If Blanchot *is* a theologian, it is because he reflects on the counter-spiritual life from the perspectives of the unknown and atheism; and he is enough of a Hegelian theologian to know that this life can never entirely remove itself from Spirit understood as the realm of the possible in which meaning and truth reign: *counter* can also point us to a reciprocity between two forces (as in "counter-offer"). In his old age he admits that "there must always be at least two languages, or two requirements: one dialectical, the other not; one where negativity is the task, the other where the neutral remains apart, cut off both from being and from non-being."[14] These two languages do not balance one another—in fact, the latter interrupts the former—yet Hegel, or at least some-thing he represents, is never far from Blanchot. The Frenchman's essays, nov-els, and *récits* are not so much a counterplot in the life of Spirit as a counter-point to it, another melody we can hear if we are sensitive to our ontological attunements.

When Blanchot reviewed *L'expérience intérieure* on May 4, 1943, he had been using the expressions "inner experience" and "contestation" for months be-fore, not only in conversations with Bataille but also in his weekly column for *Journal des Débats*. On November 4, 1942, he reviewed two recent editions of Meister Eckhart's works—*Œuvres de Maître Eckhart: Sermons-traités* and *Maître Eckhart: Traité et sermons*—praised their author lavishly, and drew attention to the contemporary relevance of the homilies and treatises. That wartime France has at best only a "gross curiosity" in mysticism is readily conceded by him, but we are asked to see in Eckhart's work something far deeper, "the sign of an authentic community of mind."[15] Moreover, "It seems that there is in the experience of the Thuringian master, as it appears to us through his works, a profundity that poses in a concrete manner exactly the problems that we constantly make our own subjects" (23; 31). Kierkegaard and Jaspers are cited in this regard, and perhaps Blanchot has Bataille also in mind; if so, he does not mention him by name. What distinguishes Eckhart from Kierkegaard and Jaspers (and, I would add, Bataille) is the lack of apparent anguish in his thought. Rather, the Meister's writing is marked by a "perfect detachment" (27; 35).

There are parallels between Eckhart's doctrines and what Bataille has called the "spiritual" life. The first of these is contestation, here grasped as the excess of experience over understanding. "Master Eckhart feels fully that if he has the right to use understanding to transcribe an experience before which thought is broken up, it is by causing it to follow one of its roles, which is to contradict itself without however being swallowed up in contradiction" (25–26; 34). That final clause is directed to the Hegel who had come across Eckhart's writings possibly as early as 1795, long before he talked with Franz von Baader about them, and who sought to suborn them to the negativity of the dialectic.[16] Eckhart may write of the *negatio negationis,* the negation of negation, but he does not simply contribute to the life of the Spirit; he also marks a moment of rupture with it, an affirmation of counter-spirit.[17] Reason is to be used, Eckhart thinks (at least according to Blanchot), to express belief "in the language of impossibility" (26; 34); and one must accept an inevitable compromise. "It is always a question of translating the most immediate experience by the movement of dialectics" (26; 34). I will return to this question of translation in a moment. But before doing so, I would like to glance at another element of Eckhartian contestation: the loss of the "I."

One thing that attracts Blanchot to Eckhart is the thought that for the German the "I" is not closed upon itself, like the *substantia cogitans,* but that "the most secret interiority opens onto the Other" (26; 34). The Meister's "I" is relinquished "by deepening itself beyond all determination" and so "is confused with the divine 'Thou' in a union that breaks the structures proper to subject and object"; and we are told that "this experience is properly that of the fact of existing" (26; 34). Blanchot does not put words into Eckhart's mouth. *The Book of Divine Consolation* tells ordinary folk that "they must lose their own image [*entbildet*], and be transformed above themselves [*überbildet*] into the image of God alone, and be born in God and from God."[18] This loss of oneself as subject is a part of what Blanchot means by "inner experience." The first readers of "Maître Eckhart," those who turned the pages of the *Journal des Débats* in early November 1942, would not have known what "inner experience" means; the expression is not defined in the column and the book bearing that title and explicating its meaning was not to appear until the following year. We who know that book might be inclined to think that "inner experience" converges with the very word Blanchot gives Eckhart to speak: "experience." Eckhart's experience supplies its own authority, since as the Meister says in several places life needs no ground other than itself.[19] In fact Blanchot does not hesitate to identify "experience" and "inner experience" for the German whose works he is reviewing. Eckhart may tell us "nothing of the inner experience of which his doctrines are only the speculative fruits," Blanchot says, yet the Frenchman has no doubt that the great Dominican enjoyed an extremely rich "spiritual experience."[20] No purely speculative theologian, Eckhart is also a mystic, albeit one unlike any other before him in the braided traditions of Western mysticism and apophatic theology. When he is called *doctor ecstaticus,* as he is by scholars from time to time, it is to signal both his learning and the character of his experience.

Readers familiar with Blanchot's works as a whole will be puzzled to find him lauding a devout Christian and a mystic, finding inner experience in a believer, and to hear him saying of Eckhart that "faith's supreme experience" is "beyond all measure and all end" (27; 36). We might be more used to him in the role of a latter-day reformist, one captivated by writing rather than scripture, so that he can recast Martin Luther's famous words at Worms to read, "In the space of writing—writing, not writing—here I stand, bent over, and I do not wait for help from the benign powers."[21] And would we not, rather, expect to hear him mark a clear difference between mysticism and inner experience, and to do so precisely because the mystic limits the movement of contestation by affirming God as its end? That is what Blanchot's review of *L'expérience intérieure* on May 4, 1943, would lead us to suppose. There he makes it plain that "inner experience" would "in every respect be similar to mystical ecstasy if it were disengaged from all the religious presuppositions that often change it and, by giving it a meaning, determine it" (39; 49–50). Notice Blanchot's phrasing: "that often [*souvent*] change it and, by giving it a meaning [*un sens*], determine it." If religious presuppositions *often* change inner experience, there must be occasions when they do not do so. For Blanchot, Eckhart presents one such occasion: he does not ascribe a direction or a meaning to his experience. Could it be that Eckhart's experience is an ecstatic "loss of knowledge [*connaissance*]"? The question is answered some months after Blanchot reviews Bataille's irruptive book. The occasion: a column on the seventeenth-century mystical poet Angelus Silesius, published on October 6, 1943. He asks there what the expression "knowledge [*connaissance*] of God" signifies; and he says in reply, "to become identical to God demands of man not only that he lose all that which makes him man, but, still more, that he annul all that which makes him believe he knows God." And he adds, "To lose oneself in all the senses of the word, to find death and to kill what one has and what one is; this is the only path of knowledge [*connaissance*]."[22]

These remarks become clear only when we remember Eckhart's distinction between God and the Godhead. Before the world was created, the deity was "absolutely undetermined," as Blanchot renders a teaching he regards as common to Eckhart and Angelus Silesius, and the act of creation not only brings creatures into being but also causes the deity to create "himself as God."[23] Only the poorest in spirit, those who are free from God's will as well as their own, can be joined to the Godhead, for one must first divest oneself of all images, all attachment to anything that is not truly divine. When a person does that he has achieved the *imitatio Christi*, for "he is more dead than death, he is exactly this dead God, to which Christ has been given as the model; he is the one who is refused everything, even the ecstasy where love is united with love in a preliminary duality."[24] The Godhead is utterly passive, Eckhart says; it allows for no transcendence in itself, has therefore no experience, and is pure no-thingness. It cannot be known because it *is*. The whole of Eckhart's teaching is directed toward showing that being and knowing form two distinct and irreducible orders, and that since being is divine it is impossible for the deity ever to be known. The soul endlessly pursues the Godhead, contesting all images of the deity, yet never arrives at her goal. It is an endless quest, not from the soul to God, but to the *unitas indistinctionis* where the soul and the Godhead are one. Only if one accepts that God cannot be known or understood, and is content to find one's peace and happiness in that eternal darkness, can one ever hope to become one with Him. For Blanchot's Eckhart, "notions of salvation, hope, and bliss no longer count" (27; 36); experience is "beyond all measure and all end" (27; 36); and the soul, having prayed for God to rid herself of God, has achieved non-knowledge.

Had Blanchot been reading Eckhart when he suggested that the "spiritual" life must "be contestation of itself and non-knowledge"? Perhaps: Blanchot must have been absorbed in the homilies and treatises in October of 1942 at the latest, and they might well have influenced the way in which he outlined the conditions for all "spiritual" life. He might well have read Eckhart in Middle High German before the French translations came across his desk. Or had Blanchot come to Eckhart with Bataille's notion of contestation in mind? That also is possible. I should add that Bataille had been reading Eckhart as well:

Pierre Prévost recalls enthusiastic conversations with Bataille about the Meister after *Oeuvres de Maître Eckhart: Sermons-traités* appeared in 1942.[25] From Blanchot's viewpoint, Bataille and Eckhart, the author of the *Summa atheologica* and the Dominican theologian, are far closer than one might suppose. Just how close they are can be judged by comparing Blanchot's response to Eckhart with his thoughts on Cardinal Nicholas de Cusa, who "remains foreign to all inner experience in the strict sense":

> The non-knowledge [*non-savoir*] which he leads us to is not, as with Meister Eckhart, the result of the complete deprivation of the soul; it does not signify the anguished death by which it renounces everything, even God and throws itself in an abyss where it is ready to lose itself. Non-knowledge [*non-savoir*], "learned ignorance" of Master Cusa is the term of a dialectical process where discursive knowledge [*connaissance*], having been affirmed, denied, then reunited in a synthesized affirmation and negation, and finally this synthesis suspended in order to overcome it, comes naturally to the Unknowable.[26]

Blanchot moves very quickly here, and we would do well to take this passage at a slower pace, if only to identify some issues that could not be considered in a newspaper column.

We should be aware that to talk about just two people, Cusa and Eckhart, is to give a stripped-down version of an important and complicated debate. First of all, there is someone standing in the background: it is Augustine. In Letter 130 he tells Proba that "there is in us a certain learned ignorance [*docta ignorantia*], if I may say so, but it is learned in the Spirit of God, who helps our infirmity."[27] That great reader of Augustine, Eckhart, speaks of *diz unbekante bekantnisse*, the unknown knowing.[28] And in homily eighty-three, *Renovamini spiritu*, the preacher goes so far as to tell his congregation, "You should love God unspiritually [*ungeistig*], that is, your soul should be unspiritual and stripped of all spirituality [*Geistigkeit*]."[29] This is the renunciation that Blanchot admires in Eckhart, a counter-spirituality that abandons "the means of its power and the method of its progress," as he says with regard to Cusa.[30] Eckhart is on center stage for Blanchot, although he does not mention here, as he does several months later, that Eckhart's thought is "prolonged by the philosophy of Nicolas de Cusa."[31] Nor does he mention Johannes Wenck, who challenges Cusa's *De Doctrina Ignorantia* and, covertly, Eckhart's mystical theology, and against whom Nicholas defends himself and the Meister.[32] In terms of that debate it is Cusa who affirms the inability of the intellect ever to be satisfied with an account of God and who speaks of an endless movement toward Him, while Wenck insists on the proper use of analogy, a strategy that would freeze this endless movement in the form of proportion.

What Blanchot rightly sees is that there are two species of non-knowledge, one coordinate with the nakedness of inner experience, and another leagued with dialectics. The former is associated with Eckhart; the latter, with Cusa. Reading the Cardinal allows us to see what is valuable in Eckhart:

> The interest of this thought is that while pretending to safeguard absolute tran-scendence it seeks to determine the channels of access which remain open in order to attain it; it wants spirit, through the activity which is proper to it, to have the same experience of God for which the mystics assign a total passivity to the soul; it substitutes non-knowledge [*non-savoir*] which is rupture with discourse and sacrifice of all thought with a discursive non-knowledge [*non-savoir*] which is the crowning of progress and the expression of a continued development.[33]

A word or two of clarification is in order. Eckhart affirms the transcendence of the deity: God is *esse absolutum,* and we have being only insofar as we are one with God. Yet this affirmation is part of a dialectic, for he also maintains that, if we consider creatures as having being, *esse formaliter inhaerens,* then God is above or beyond being. The soul longs to reach the groundless ground where she and the Godhead are one. This is not a dialectic that actively moves the soul forward along a spiritual path; on the contrary, it contests—Eckhart's verb is *entbilden,* "unforms"—that very idea. The soul proceeds along its path in darkness, by unknowing, and its passivity is prior to the distinction between active and passive. Cusa, however, accents the activity of the soul, its willing-ness to contest images of the deity. Rhetorically at least, this makes Cusa seem closer than Eckhart to what Bataille and Blanchot mean by "contestation." The closeness is more apparent than real: for all its apparent muscularity, contesta-tion is a peculiar sort of power in that it turns on itself. Once that is grasped, it should not be surprising to find Blanchot viewing Cusa as already on the way to a dialectics that will find its apogee in Hegel: a philosophy that excludes contestation or, if you like, philosophy as onto-theology.

Is there is a passage from that which disrupts discourse to that which thrives on it? There is. "It is always a question of translating the most immediate experience by the movement of dialectics," Blanchot writes of Eckhart, and to be sure there is a movement in the Meister's works that links *unwizzen,* un-knowing, and dialectics. Considering *L'expérience intérieure,* Blanchot says the same thing but teases out the thought: "In a sense, however, discourse is not forbidden to try to account for that which escapes discourse; on the contrary, it is even necessary, since translation, although never being satisfying, still keeps an essential part of authenticity insofar as it imitates the movement of challenge [*récusation*] that it borrows and, by denouncing itself as unfaithful guardian, doubles its text with another that supports it and erases it by a kind of permanent half-refutation."[34] In Eckhart, the translation of experience into discourse maintains a rapport with experience by dint of the sheer radicality and fecundity of the Meister's figures: God is beyond God, the Son is born in the soul, I am a cause of God, and so forth. In Bataille, one finds a similar extremity, and Blanchot finds that the literary form of *L'expérience intérieure* imitates the movement of contestation.

Kafka wrote unfinished and unfinishable fragments, and his style, Blanchot says, is "the almost naked manifestation" of the "struggle" (*contestation*).[35] Without reducing the differences between Kafka and Bataille, one could say the same of the Frenchman's style. Both writers communicate in their very writing a passion that does not serve a definite end or a particular value. There is no doubt that for Bataille contestation precedes any and all distinctions between "mysticism" and "literature," although it must be added that there can be no contestation before its object appears and the form or forms it takes with respect to its object cannot be foretold. Blanchot agrees but shows more interest than his friend in the relations between inner experience and the texts that try to account for it. When he considers French poetry, a month after reviewing Bataille's book, he observes that the path leading "from Maurice Scève to Rimbaud is marked by works which are religious through the inner experience they seek to communicate."[36] Yet the very experience of these poets marks "their escape from religion." The poet "makes himself his own sacrificer," Blanchot says, in all likelihood alluding to Hölderlin's hymn "Wie wenn am Feiertage. . ." (1799?), a poem that will continue to fascinate him. These remarks about French poetry could be rephrased in terms that would harmonize with Eckhart; but Blanchot is already moving in another direction, seeking another "beyond," one in which literature will be his main concern.

When contemplating a new edition of André Gide's *Les Nourritures terrestres* in his column for November 11, 1942, just a week after his article on Meister Eckhart, Blanchot treats the book as a prime instance of a modern literary form, one that draws from Novalis and Rimbaud, and that he dubs the "literature of experience."[37] Of course, the word "experience" refers us to the author's personal encounters with the world, but more importantly it points us to how the author is changed by what he or she writes. "It represents an adventure or, more precisely, an actual experience whose results, as elaborate as the givens were, as carefully thought out its operation, cannot be measured in advance, one that must be followed to the end to know where it leads its author, in what transformations of self it culminates" (298; 338). The risk at work here can stem from deep instincts, although equally it can be broached by a writer trying to fulfill the demands of a strict form. When Lautréamont began composing *Les Chants de Maldoror*, Blanchot says in 1948, he did not have those six strange songs in his mind, for "this mind did not yet exist, and the sole end that he could have had was this distant mind, this hope of a mind which, at the moment when *Maldoror* would be written, would bring to him all the desired force to write it."[38]

Just a year before, in 1947, Blanchot was speaking of writers opening themselves to change through writing, this time with Michel Leiris in mind. "Writing is nothing if it does not involve the writer in a movement full of risks that will change him in one way or another."[39] That same year he returned to Gide and expanded his comments on the literature of experience, yet this time he phrased them in another register. Literature, he tells us, "is an experience that is essentially deceiving, and that is what creates all its value." Deception as ground of value? Yes, "for anyone who writes enters into the illusion, but this illusion, deceiving him, carries him away and, carrying him away by the most ambiguous movement, gives him, as he chooses, a chance either to lose what he had already thought he found, or to discover what he can no longer lose."[40] Literature is *essentially* deceptive because it prizes itself while calling itself into question. Even when it presents itself as a force of negation, as when condemning the art of an earlier generation, it never goes so far as to denounce art as "mystification or deception."[41]

So the writer is borne away by the very words that appear on the page, and in that process two things happen, Blanchot thinks. First, the writer loses grip on the self as subject: the very act of writing presumes a movement from the first to the third person, even if one always elects to use "I." And second, the writer communicates with the realm of the imaginary: not a fund of creative potential as one typically associates with the Romantics but a suffocating space where being perpetuates itself as nothingness. In writing a great work, Blanchot thinks, an author does not overcome death by dint of producing a monument that will outlast him or her. *Exegi monumentum aere perennius:* Horace's claim in Ode III.xxx is true so far as it goes—we do still read the *Carmen,* and with great pleasure—but the old boast is also completely misplaced, Blanchot implies. For writing invites the approach of the imaginary: in Ode I.v Pyrrha will never emerge from her bower of roses, her slim lover will forever smell of the same perfume, and the narrator will murmur, again and again, *Quis multa gracilis.* . . . Put more abstractly, art points us to a realm, or—better—a non-realm, where no event truly begins but only begins again and where no event ever concludes. It is not a space of death, for there is no traction for the dialectic to take hold. Nor is it a space of eternal life, since art does not manifest being but the absence of being. It is a space of endless dying: in art, the dark shore is never reached.

Needless to say, Horace's ode "*Quis multa gracilis.* . ." remains in the world of meaning, truth, and value; and the many poems that draw from it, as well as the many translations it has spawned, bear testimony to that. For the reader, though, as perhaps for Horace himself, the ode slips away from meaning, truth, and value. To read it well would be to slide toward sheer alterity—a neutral state in which nothing begins or ends but only repeats itself—to be exposed to a "beyond" which is not subsequent to death but is co-ordinate with dying. One could say the same of poems by Po Chü-I and Tu Fu, by Keats and Browning, by. . . . Names can be added at will, but not just any names, since Blanchot believes that some books foreclose in advance on the "beyond" and, in doing so, merely serve the established cultural order.[42] I have chosen to talk about Horace partly because the theme of literary survival is associated preeminently with his name and partly because many of Blanchot's comments on art are so general in their scope that they reach back to Horace and before him. Yet Blanchot came to think that there has been a change of epoch, and that after Lautréamont and Mallarmé we can see, more clearly than their predecessors could, that art maintains a special relation with alterity, one that in time he will phrase as a "relation without relation." The historical scope of Blanchot's judgments about art is not a question I can examine in any detail here, although it will surface again in a little while. Of more importance now is the question of contestation. Needless to say, what is contested, how the act occurs, and what results from it will differ from age to age and from writer to writer. If art leads to an "original experience" that opens onto a neutral realm, however, we might ask in what sense can we associate art and contestation.

Would it not be that we would see art stalled in the imaginary rather than contesting anything at all?

For the Blanchot of *L'espace littéraire* the question would seem to be badly put. Or at least it would appear to be phrased uncritically in terms of a philosophical framework that can be identified with three familiar and exalted names: Hegel, Nietzsche, Heidegger. What links the people in this unlikely triad, more known for their mutual disagreements than for their agreements, is that they all attempt "to make death possible."[43] Certainly, in their very different ways these three thinkers construe human being by way of death, and accordingly view death in terms of possibility. And certainly all three value art, far more than most modern philosophers have shown a willingness to do. That said, Blanchot's point is at odds with all philosophy of art, which by and large tends to be an extension of an epistemology, ontology, or metaphysics that has already been worked out. His claim is that art reveals something other than the truth of the philosophers. It is "exile from the truth . . . the risk of an inoffensive game" and it affirms the neutrality of the imaginary that I have evoked.[44] Rather than art being something which philosophy must master, it is precisely that which calls modern philosophy's determination of "human being" into question.

Art contests the view that "human being" appears only in the space that the dialectic makes available for it. Something in "human being," art suggests, inclines us both to name the possible and to respond to the impossible. Like his close friend Emmanuel Levinas, Blanchot develops an account of the imaginary in which an event presents both itself and its image. "Being is not only itself, it escapes itself . . . the thing is itself and its image," says the one; "distance [*l'éloignement*] is in the heart of the thing . . . having become image, instantly it has become that which no one can grasp, the unreal, the impossible," says the other.[45] No sooner does something appear, then, than it becomes possible for it to withdraw into the non-world of the imaginary, a "beyond" where being is utterly evacuated and from which we can neither enter nor remove ourselves. Viewed one way, art appears as gnostic excarnation; viewed another way, art lead the way to a radical nihilism. It is this view of art contesting philosophy and opening the way to nihilism that characterizes *L'espace littéraire* (1955). Only a few years later, in the early 1960s, when he is doing the groundwork for the *Revue Internationale,* a journal that barely saw the light of day, Blanchot adopts a different vocabulary.[46] Here there is no talk of art indicating "the menacing proximity of a vague and vacant outside, a neutral existence, nil and limitless," no evocations of art pointing "into a sordid absence, a suffocating condensation where being ceaselessly perpetuates itself as nothingness."[47] Rather, there is talk about power.

I do not think that Blanchot changed his mind about the relation of art and the impossible or that he stopped thinking about it in the 1960s, but round about that time he starts to place a different accent on things. He takes care to stress that "literature and the arts" have a strange ability to question everything. They can "readily be inspected by a Marxist-style critique," he writes, and "that is certainly admissible, even necessary, so long as this critique is fresh and does not rehash tired commonplaces." Having addressed Jean-Paul Sartre and other communists of one stripe or another, including himself, he turns to his main point:

> But we must also admit that, still for us at least, literature constitutes not only its own experience but also a fundamental experience, calling everything into question, including itself, including the dialectic, since, if it is true that the dialectic can and should seize literature and use it for its own purposes, it is also true that the mode of literary affirmation escapes the dialectic, does not belong to it. Literature represents a power of a particular sort that does not concern possibility (something that the dialectic now enables us to see): art is infinite contestation, contestation of itself and contestation of other forms of power—not simple anarchy, but in the free search for the original power that art and literature represent (*power without power*).[48]

Literature cannot be suborned by the dialectic; it answers to something that runs counter to Spirit, something that Blanchot calls "power without power." We can only respond to this counter-spirit, as I call it, never direct it to an end or ascribe a value to it. We cannot use it; we can only be put to the test by it, as when I lose myself as subject in the experience of writing a poem or a story. If the Blanchot of *L'espace littéraire* attends to the experience of an event appearing both as itself and as image, he soon begins to pay more attention to that which exceeds experience in an event. There is always more to an event than what it gives to lived experience, for the event opens up other possibilities that can be lived; it indicates a role for *Erfahrung*, not only *Erlebnis*.[49] Such is the "power without power" that he calls contestation and that he finds not working but unworking in literature.

If we move a few years ahead, from the deliberations over the *Revue Inter-*

nationale to the presentation of *L'entretien infini* (1969), we find the same thoughts about contestation recast in a more apocalyptic tone. His quarry here is "the Book," a notion that presumes "the primacy of speech over writing, of thought over language, and the promise of a communication that would one day be immediate and transparent"; and it is not literature as such that calls these values into question. It is writing, *écriture*, that can take us "beyond" history:

> Writing, in this sense—in this direction in which it is not possible to maintain oneself alone, or even in the name of all, without the tentative advances, the lapses, the turns and detours of which the texts assembled here are the trace (and their interest, I believe, lies in this)—supposes a radical change of epoch: inter-ruption, death itself—or, to speak hyperbolically, "the end of history." In this way writing passes through the advent of communism, recognized as the ultimate affirmation—communism being still always beyond communism. Writing thus becomes a terrible responsibility. Invisibly, writing is called upon to undo the discourse in which, however unhappy we believe ourselves to be, we who have it at our disposal remain comfortably installed. From this point of view writing is the greatest violence, for it transgresses the Law, all law, and also its own law.[50]

Literature may expose us to the imaginary and in doing so can make us realize that "human being" presumes a relation with the impossible as well as with the possible, the neutral as well as the negative. Writing, however, takes us to a different "beyond," one that abides on the hither side of history understood as the history of meaning. Blanchot's verb for describing what writing does is "transgress," and it indicates his third and final formulation of contestation. If the word recalls Bataille, and specifically his interest in the relations of religion and society, that is entirely appropriate.

In no sense does Blanchot replace "literature" with "writing." The very first page of the "Note" that presents *L'entretien infini* reminds us of Blanchot's central question—"What would be at stake in the fact that something like art or literature exists?"—and reminds us that it is "extremely pressing, and histor-ically pressing" (xi; vi). The phrasing deserves a second look: " something like [*quelque chose comme*] art or literature," he writes, suggesting that what is truly important in art and literature is not the specific historical forms they have assumed or their aesthetic properties but a relation with the imaginary that would occur by dint of the doubleness unworking in the very presentation of a phenomenon. What would be at stake in the fact that we have art, however we delimit it? If the answer is the ontological status of "human being," as I have suggested, then it is bound to be philosophically and theologically important in ways that literary and art criticism shy away from. And if it is true, as Blanchot thinks it is, that we are in the midst of a "radical change of epoch" (xii; vii), then those philosophical and theological questions intersect with historical, social, and political concerns. Those concerns are, it seems, best articulated by way of writing rather than literature. To grant *écriture* such a formidable role is to live in the wake of Mallarmé ("this mad game of writing"), and to do so expressly in 1969 is to have been touched by Jacques Derrida's first publications. That Blanchot was affected by the essays later collected in *L'écriture et la difference* (1967) and *De la grammatologie* (1967) is clear from a comparative study of the vocabulary of his essays when they appeared in journals and when they were revised for inclusion in *L'entretien infini*.[51] "Writing" here, though, is not phenomenal script nor is it exactly the same as the quasi-transcendental movement of *la différance*. It is "plural speech" or what Blanchot glosses as "the speech of writing."

What interests Blanchot in writing is that it brings forth "possibilities that are entirely other: an anonymous, distracted, deferred, and displaced way of being in relation" (xii; vii). As evoked, this being in relation is social, but the specific contestations appear to be presented as addressed to metaphysics—"the idea of God, of the Self, of the Subject, then of Truth and the One"—and then as engaging the literary: "then finally the idea of the Book and the Work" (xii; vii). It is an odd sequence, especially because the main quarry is the One that, like Greeks from Parmenides to Plotinus, Blanchot recognizes as transcendent. Indeed, he goes further than any Greek in affirming that the One is above the deity: "Not the One God but Unity, strictly speaking, is God, transcendence itself" (433; 635). How to contest unity? Why, by re-thinking the fragment, and therefore, first of all, by returning to the Jena Romantics. That said, the fragment we associate with Friedrich Schlegel and Novalis remains tied to a sense of the whole and unity whereas Blanchot seeks to go further and, by a fragmentary writing, make possible "new relations that except themselves from unity, just as they exceed the whole" (359; 527). The fragmentary would therefore be neither a whole nor a part, and the very phrasing suggests that for Blanchot it would be neutral. Yet if understanding involves a play of part and whole, no fragmentary writing could be understood: it would always exceed or interrupt its contexts. One can put an affirmative spin on this and argue that, because it cannot be mastered, our experience of the fragmentary leads us to an experience of the impossible. Hans-Jost Frey goes so far as to see the fragmentary inviting us "to live without indications about how one should live," for "one lives fragmentarily when one cannot go on any more, when one has nothing to expect from the future except that one has none. One lives posthumously and above all without asking how one lives."[52]

We have passed from Eckhart's preaching of living without a why to Frey's resignation to living without a how. The former is affirmative—one is released from pointless cares—while the latter would seem to operate without a social conscience. Blanchot must be set apart from this style of nihilism, if only because he regards the fragmentary as exposing us to a more profound fraternity than we have known, a communism "beyond communism" (xii; viii).[53] Even if the fragmentary leads us away from a unity of parts or phases and invites us into a world of plural speech, it cannot entirely suspend unity as a horizon of intelligibility. One can be disoriented or surprised by the fragmentary, but only relative to that horizon. Of course, that horizon can be disrupted or interrupted: modern literature could be read as the history of such occasions. But it cannot be eliminated altogether. Were it to be erased, events would be experienced (if the word can even be used here) as chaos at best. Blanchot appears to anticipate this objection when he speaks, with regard to Paul Celan's final poems, of "a union that does not make a unity," though it is unclear what the relation of "union" and "unity" would be.[54]

Let us go back a step or two, from the last item in Blanchot's first list of what is to be contested, "the One," to the first, "the idea of God." It is entirely appropriate that Blanchot begin with the idea of God, and not just any idea of God but the Jewish one. In "Être Juif" (1962) we are told that Israel's most significant bequest to us has been an anticipation of plural speech or "first writing": "Here we should bring in the great gift of Israel, its teaching of the one God. But I would rather say, brutally, that what we owe to Jewish monotheism is not the revelation of the one God, but the revelation of speech [*parole*] as the place where men hold themselves in relation with what excludes all relation: the infinitely Distant, the absolutely Foreign. God speaks, and man speaks to him. This is the great feat of Israel."[55] As it happens, this view emerges by contesting an idea of Martin Buber's that he had considered three years before, in 1959. Buber does not suggest that monotheism is less important than dialogism; rather, what is decisive about it is the Jewish people's trusting relation with YHWH, not the metaphysical claim that the deity is a unity.[56] Buber's claim is that Israel "pointed out that this God [i.e., "the one real God"] can be addressed by man in reality, that man can say Thou to Him."[57]

Blanchot rephrases Buber, and it is worth following the passage carefully, for contestation often occurs with Blanchot in an almost imperceptible passage from faithful paraphrase to a twisting away from the frame of reference:

> Speech alone can cross the abyss; the voice of God alone, God as voice, as power that addresses without letting itself be addressed in turn, makes this separation the locus of understanding. In every religion, no doubt, there have been relations between Creator and creature through sacrifice, prayer, inner rapture [*ravissement intérieur*]. But in Israel, a unique relation of familiarity and strangeness, of proximity and distance, of freedom and submission, of simplicity and ritual complication comes to light, a relation whose speech—the mystery and friendship of speech, its justice and reciprocity, the call it conveys and the response it awaits—constitutes the principle of the substance.[58]

Not only does Blanchot move away from Buber in repeating him but also he reworks contestation itself. We can glimpse in these lines a passage from thinking contestation by way of inner experience, similar to yet distinct from the ecstasies of the Christian mystics, to rethinking it along the lines of plural speech, understood as a specifically Jewish approach to spirituality. What Blanchot will come to call "being Jewish" three years after writing on Buber turns on the uniqueness of a "relation of familiarity and strangeness." If a Jewish spirituality is involved in Blanchot's later thought, it runs counter to the affirmation of the one true God.

Were one to stand several giant steps away from debates about French criticism and philosophy, one could regard Blanchot's later thought as an endless contestation of the Bible. "The Book begins with the Bible," he tells us, some years before saying that it speaks of the "nearness of the Eternal"; and that proximity is not something he will readily abandon.[59] In order to put pressure on the link between the Bible and unity, Blanchot goes first to the Jerusalem Talmud. There he reads that Torah existed before Creation: "It was written with letters of black fire upon a background of white fire" (*Tractate Shekalim*, fol. 13b). Seeking to interpret this passage of haggadah, he turns to Rabbi Isaac the Blind, father of Kabbalah, who ventures to say that the true written Torah is to be found in the white fire, and that the black fire is the oral Torah.[60] On this understanding, the first five books of the Bible constitute the *oral* Torah, while the true *written* Torah exists illegibly in the white spaces between the letters. "First writing," the mystical Torah that only Moses could begin to decipher, interrupts and transgresses "second writing," the Torah that gives us the Law and that binds us to Unity. "God," we are told in *L'entretien infini*, "is God only in order to uphold Unity and in this way designate its sovereign finality."

It will be objected that Blanchot allegorizes scripture out of history, much like Philo Judaeus before him, and that he does so on highly dubious historical and hermeneutical grounds. It will be urged that the "first writing" or plural speech he finds in the Bible is not there at all, except to the eyes of certain Kabbalists, and to import it there in order that it might contest the "second writing" or Law of Unity, undercuts the Shema—"Hear, O Israel: The LORD our God is one LORD" (Deut. 6:4)—and shakes the foundation of being Jewish for all religious Jews. And it will be pointed out that Blanchot's interpretation of "being Jewish" is no more than an ethics of relationality proposed under the title "Atheism and Writing" as much as under "Being Jewish," and that it is an abomination to associate Judaism with nihilism, such as he does in *L'entretien infini* and elsewhere. In self-defense, Blanchot would point out that "first writing," or the "relation without relation," is found in the Bible, though only if we wrest the work from the book and wear the consequences of the rupture: living not by the revelation of the Law but by a law that binds us before the Law, namely, an ethical obligation to the other person.[61] The vocation of the Jews is not that of a people elected by God to be singular and unique but rather to open what has been given to them—"first writing," the law before the Law— to all the nations.

To unfold this ur-law, the primacy of ethical obligation to the other, would be an infinite task. As it uncoils, it contests everything with which it comes in contact, including the Law and its own historical forms. For Blanchot, this "first writing" is best seen not in the chanting of Torah in the synagogue but on the streets where everyday life takes place. Why the everyday? Because it is neither a mystical fusion nor a dialectical progression but an anonymous and shifting way of being in relation with one another. To be sure, when describing the everyday one's language sometimes resembles that of negative theologians, not because the quotidian is transcendent (in the religious sense of the word) but because it is neutral. "In this consists its strangeness," Blanchot says, "the familiar showing itself (but already dispersing) in the guise of the astonish-ing."[62] Everyday life is neither that of the subject nor the object; and the distinction between true and false finds no traction there. There is no room for God in quotidian life, Blanchot assures us: "Everyday man is the most atheist of men. He is such that no God whatsoever could stand in relation to him" (245; 366). These two sentences would certainly surprise the compilers and readers of the Talmud, a text ablaze with the significance of the everyday.

Rather than rejecting Blanchot's assertion as merely pious counter-doctrine, though, we would do well to consider two points, one that he himself went on to make and one that he left ajar as an objection to his own position. The first concerns the relation of the neutral and the dialectic. As I noted at the very start, Blanchot says that we must always speak "at least two languages . . . : one dialectical, the other not; one where negativity is the task, the other where the neutral remains apart, cut off both from being and from non-being."[63] Long before he wrote those words, Blanchot had said the same thing in terms of living rather than vocabulary. It is "given to us to 'live' each of the events that is ours by way of a double relation," he says. "We live it one time as something we can comprehend, grasp, bear, and master (even if we do so painfully and with difficulty) by relating it to some good or to some value, that is to say, finally by relating it to Unity."[64] So Blanchot has no complete redescription of reality that suspends words like "Unity" and "God"; his position differs from the one commonly ascribed to him, as he makes clear when adding that we live an event "another time as something that escapes all employ and all end, and more, as that which escapes our very capacity to undergo it, but whose trial we cannot escape" (207; 308). What we cannot protect ourselves from, he suggests, is the ontological attunement of passive suffering—utter boredom, pointless waiting, wretchedness—in which we do not approach an event so much as it approaches us. It cannot be lived because it cannot be constituted by an intending consciousness; indeed, it deconstitutes the subject. This event has no meaning for the one transfixed by it because in suffering time itself has slackened, lost direction, and opened onto the non-realm of the imaginary where being appears as nothingness. In the extremity of affliction, Blanchot thinks, the self becomes the other and it is that other who is to be preserved, and in that rending we find an "inexorable affirmation": humankind is valued by individuals over and above their lives.[65] It is here, in this honoring of a species to which we all belong, that Blanchot glimpses the possibility of an ethics and a politics.

No sooner is this affirmation of humankind made, however, than the one who makes it is "placed back into a situation of dialectical struggle" (134; 197). The counter-spiritual life finds itself once again in relation with Spirit. If we return to the everyday with all this in mind, we can see that to celebrate the man and woman on the street who contest everything and therefore escape "all authority, be it political, moral, or religious" (245; 366) is not all that must be done. We must also acknowledge the role of the dialectic, the experience of Spirit. Those on the street are going to work or to vote, they are going to eat or to meet a friend, they are going shopping or to a bar, they must attend a baptism, a bar mitzvah, teach a class. . . . Each of them is going somewhere, and that movement is one of contestation as well as negation. As Blanchot himself says in one of his later reflections, "A being does not want to be recognized, it wants to be contested [*contesté*]: in order to exist it goes towards the other, which contests [*conteste*] and at times negates it, so as to start being only in that privation that makes it conscious . . . of the impossibility of being itself, of subsisting as its *ipse* or, if you will, as itself as a separate individual."[66]

Contestation always implies "exposure to some other (or to the other) who . . . [can] bring me into play," and doubtless it implies self-sacrifice.[67] The question is why Blanchot restricts this "other" to human beings and, like Levinas, runs the risk of turning ethics into ethicity. I leave aside the interesting counter-example of the animal, as vexed for Levinas as for Blanchot, and restrict myself to the deity. It is the young Blanchot writing for *Journal des Débats* who, when pondering Eckhart, leaves open the possibility of an experience of the deity the meaning of which is not determined in advance by an onto-theological understanding of God. From Eckhart's perspective, God welcomes all contestations of "God." St. Paul's figure of ἐπέκτασις in Philippians 3:13 is not one that Eckhart explicitly puts to work in his homilies and tractates although its image of an endless stretching forth of the soul is one that the Dominican could use to his advantage in affirming the Godhead. In his turn, could not Blanchot maintain that infinite contestation coheres with the infinite God, a deity beyond all dialectic? And if he rejects that possibility, and maintains that infinite contestation meets its limit with ethics, could he reasonably deny the charge of dogmatism?

Notes

Introduction

1. Georges Bataille, "Maurice Blanchot," *Une liberté souveraine*, texts and interviews collected and introduced by Michel Surya (Vendôme: Farrago, 2000), 67. The text first appeared in *Gramma* 3–4, "Lire Blanchot I," 1976.

2. In a letter to Gaston Gallimard written on December 29, 1948, Bataille proposed writing a book provisionally entitled *Maurice Blanchot et l'existentialisme*. No manuscript has been found. See Bataille, *Choix de lettres 1917–1962*, ed. Michel Surya (Paris: Gallimard, 1997), 392.

3. See Maurice Blanchot, "Traces," *L'amitié* (Paris: Gallimard, 1971), 252–58.

4. See Blanchot, *The Space of Literature*, trans. Ann Smock (Lincoln: University of Nebraska Press, 1982), 23 and 24, 194–96 respectively.

5. Roland Barthes, "The Death of the Author," *Image-Music-Text*, trans. Stephen Heath (New York: Hill and Wang, 1977); Paul de Man, *Allegories of Reading: Figural Language in Rousseau, Nietzsche, Rilke, and Proust* (New Haven: Yale University Press, 1979), 245.

6. Blanchot, *The Space of Literature*, 96.

7. See Jean-Paul Sartre, *L'imagination* (1936; Paris: Presses Universitaires de France, 1963), chap. 3.

8. See Blanchot's letter to Catherine David, "Penser l'apocalypse," *Le Nouvel Observateur*, 22 January 1988, 79.

9. Blanchot, *The Space of Literature*, 255.

10. Blanchot, *The Space of Literature*, 260.

11. Blanchot cites Rilke's letter of January 6, 1923, in *The Space of Literature*, 242.

12. For examples of Heidegger's use of *Stimmung* and *gestimmt*, see *Being and Time*, trans. John Macquarrie and Edward Robinson (Oxford: Basil Blackwell, 1973), §§ 29, 50, and *The Fundamental Concepts of Metaphysics: World, Finitude, Solitude*, trans. William McNeill and Nicholas Walker (Bloomington: Indiana University Press, 1995), pt. 1.

13. Blanchot, *The Space of Literature*, 242–43.

14. See Blanchot's reading of Broch's novel, " 'La Mort de Virgile': *La Recherche de l'unité*," *Le Livre à venir* (Paris: Gallimard, 1959), 160–72. Blanchot considers Char in several essays, most notably in "René Char and the Thought of the Neutral," *The Infinite Conversation*, trans. Susan Hanson (Minneapolis: University of Minnesota Press, 1993), 298–306. He quotes fragment thirty of "Partage formel" several times: "Le Poème est l'amour réalisé du désir demeuré désir." See Char, *Fureur et mystère* (Paris: Gallimard, 1962), 73.

15. Blanchot, *The Writing of the Disaster,* trans. Ann Smock (Lincoln: University of Nebraska Press, 1986), 66. Also see *The Step Not Beyond,* trans. Lycette Nelson (Albany: State University of New York Press, 1992), 89, 104.

16. The essay appears in *Les Temps Modernes* 38 (1948): 771–89, preceded by the editorial on pp. 769–70.

17. See Heidegger, " . . . Poetically Man Dwells . . . ," *Poetry, Language, Thought,* trans. Albert Hofstadter (New York: Harper and Row, 1975), 211–29.

18. Emmanuel Levinas, "The Poet's Vision," *Proper Names,* trans. Michael B. Smith (Stanford: Stanford University Press, 1996), 137.

19. Levinas, "The Poet's Vision," 127.

20. See Levinas, "The Servant and Her Master," *Proper Names,* 185 n. 4.

21. Levinas, "The Servant and Her Master," 148.

22. Twenty years later, in 1986, Levinas testified to Blanchot's importance to him since they had been undergraduates together at Strasbourg. "For me he stood for the very epitome of French excellence," he told François Poiré; and, thinking of May 1968, he observed that his friend "always chose the least expected, most noble and difficult path. This moral elevation, this fundamentally aristocratic nature of thinking, is what counts the most and edifies." Levinas, "Interview with François Poiré" (1986), in *Is It Righteous to Be? Interviews with Emmanuel Lévinas,* ed. Jill Robbins (Stanford: Stanford University Press, 2001), 30, 29.

23. Jacques Derrida, "Pas," *Gramma,* 3–4, "Lire Blanchot I," 1976. Revised and reprinted in *Parages* (Paris: Gallimard, 1986), 55. Several years later, Derrida reminisced about the period 1958–68: "It is also true that the living thinkers who gave me the most to think about or who most provoked me to reflection, and who continue to do so, are not among those who break through a solitude, not among those to whom one can simply feel oneself close, not among those who form groups or schools, to mention only Heidegger, Levinas, Blanchot among others whom I shall not name. It is thinkers such as these to whom, strangely enough, one may consider oneself most close; and yet they are, more than others, other. And they too are alone." "The Time of a Thesis: Punctuations," trans. Kathleen McLaughlin, *Philosophy in France Today,* ed. Alan Montefiore (Cambridge: Cambridge University Press, 1983), 41.

24. Also see Derrida, "Sauf le nom," *On the Name,* ed. Thomas Dutroit, trans. David Wood et al. (Stanford: Stanford University Press, 1995).

25. Derrida, *Aporias,* trans. Thomas Dutoit (Stanford: Stanford University Press, 1993), 77.

26. Heidegger, *Being and Time,* 307.

27. Christophe Bident notes that the special number of *Critique* "represents a turn in the critical reception" of Blanchot's work. *Maurice Blanchot, partenaire invisible: Essai biographique* (Seyssel: Champ Vallon, 1998), 457. The special number was reprinted in 1997.

28. See James Miller, *The Passion of Michel Foucault* (New York: Simon and Schuster, 1993), 82.

29. See Michel Foucault, *The Order of Things: An Archeology of the Human Sciences,* n. trans. (London: Tavistock Publications, 1970), 383–84. Deleuze clearly points out the main lines of influence running from Blanchot to Foucault in his *Negotiations, 1972–1990,* trans. Martin Joughin (New York: Columbia University Press, 1995), 97. Also see his *Foucault,* trans. Seán Hand (London: Athlone Press, 1988), 14, 87.

30. See Foucault, "Maurice Blanchot: The Thought from Outside," in *Foucault/ Blanchot*, trans. Jeffrey Mehlman and Brian Mussumi (New York: Zone Books, 1999), 9–19.

31. For studies in French, see Brian T. Fitch, *Lire les récits de Maurice Blanchot* (Amsterdam: Éditions Rodopi, 1992); Roger Laporte, *A l'extrême pointe: Bataille et Blanchot* (Montpellier: Fata Morgana, 1994); Anne-Lise Schulte Nordholt, *Maurice Blanchot: L'écriture comme expérience du dehors* (Geneva: Libraire Droz, 1995); Philippe Mesnard, *Maurice Blanchot: Le Sujet de l'engagement* (Paris: L'Harmattan, 1996); Chantal Michel, *Maurice Blanchot et le déplacement d'Orphée* (Saint-Genouph: Libraire Nizet, 1997); Manola Antonioli, *L'écriture de Maurice Blanchot: Fiction et théorie* (Paris: Éditions Kimé, 1999); Philippe Fries, *La "Théorie fictive" de Maurice Blanchot* (Paris: L'Harmattan, 1999); Marie-Laure Hurault, *Maurice Blanchot: Le Principe de fiction* (Saint-Denis: Presses Universitaires de Vincennes, 1999); Marlène Zarader, *L'être et le neutre: À partir de Maurice Blanchot* (Lagrasse: Verdier, 2001); and Christophe Bident and Pierre Vilar, eds., *Maurice Blanchot: Récits critique* (Tours: Éditions Farrago/ Éditions Léo Scheer, 2003). In 1990 *Lignes* 11 gathered together a variety of texts relating to Blanchot; in 1997 *Ralentir Travaux* 7 did the same, as did *L'Œil de Bœuf* in its double number 14–15 in 1998, while in 1999 the *Revue des Sciences Humaines* followed suit. Digests of Blanchot's thought were prepared by Laure Himy, in *Maurice Blanchot: La Solitude habitée* (Paris: Bernard-Lacoste, 1997), and Jean-Philippe Miraux, in *Maurice Blanchot: Quiétude et inquiétude de la littérature* (Paris: Éditions Nathan, 1998).

32. See *Magazine Littéraire* 424 (2003).

33. Zarader, *L'être et le neutre*, 20.

34. Two photographs of the young Blanchot appeared in François Poiré, *Emmanuel Lévinas: Qui êtes-vous?* (Lyon: La Manufacture, 1987), and a third, taken without Blanchot's knowledge or permission, appeared in *Lire* 117 (June 1985): 46.

35. Denis Hollier, "Foreword," *The College of Sociology, 1937–39* (Minneapolis: University of Minnesota Press, 1988), xxiii.

36. Foucault, "The Thought from Outside," 19.

37. See Blanchot, "Thought and the Exigency of Discontinuity," *The Infinite Conversation*, 3–10.

38. Ramon Fernandez, "The Method of Balzac," *Messages: Literary Essays*, trans. Montgomery Belgion (New York: Harcourt, Brace, 1927), 63. The essay, "La Méthode de Balzac," appeared in *Messages: Première série* (Paris: Gallimard, 1926).

39. Blanchot, *The Infinite Conversation*, xii.

40. See Blanchot, "Discours sur la patience," *Le Nouveau Commerce* 30–31 (Spring 1975): 19–44. With a few revisions, the text was taken up into *L'écriture du désastre* (Paris: Gallimard, 1980).

41. Blanchot, "Our Clandestine Companion," *Face to Face with Levinas*, ed. Richard A. Cohen (Albany: State University of New York Press, 1986), 48. A similar point is made with regard to Merleau-Ponty in "Le 'Discours Philosophique,'" *L'Arc* 46 (1971): 4.

42. See Blanchot, "Le Terrorisme, méthode de salut public," *Combat* 7 (July 1936): 106.

43. See Bident, *Maurice Blanchot, partenaire invisible*.

44. See Claude Mauriac, *Et comme l'espérance est violente* (Paris: Grasset, 1986), 530; Foucault, "L'homme est-il mort?" *Arts et loisirs* 38 (June 1966): 8.

45. Blanchot, "Reflections on Hell," *The Infinite Conversation*, 173.
46. Derrida, "Unsealing ('the old new language')," *Points . . . : Interviews, 1974–1994*, ed. Elisabeth Weber, trans. Peggy Kamuf et al. (Stanford: Stanford University Press, 1995), 122.
47. See Richard Macksey and Eugenio Donato, "Preface," *The Structuralist Controversy: The Languages of Criticism and the Sciences of Man* (Baltimore: Johns Hopkins University Press, 1970), xv.
48. See Paul de Man, "The Dead-End of Formalist Criticism," *Blindness and Insight: Essays in the Rhetoric of Contemporary Criticism*, 2d ed., intro. Wlad Godzich (London: Methuen, 1983).
49. See *The Structuralist Controversy*, 150, 184.
50. See Juliet Flower MacCannell, "Portrait: de Man," *Genre* 17, nos. 1–2 (1984): esp. 53. Also see Derrida, *Memoirs: For Paul de Man*, trans. Cecile Lindsay et al. (New York: Columbia University Press, 1986), esp. "Mnemosyne."
51. See Georges Poulet, "Criticism and the Experience of Interiority," *The Structuralist Controversy*, 66–68.
52. De Man's essay on Derrida is entitled "The Rhetoric of Blindness: Jacques Derrida's Reading of Rousseau"; his essay on Blanchot in *Critique* was translated into English and retitled "Impersonality in the Criticism of Maurice Blanchot." Both pieces are in *Blindness and Insight*. The papers by Derrida to which we allude are gathered in *Parages*.
53. We quote from her endorsement of Lydia Davis's translation of Blanchot's *When the Time Comes* (Barrytown, N.Y.: Station Hill Press, 1985).
54. Geoffrey Hartman, "Preface," *The Gaze of Orpheus and Other Literary Essays* (Barrytown, N.Y.: Station Hill Press, 1981), xi.
55. See Gerald L. Bruns, *Maurice Blanchot: The Refusal of Philosophy* (Baltimore: Johns Hopkins University Press, 1985), and Leslie Hill, *Blanchot: Extreme Contemporary* (London: Routledge, 1997). Ullrich Haase and William Large have attempted to simplify Blanchot even more in their *Maurice Blanchot* (London: Routledge, 2001).
56. Bataille, *Inner Experience*, trans. and intro. Leslie Anne Boldt (Albany: State University Press of New York, 1988), 12.
57. Bataille, "Autobiographical Note," *My Mother, Madame Edwarda, The Dead Man*, trans. Austryn Wainhouse, intro. Yukio Mishima (New York: Marion Boyars, 1989), 221.
58. Blanchot, "Mahatma Ghandi," *Les Cahiers Mensuels*, 3d series, 7 July 1931.
59. Blanchot, "On demande des dissidents," *Combat*, 20 December 1937, trans. Leslie Hill, in his *Blanchot: Extreme Contemporary*, 40.
60. Blanchot, "Inner Experience," *Faux pas*, trans. Charlotte Mandell (Stanford: Stanford University Press, 2001), 38.
61. Blanchot, "Our Clandestine Companion," 42.
62. Blanchot, "Humankind," *The Infinite Conversation*, 135.
63. Blanchot, "Our Clandestine Companion," 42.
64. Blanchot, "From Anguish to Language," *Faux pas*, 1.
65. G. W. F. Hegel, *The Phenomenology of Mind*, trans. and intro. J. B. Baillie, 2d ed. (London: George Allen and Unwin, 1931), 237.
66. Blanchot, *The Unavowable Community*, trans. Pierre Joris (Barrytown, N.Y.: Station Hill Press, 1988), 9.

67. On this theme see David Carroll, *French Literary Fascism: Nationalism, Anti-Semitism, and the Ideology of Culture* (Princeton, N.J.: Princeton University Press, 1995), pt. 1.

68. Blanchot, *The Infinite Conversation,* xii.

69. Blanchot, "The Limit-Experience," *The Infinite Conversation,* 212.

70. Blanchot, "Communism without a Heritage," in *The Blanchot Reader,* 203.

71. For further discussion, see Kevin Hart, *The Dark Gaze: Maurice Blanchot and the Sacred* (Chicago: University of Chicago Press, 2004), chaps. 6 and 7.

CHAPTER ONE: An Event without Witness

1. "Cette philosophie de l'affirmation non-positive, . . . c'est elle, je crois, que Blanchot a défini par le principe de contestation." "Préface à la transgression," *Critique* 195–96 (August–September 1963), in Michel Foucault, *Dits et écrits,* vol. 1 (Paris: Gallimard, 2001), 266.

2. "Il y a quelque chose qui me préoccupe actuellement, c'est le sens qu'on peut donner à cette notion si importante de contestation qu'on trouve chez Bataille, qu'on trouve un petit peu chez Blanchot. . . . [C]ette notion de contestation . . . . est . . . l'une des notions les plus problématiques, les plus difficiles, les plus obscures d'un minuscule courant philosophique . . . mais dont on trouverait au moins la source chez des gens comme Blanchot et Bataille." "Débat sur la poésie," *Tel Quel* 17 (Spring 1964), in *Dits et écrits,* vol. 1 (Paris: Gallimard, 1994), 423–24. All translations are my own, unless otherwise specified.

3. "est la manière dont *s'affirme* la négation radicale qui n'a plus rien à nier. Ce que nous venons d'essayer d'éclairer en précisant que l'expérience ne se distingue pas de la contestation. Mais de quelle espèce est alors l'affirmation qu'il revient à un tel moment de mettre en place?" Maurice Blanchot, *L'entretien infini* (Paris: Gallimard, 1969), 309.

4. "Il ne s'agit pas là d'une négation généralisée, mais d'une affirmation qui n'affirme rien: en pleine rupture de transitivité." "Préface à la transgression," 266.

5. "Une affirmation qui, pour la première fois, n'est pas un produit (le résultat de la double négation), et ainsi échappe à tous le mouvements, oppositions et renversements, de la raison dialectique . . . . Evénement difficile à circonscrire. L'expérience intérieure affirme, elle est pure affirmation, elle ne fait qu'affirmer. Elle ne s'affirme même pas, car alors elle se subordonnerait à elle-même: elle affirme l'affirmation. C'est en cela que Georges Bataille peut accepter de dire qu'elle détient en elle le moment de l'autorité, après avoir dévalué toutes les autorités possibles et dissous jusqu'à l'idée d'autorité. C'est le Oui décisif." *L'entretien infini,* 310.

6. "est la mise en question (à l'épreuve), dans la fièvre et l'angoisse, de ce qu'un homme sait du fait d'être." Georges Bataille, *L'expérience intérieure* (Paris: Gallimard, 1943), 16.

7. "S'en apercevoir est, sans rien autre, contester avec assez de suite les faux-fuyants par lesquels nous nous dérobons d'habitude. Plus question de salut: c'est le plus odieux des faux-fuyants. La difficulté—que la contestation doit se faire au nom d'une autorité—est résolue ainsi: je conteste au nom de la contestation qu'est l'expérience elle-même (la volonté d'aller au bout du possible). L'expérience, son autorité, sa méthode ne se distinguent pas de la contestation." Ibid., 24.

8. "ne pouvant et ne voulant pas recourir à l'ascèse je dois lier la contestation à la *libération du pouvoir des mots*." Ibid., 28.

9. "L'esprit de contestation en arrive maintenant à formuler l'affirmation dernière: '*Je ne sais qu'une chose: qu'un homme ne saura jamais rien.*'" Ibid., 125.

10. "Je traîne en moi comme un fardeau le souci d'écrire ce livre. En vérité je suis *agi*." Ibid., 75.

11. "Le *tiers,* le compagnon, le lecteur qui m'agit, c'est le discours, c'est lui qui parle en moi, qui maintient en moi le discours vivant à son adresse. Et sans doute, le discours est projet, mais il est davantage cet *autre,* le lecteur, qui m'aime et qui déjà m'oublie (me tue), sans la présente instance duquel je ne pourrais rien, je n'aurais pas d'expérience intérieure." Ibid., 75.

12. "Il n'y a plus sujet = objet, mais 'brèche béante' entre l'un et l'autre et, dans la brèche, le sujet, l'objet sont dissous, il y a passage, communication, mais non de l'un à l'autre: *l'un* et *l'autre* ont perdu l'existence distincte." Ibid.

13. "D'une façon toute indépendante de son livre [*Thomas l'obscur*], oralement, de sorte cependant qu'en rien il n'ait manqué au sentiment de discrétion qui veut qu'auprès de lui j'ai soif de silence, j'ai entendu l'auteur poser le fondement de toute vie 'spirituelle,' qui ne peut:

— qu'avoir son principe et sa fin dans l'absence de salut, dans la renonciation à tout espoir,

— qu'affirmer de l'expérience intérieure qu'elle est l'autorité (mais toute autorité s'expie)

— qu'être contestation d'elle-même et non-savoir." Ibid., 120.

14. "L'un de ceux sur lesquels Maurice Blanchot insiste comme sur un fondement." Ibid., 24.

15. A more detailed study would show that on the occasions when the term does surfaces in Blanchot's writing over the years, it almost always refers either explicitly or implicitly to Bataille's use of it.

16. "Blanchot me demandait: pourquoi ne pas poursuivre mon expérience intérieure comme si j'étais le *dernier homme?* En un certain sens . . ." Ibid., 76.

17. "le régime démocratique qui se débat dans des contradictions mortelles, ne pourra pas être sauvé." Advertisement for "Front populaire dans la rue," *Les Cahiers de CONTRE-ATTAQUE* 1 (May 1936), in Georges Bataille, *Œuvres complètes,* vol. 1 (Paris: Gallimard, 1970), 385.

18. "Non seulement le régime, mais la France même semble se dresser contre la France." "Il ne suffit pas de dire: Ni Berlin ni Moscou," *L'Insurgé* 25 (30 June 1937): 3.

19. "une force périssable . . . grandie par la conscience de la mort possible." "Le Problème de l'Etat," *La Critique Sociale* 9 (September 1933): 105–7. In *Œuvres complètes,* vol. 1, p. 333.

20. "Notre plus grande espérance aujourd'hui, c'est que, pour une nation libre . . . se lève la promesse magnifique de la révolution." "La Révolution nécessaire," *Le Rempart,* 22 June 1933, 2.

21. "Le *Collège de sociologie* regarde l'absence générale de réaction vive devant la guerre comme un signe de *dévirilisation* de l'homme." "Déclaration du *Collège de sociologie* sur la crise internationale," *Nouvelle Revue Française* 302 (November 1938):

874–76. In Denis Hollier, ed., *Le Collège de sociologie* (Paris: Gallimard, 1979), 98–104 (103).

22. "La Crise qui va s'ouvrir," *L'Insurgé*, 10 February 1937, 4.

23. "Il ne suffit pas de dire: Ni Berlin, ni Moscou," 4.

24. "une nation . . . attérée . . . par une étrange inertie morale et sociale." "Pour une diplomatie révolutionnaire," *L'Insurgé*, 27 October 1937, 8.

25. "la proximité du désastre transforme leur lâcheté en angoisse et pourrisse leur confiance en désespoir." "Ce qu'ils appellent patriotisme," *L'Insurgé*, 3 March 1937, 4.

26. "Les Vraies traditions de la France profonde," "Les Français et le couronnement," *L'Insurgé*, 19 May 1937, 4.

27. "Demain la guerre," *L'Insurgé*, 5 May 1937, 4.

28. The OED provides the following quotation to illustrate this original usage: "Contestation is when both parties exclaim: 'Give your attestation.' It marks the definitive settlement of the issue to be tried." *Gaii institutionum juris civilis comentarii quatuuor*, or *Elements of Roman Law by Gaius*, with a translation and commentary by E. Poste, 2d ed. (Oxford, 1875). J. A. C. Thomas describes *litis contestatio* as "a joint formal declaration to witnesses of the proceedings, *Testes estote* (Be you witnesses)." J. A. C. Thomas, *Textbook of Roman Law* (Amsterdam: North Holland Publishing Company, 1976), 75. I am grateful to Mike Macnair for his advice on this issue.

29. "Etymologically *testis* is he who is present as a 'third party' (**terstis*) to an affair in which two people have an interest; and this conception can be traced back to the common Indo-European period [*Etymologiquement testis est celui qui assiste en "tiers" (*terstis) à une affaire où deux personnages sont intéressés; et cette conception remonte à la période indo-européenne commune*]". Emile Benveniste, *Le Vocabulaire des institutions indo-européennes* (Paris: Editions de Minuit, 1969), vol. 2: "Pouvoir, droit, religion," 277.

In "Demeure," Jacques Derrida refers to this etymology when he evokes "the immense question of the third party, the witness as third party (*testis, terstis*) [*l'immense question du tiers, du témoin comme tiers* (testis, terstis)]." ("Demeure," in *Passions de la littérature. Avec Jacques Derrida,* edited by Michel Lisse (Paris: Galilée, 1996), 13–73 (25).

30. St. Thomas Aquinas, *Summa Theologica*, SSQ89 A1 Ra3, in *S. Thomae Opera*, vol. 2 (Stuttgart: Richard Fromm Verlag, 1980), 642.

31. For a detailed study of the rise of "ocularcentrism" in Western culture and the concomitant crisis of vision to which it gives rise in the modern era, see Martin Jay, *Downcast Eyes: The Denigration of Vision in Twentieth-Century French Thought* (Berkeley: University of California Press, 1993). It would be possible to argue that it is the displacement of voice by vision in the Christian relation to God which is at the heart of the crisis of witnessing that is reflected in the history of "contestation."

32. Oreste Ranum, "Contestation and Its Boundaries in Seventeenth-century France," Donma C. Stanton, "On *la contestation* and *le carnaval*: A Paradoxical Preface," and Michel Bareau and Judith Spencer, "Avant-propos," *Les Contes de Perrault. La Contestation et ses limites. Furetière*. Actes de Banff, 1986, edited by Michel Bareau, Jacques Barchilon, Donma Stanton, and Jean Alter (Paris-Seattle-Tübingen: Papers on French Seventeenth-century Literature, 1987), 143–67 (144), 123–42 (126), and 7–10 (9): "les Réformés sont perçus comme des 'contestataires': dénoncés comme entretenant un Etat dans un Etat."

33. Sandy Petrie, *Realism and Revolution: Balzac, Stendhal, Zola, and the Performances of History* (Ithaca, N.Y.: Cornell University Press, 1988), 24.

34. Petrie characterizes this tautology thus: "The National Assembly . . . declares its own authority while at the same time justifying its right to do so on the basis of the authority that it is in the process of declaring." Ibid., 23.

35. Georges Sorel, *Réflexions sur la violence* (1908; Paris: Editions du Seuil, 1990), 64.

36. Carl Schmitt, *The Concept of the Political,* trans. George Schwab (1932; Chicago: Chicago University Press, 1996), 36.

37. In an article entitled "Tu peux tuer cet homme" (You may kill this man), which he wrote in 1954 (and which incorporated another one, "Les Justes" [The Just], from *France-Observateur* [20 July 1950, 17]), Blanchot approaches the issue that Schmitt raises, but by way of Brice Parain, Albert Camus, and the Russian nihilists. In a number of respects, not least for the tentative engagement with Levinas's notion of the face-to-face encounter that it contains, this text marks a crucial phase in the development of Blanchot's postwar thinking.

38. Nevertheless, as Jean Baudrillard observed in 1969, the contestation that marked the events of May 1968—and which Blanchot never evoked at the time in other than negative terms (e.g., "Rectors, deans, professors, students, *contestataires* and counter-*contestataires,* all of that amounts to an agitation aimed at concealing nothingness, a nothingness governed by a time which is dead [*Recteurs, doyens, professeurs, étudiants, contestataires, contre-contestataires, tout cela s'agite pour couvrir le néant, un néant que régissent les règles d'un temps mort*]," "Sur le mouvement" [December 1968], in *Lignes,* 33 [March 1998]: 177–80 [179])—gave rise to an entirely new political situation, which he characterizes as "a transpolitical intervention [*une intervention transpolitique*]": "In May . . . we witnessed the eruption of a principle which comes before (or after) the reality principle, intervening *en bloc* as contestation living in the system, and thereby denouncing it, putting it out of action, with the aim of subverting it, of blocking it rather than of bringing its contradictions to a head in order to resolve them dialectically. In opposition to the principles . . . of the repressive Power of Revolution, there arose a third principle: that of Subversion [*Au mois de mai . . . on a vu l'irruption d'un principe antérieur (ou ultérieur) au principe de la réalité, intervenant en bloc comme contestation vivant dans le système, et par cela même le dénonçant, le détraquant, visant bien plus à le subvertir, à le bloquer qu'à en faire éclater les contradictions pour les résoudre dialectiquement. Face aux principes . . . du Pouvoir répressif de la Révolution, s'est dressé un troisième principe: celui de la Subversion*]." Jean Baudrillard, "Le Ludique et le policier," *Utopie* 13 (May 1969), in *Le Ludique et le policier* (Paris: Sens and Tonka, 2001), 15–38 (33–34).

39. *L'expérience intérieure,* 76.

40. "Dans la mesure où ce n'est pas un enfant dans le drame ou une mouche sur le nez, il est *conscience d'autrui* . . . ; se faisant *conscience d'autrui,* et comme l'était le choeur antique, le témoin, le vulgarisateur du drame, il se perd dans la communication humaine, en tant que sujet se jette hors de lui, s'abîme dans une foule indéfinie d'existences possibles." Ibid.

41. The Greek term *martus,* from which "martyr" derives, means "witness." In the New Testament, *marturein* signifies "bearing witness to God's presence in the world."

42. "The witness is the person who speaks . . . in such a way that God, in sovereign

judgment, declares it 'True, worthy of attention, really faithful' (Barth)." Jacques Ellul, *The Humiliation of the Word* (Grand Rapids, Mich.: Eerdmans, 1985), 107.

43. Jamie S. Scott, "Dietrich Bonhoeffer, *Letters and Papers from Prison* and Paul Ricoeur's Hermeneutics of Testimony," in *Paul Ricoeur and Narrative: Context and Contestation,* ed. Morny Joy (Calgary: University of Calgary Press, 1997), 13–24 (14, 18).

44. Jean-François Lyotard formulates this condition as follows: "In the republic, the first person plural pronoun is in fact the kingpin of the discourse of authorization. Substitutable for a proper noun: *We the French people . . . ,* it is supposed to be capable of linking prescriptions and their legitimacy. The principle of legitimacy of the republican regime is the fact that the addresser of the norm and the addressee of the obligation are one and the same. But this construction of a homogeneous We conceals a double heterogeneity. On the one hand: *I declare;* on the other: *You must.* The proper name masks this displacement, as does the *we,* since it can brings together *I* and *you.* You can make the law and obey it, but not in the same sentence. [*Dans la république, le pronom de la première personne du pluriel est en effet la cheville du discours de l'autorisation. Substituable à un nom propre:* Nous peuple français . . . , *il est censé pouvoir enchaîner . . . des prescriptions . . . avec leur légitimation. . . . Le régime républicain a pour principe de légitimité que le destinateur de la norme . . . et le destinataire de l'obligation . . . soient le même. . . . mais cette construction d'un nous homogène cache une double hétérogénéité. . . . D'un côté :* Je déclare; *de l'autre:* Tu dois. *Le nom propre masque ce déplacement, et le* nous *aussi, puisqu'il peut réunir* je *et* tu. *. . . On peut faire la loi et la subir, mais pas dans la même phrase*]." *Le Différend* (Paris: Editions de Minuit, 1983), 146–47.

45. "L'expérience, cela doit être tout de suite dit, ne se distingue pas de la contestation, dont elle est l'expression fulgurante dans la nuit." It is "ce déchirement total qui est comme l'extrême de la négation," and it takes place as "un état qui a un caractère positif, qui est l'autorité, que l'être affirme en se séparant de soi." "L'expérience intérieure," in *Faux pas* (Paris: Gallimard, 1943), 47–52 (50).

46. "L'expérience est donc essentiellement paradoxe, . . . elle est la contestation s'exprimant dans une situation originale, dans une situation qu'on peut vivre." Ibid.

47. "arrache l'homme à sa suffisance et le *communique à rien.*" Ibid.

48. "Contestation, expérience, communication sont des termes qui s'appellent étroitement—pour ne pas dire plus." Ibid.

49. In a chapter devoted to Hindu thought, he writes that there is error "each time discursive reason calmly enters an order, the sole mode of access to which should be struggle with contradiction, infinite contestation of itself and the passion of paradox [*chaque fois que la raison discursive entre tranquillement dans un ordre où sa seule manière d'accéder devrait être la lutte avec la contradiction, la contestation infinie d'elle-même, la passion du paradoxe*]." Ibid., 43.

50. *La Part du feu* (Paris: Gallimard, 1949), 31.

51. "Si l'on comparait cette patience à la dangereuse mobilité de la pensée romantique, elle en apparaîtrait comme l'intimité, mais aussi comme la pause intérieure, l'expiation au sein même de la faute." *L'espace littéraire* (Paris: Gallimard, 1955), collection "Idées," 162.

52. "Ce jugement n'est pas le simple châtiment de la démesure du langage, mais expiation et langage, c'est la même chose: le poète se detruit . . . Ruine, contestation,

division pure, réellement *jedem offen* comme il est dit, ouvert à tous, parce qu'il n'est plus qu'absence et déchirement, c'est comme tel qu'il parle." *La Part du feu,* 130–31.

53. "La Révélation de la parole comme du lieu où les hommes se tiennent en rapport avec ce qui exclut tout rapport." *L'entretien infini,* 187.

54. "Parler inaugure une relation originale, celle par laquelle les termes en présence n'ont pas à expier cette relation . . . , mais demandent et reçoivent accueil en raison même de ce qu'ils ont de non commun." Ibid.

55. Friedrich Nietzsche, *Also Sprach Zarathustra,* in *Nietzsche Werke: Kritische und Gesamtausgabe,* ed. Giorgio Colli and Mazzino Montinari (Berlin: Walter de Gruyter, 1968), vol. 6, p. 13.

56. The dying insect whose approaching end coincides with the death of Henri Sorge, the protagonist of *Le Très-haut* (Paris: Gallimard, 1948, pp. 239ff.), recalls the "fly on someone's nose" which Bataille evokes to illustrate what it is that he cannot accept about Blanchot's invitation to be the last man.

57. "Docile, presque obéissant, et niant très peu, ne contestant pas, [. . .] et, dans tout ce qu'il fallait faire, prêt à un assentiment naïf." *Le Dernier homme* (Paris: Gallimard, 1957), 11.

58. "Un Dieu lui-même a besoin d'un témoin. L'incognito divin, il faut qu'il soit percé ici-bas. J'avais longuement évoqué ce que serait son témoin. Je devenais comme malade à la pensée qu'il me faudrait être ce témoin . . . . Mais lentement—brusquement—se fit jour la pensée que cette histoire était sans témoin: j'étais là—le 'je' n'était déjà plus qu'un Qui? Une infinité de Qui?—pour qu'il n'y eût personne entre lui et son destin. . . ." Ibid., 23–24.

59. "[Ces] témoins qui ne recontrent jamais l'audience capable de les écouter et de les entendre." Paul Ricoeur, *La Mémoire, l'histoire, l'oubli* (Paris: Seuil, 2000), 208.

60. Shoshana Felman and Dori Laub, M.D., *Testimony: Crises of Witnessing in Literature, Psychoanalysis, and History* (New York and London: Routledge, 1992), 29, 160.

CHAPTER TWO: Maurice Blanchot

1. *Negative Dialectics,* trans. E. B. Ashton (New York: Continuum, 1992), 360.

2. This is now clearly documented by Christophe Bident, *Maurice Blanchot: Partenaire Invisible* (Paris: Camp Vallon, 1998). The book, which calls itself modestly an "Essai biographique," includes a full bibliography of Blanchot's early and voluminous journalistic writings. Blanchot does not give up all political writing in 1938 but rather in the fall of 1940; and he continues to conduct a literary chronicle for the Vichyist *Journal des Débats* till August 1944. There is a less complete bibliography of his early essays in a special Blanchot ("Flying White") issue of *substance* 14 (1976). See 142–59.

3. Bident, *Blanchot,* 73–75. During the war he directly helped Paul Lévy and the family of Levinas.

4. He returned to political journalism from his "retrait littéraire" between 1958 and 1969. But in his edition of *Thomas l'obscur* (new version) (Paris: Gallimard, 1950), Blanchot says in a prefatory note that the pages under that title were first composed in 1932, so that his political journalism and literary activity run parallel, as Bident's biography also shows. Whether there was a distinctive "transformation of convictions" remains uncertain. It may have come about through his friendship with Robert

Antelme and discovery of the concentration camps. The most thorough account of his engagements and withdrawals, before Bident's biography, which gives a balanced interpretation of his activity between 1938 and 1943, is by Philippe Mesnard: *Maurice Blanchot: Le Sujet de l'engagement* (Paris: L'Harmattan, 1996).

5. The question of how to understand Blanchot's biography has been raised in many articles by Jeffrey Mehlman, who draws a fascinating picture of what it might mean for a protofascist and sometimes anti-Semitic writer to change totally into a philo-Semitic thinker concerned with preserving the possibility of unmediated vision within the "passivity" of a writing-culture. See especially "Writing Lives: Speculations of a Biographer-in-Waiting," *Common Knowledge* 4 (1995): 97–112. Mehlman traces Blanchot's identification with not only literary friends but also literary revenants and outlines an intricate intertextual psychobiography.

6. *L'amitié* (Paris: Gallimard, 1971), 254. "C'est d'une parole toujours déjà détruite que l'homme apprend à tirer l'exigence qui doit lui parler: pas d'entente vraiment première, pas de parole initiale et intacte, comme si l'on ne parle jamais que la seconde fois, après avoir refusé d'entendre et pris ses distances à l'égard de l'origine." (All translations are mine unless otherwise specified.)

7. Since what we have in Blanchot's books is not speech ("la parole") but written speech, while he admits that "writing seems to have been invented to make more durable what is not durable or to prevent that loss of speech which speech always is," he adds: "Writing is always second, in the sense that even if nothing precedes it, it does not posit itself as a first, ruining rather by an indefinite deferral, which does not leave any place to the void, all primacy." *Le Pas au-delà* (Paris: Gallimard, 1973), 124–25.

8. Steven Shapiro quotes Emerson's "Nature": "All mean egotism vanishes, I become a transparent eyeball; I am nothing; I see all." He adds, "The narcissistic integrity of the ego is less important than the purity of sight itself." Steven Shapiro, *Passion and Excess: Blanchot, Bataille, and Literary Theory* (Tallahassee: Florida State University Press, 199), 5. Shapiro is especially good on links between Bataille and Blanchot.

9. All quotations in English, unless otherwise noted, are from Robert Lamberton's translation of *Thomas the Obscure: New Version* (New York: David Lewis, 1973). These lines evoke an ecstatic experience, which Blanchot will later argue is not simply an "expérience intérieure" but must be exteriorized, must be exposed to others, creating not something more objective and stabilizing but a community—of such experiences—which, as in Bataille, dissolves or is reticent, even "inavouable." See *La Communauté inavouable* (Paris: Editions de Minuit, 1983), 33–39.

10. *Le Pas au-delà*, 101–7.

11. There may be three persons, since, surprisingly, the dialogue between "il" and "elle" is interrupted on a few occasions by an authorial "je" ("Un instant, je me mêlais à leur dialogue"), a voice which the protagonists in this dialogue of one react to as if the intervention were by a "new god." See *L'attente l'oubli* (Paris: Gallimard, 1962), 63, 75.

12. In *Le Pas au-delà* (e.g., 167–71), there are also fragmentary thoughts (more coy still) suggesting the author's relation to unspecified characters, "young names" (126) who tempt him, despite "le jeu qui lui est propre" and the " 'pas' du tout à fait passif," toward a still deeper passivity or impassibility, one that is a dying rather than death. At the same time and "*peut-être*" an affirmation is suggested. If "thought . . . in its most passive passion, unhappier than all unhappiness," could remain thought in the face of such unhappiness, which reaches it in / from the other [*en l'autrui*]," then "il s'affirme

dans sa souveraineté sombre, en ruine." (What the "il" refers to grammatically is not totally clear to me, but it seems to conflate "malheur" and "autrui." There is often a similar problem with the author's "ils": the referent sometimes seems to be words themselves, as if "they" were words talking with words, like characters in fiction, or taking over that role.) I cannot but feel here the ever-so-cautious representation ("parole non prononcée mais à jamais dite") of a *second* Christianity without a first—a spirituality that must and cannot completely forget, as allusion, what went before.

13. Given the importance of the drama of mutual acknowledgment in the "Herr" and "Knecht" dialectic of Hegel's *Phenomenology,* which (after Kojève) pervades French thought, one could view *L'attente l'oubli* as an exhaustive playing out or working through of the attempt to achieve *Anerkennen* in a perfectly ordinary situation, one deprived both of issues of dominance and the support (as in Beckett) of a high unseriousness. The subtlest critique of "acknowledgment" as an ethical criterion, especially in matters of multiculturalism, can be found in Alexander Garcia Duetmann, *Zwischen den Kulturen* (Frankfurt am Main: Suhrkamp, 1997). His chapter "Kulturmüll" is particularly relevant. I cite only his question: "Gehört nicht der Begriff der Anerkennung zu [Adornos] den 'vom Hohen getönten' Wörtern, die nach Auschwitz kein Recht mehr haben, unverwandelt gebraucht zu werden?" (44)

14. In *Pour l'amitié* (Paris: Fourbis, 1996), first published in 1993, he finally talks directly about his role in the Declaration of the 121 during the Algerian crisis, and the events of May 1968. He remains suspicious, however, of historical reconstructions of this kind, and his overall purpose is to continue his reflection on friendship and its limits. (It is unclear to what degree Christophe Bident's "essay biographique" is an authorized biography, but it is the best informed source for Blanchot's intellectual itinerary.) By publishing *L'instance de ma mort* (1994), however, Blanchot has stimulated a fascinating discussion of a near-death experience that, while seemingly avoiding myth itself, suggests that life-writing, and perhaps mimetism generally, is anchored in a consciousness surviving death, and necessarily, therefore, in the mythic—including the myth of descending to and returning from the dead. See, on this, a paper by Phillipe Lacoue-Labarthe given at Cérisy, July 1997, printed in translation as "Fidelities," *Oxford Literary Review* 22 (2000): 132–51.

15. Bident, *Blanchot,* 55.

16. See his article "Le Refus," published first in 1958, during the Algerian crisis, and republished in *L'amitié,* 130–31. The refusal refers to Blanchot's rejection of the return of De Gaulle; but it leads me to wonder whether something like it occurred already in 1938. The article begins: "At a certain moment, faced with public events, we know we must refuse." This seems to differ from the prototype of "the great refusal" (a refusal of death, i.e. of death considered as unredeemable) that Blanchot ascribes to Hegel's systematic quest for permanence and totality, and which must be reaffirmed although we know it to be an illusion ("Le Grand refus," *L'entretien infini* [Paris: Gallimard, 1969] 46ff.). By refusing a certain kind of political action, fixated on the "now," and verging on apocalyptic or heroic expectation—on hope in a future brought into being by terror, by an absolute disruption—Blanchot could be said to refuse this further refusal of death as unredemptive. These intricacies are carefully followed by Gerald Bruns, who integrates them under the heading of "The Refusal of Philosophy" and "anarchism." Mehlman, "Writing Lives," 110, sees the refusal as Blanchot's forswearing fas-

cism in 1938, when he realizes that, though fervently French, it would lead to collaboration in case of a German occupation. This context, moreover, involves a French "fascism of the spirit," whose most eminent proponent was Blanchot's friend Thierry Maulnier. Perhaps Blanchot understood that the French version of fascism was not as distinctive as believed by those who contrasted it to German fascism. For French fascism, see Zeev Sternhell, *Neither Right nor Left: Fascist Ideology in France* (Los Angeles: University of California Press, 1986), especially chap. 7, "Spiritualistic Fascism." For Blanchot's very early reflection on refusal as a spiritual force, see note 85, below.

17. John Gregg, in *Maurice Blanchot and the Literature of Transgression* (Princeton: Princeton University Press, 1994), 37ff., has interesting remarks on Blanchot's conception of autobiography as an (invalid and fallible) defense against the "rapport with passivity, indecision, and the fascination of the image." Mesnard talks of "une chute d'éléments biographiques dans l'oubli" (86) and associates this not only with Blanchot's "retreat" into literature but also with his acceptance of the Hegelian discourse of negativity between 1947 and 1949. As Mesnard points out, the identitarian issue already surfaced in Blanchot's early fiction with the theme of the stranger, and outsideness or outsiderness. (From there a thematic line leads to the Jew as stranger.) In a previous essay, based on Blanchot's writings to 1960, I described his dilemma as that "of a mind that seeks to overcome itself from within, to pass into reality rather than more and more consciousness"; through art (or as Blanchot would say *écriture*) it intended to become real rather than more conscious. See "Maurice Blanchot: Philosopher-Novelist" in *Beyond Formalism* (New Haven: Yale University Press, 1970), 93–110. It is possible that Blanchot alludes to the identity-unity complex demanded by political engagement, and the contrary pressure exerted by "writing," one that leads to an indirect or nontransparent self-inscription, in two axioms following each other in *L'écriture du désastre* (Paris: Gallimard, 1980): "The 'false unity,' the simulacrum of unity, compromises more than its direct contestation [*mise en cause*] which, moreover, is not possible" (8). "To write, could it be, in this book, to become readable for everyone, and for oneself indecipherable?" (8) (Translations mine.) Not even Mesnard has managed to totally disentangle concepts that Blanchot melds: contestation / (Hegelian) negation / autonomous literary space / the expenditure of self as depersonalization / asceticism. Blanchot's prewar fiction, of course, had already jettisoned realism of the conventional sort and was experimenting with a mode of cryptic self-estrangement close to Kafka as well as the *Kunstmärchen* of the German Romantics.

18. *L'espace littéraire* (Paris: Gallimard, 1955), 48. My translation.

19. *Après coup, précédé par Le ressassement éternel* (Paris: Éditions de Minuit, 1983), 86. My translation.

20. Martin Jay, *Downcast Eyes: The Denigration of Vision in Twentieth-Century French Thought* (Los Angeles: University of California Press, 1993).

21. *L'entretien infini*, 35–45, and *The Writing of the Disaster*, 20. Blanchot even calls the "abolition" of the writer by what he writes a "death" or a "suicide." He talks of the "nudity" of the word *écrire*, comparing it to the sexual exhibition of Georges Bataille's "Madame Edwarda," and insists at the same time that the writer is the most discreet person, or one who has no secrets, no intimacy to protect. A road I have not taken is to connect Blanchot's reversal with what Jonas Barish has documented in the history of thought from Plato on as "the anti-theatrical prejudice." His writing life, moreover,

seems to span pressures coming from both "the logosphere" and "the videosphere." See Régis Debray, *Vie et mort de l'image: Une histoire du regard en Occident* (Paris: Gallimard, 1992).

22. For the complexity of the *pathos* concept, see the article by R. Meyer-Kalkus in *Historisches Wörterbuch der Philosophie,* ed. Joachim Ritter and Karlfried Gruender, vol. 7 (Basil: Schwabe, 1971), 193–99.

23. This emphasis may be a sign of Levinas's influence on or interaction with Blanchot. I cannot do better than quote Susan A. Handelman on Levinas and "passivity." It is a word, she comments, "which is part of the 'trauma' to the willing, enjoying, egoistic self. Perhaps [Levinas] employs this highly unfashionable term to administer a shock to the ego of the Western reader. . . . The term *passivity* is used to describe the subject as opened, hollowed out, traumatized, wounded, deposed, and subject to the other." *Fragments of Redemption: Jewish Thought and Literary Theory in Benjamin, Scholem, and Levinas* (Bloomington: Indiana University Press, 1991), 259. One of the most eloquent passages in Blanchot connects this passivity with the idea of suicide (which is not the case in Levinas), when Kleist is discussed in *L'espace littéraire,* 102: "that passion which seems to reflect the immense passivity of death, which escapes the logic of decisions, which certainly can speak but remains secretive, mysterious, and undecipherable, because it has no relation to the light. It is, then, that *extreme passivity* we also observe in voluntary death, the fact that action there is but the mask of a bewitched dispossession." (My translation.)

24. See also *L'espace littéraire,* the many pages on Mallarmé, including p. 36, n. 1, where Blanchot cites Georges Poulet on "philosophical suicide" in *Igitur,* and chapter 4 on "The Work and the Space of Death."

25. The condition of literary impersonality, of being an outsider to one's own work, is not always seen as tragic: Blanchot sometimes alludes to a "happiness [*bonheur*] of speaking" that precedes and survives the most radical misfortune [*malheur*]. Despite qualms (see below), he affirms this even after Auschwitz, modifying Adorno's notorious axiom about the impossibility of poetry. "Whatever the date it was written, every story henceforth will be as if written before Auschwitz." *Après coup, précédé par Le Ressassement éternel* (Paris: Éditions de Minuit, 1983), 98–99, my translation.

26. For a full description of the effects of this shame on speech and representation, see Claudine Kahan, "La Honte et le poète," in Philippe Mesnard and Claudine Kahan, *Georgio Agamben à l'épreuve d'Auschwitz: Témoignages, intérpretations* (Paris: Kimé, 2001), 108–23. I should add that Blanchot rejects art's striving for (realistic) resemblance from early on. This anti-iconic vein may have been fortified by his encounter with Levinas. On the question, and questionability, of (Aristotle's) concept of mimesis, see especially the work of Phillipe Lacoue-Labarthe.

27. *Après coup,* 98.

28. *Après coup,* 98–99. My translation.

29. This aspect of Judaism runs parallel in Blanchot, as in Mallarmé and Heidegger, with giving priority to the "parole essentielle" over the "parole brute."

30. *L'amitié,* 254–55, including note 1 to Levinas's *Difficile liberté.*

31. *L'amitié,* 252ff. The large claim about "history" shows that Blanchot remains within a Hegelian perspective. But this passage foreshadows the post-Holocaust "rupture" he describes in *Après coup.*

32. 11. *L'entretien infini,* 187.

33. So, alluding to Israel, he asks (the italics are in the original): "*Why did all the afflictions—finite, infinite, personal, impersonal, current, timeless—imply and ceaselessly recall, the historically dated affliction, which is nevertheless without any date, of a country already so reduced that it seemed almost effaced from the map and whose history nonetheless exceeded the history of the world? Why?*" *The Writing of the Disaster*, trans. Ann Smock (Lincoln: University of Nebraska Press, 1995), 37. The translator has chosen to render "malheur" as "affliction." Blanchot does have an essay on "Être-Juif," which transvalues the anti-Semitic charge that the Jew is an exploitative alien, coldly intellectual, without national feeling or roots, by idealizing that "exteriority" and calling his status as diasporic stranger an "irreducible relation." See *L'entretien infini* (1967), trans. as *The Infinite Conversation* by Susan Hanson (Minneapolis: Minnesota University Press, 1993), 123–30.

34. In *La Communauté inavouable,* talking of an ecstasy without object or certainty, Blanchot does mention John of the Cross (37). But the "passive" righteousness, so important to Luther's Reformation breakthrough, directed against justification by works, and prominently mentioned in his *Retrospect,* plays no overt role in Blanchot's thinking. He does make a reference, however, to Lurianic messianism's concept of God withdrawing in order to create ("Retirement et non pas dévelopement. Tel serait l'art, à la manière du Dieu d'Isaac Louria qui ne crée qu'en s'excluant." *L'écriture,* 27). See also his more explicitly Heideggerian reference on p. 208 to what "retires, slips away in the exigence of unveiling: the obscurity of the clearing or the error of truth itself" (my translation). Moreover, his important essay on Simone Weil in *L'entretien infini,* 153–79, contains crucial remarks on her refusal to convert and especially her projection of a new or different kind of Christianity, based on a "*regard*" directed toward God that maintains her in a totally attentive and receptive position. Finally, though, Blanchot claims that, even for Weil, "Le Langage est le lieu de l'attention."

35. *La Part du feu* (Paris: Gallimard, 1949), 37. My translation. The shock to signification, however, as John Gregg remarks, enhances the material, languagy presence of the word.

36. See, e.g., the play with numbers and dates at the beginning of *L'arrêt de mort* (Paris: Gallimard, 1948), 7–8, when the author discusses his "giving a form to these events" that happened around the time of Munich. Bident points out that the "events" dated so precisely by Blanchot in the opening pages actually took place in 1937, so that the precision of dating is a ruse. Bidet, *Blanchot,* 105–6.

37. Since my tenor in this essay is more expository than critical, I should indicate here that Blanchot, in theory, renounces *any* instrumental use of words as if that would fatally lead to their becoming instruments of power. This clearly does not follow; yet it inclines him toward absolutizing Mallarmé's concept of differentiating verbal discourse into the radical types of poetry (including literary prose) and . . . all the rest, or journalism. When Blanchot writes "Language is the undertaking through which violence agrees not to be open, but secret, agrees to forgo spending itself in a brutal action in order to reserve itself for a more powerful mastery" (*The Infinite Conversation,* trans. Susan Hanson, 42), he remains caught in the power dialectic, even if he intends by "powerful mastery" a more radical withdrawal or refusal that opens onto the impossible horizon where conversation is so selfless that each companion is "Celui qui ne m'accompagnait pas."

38. "Entre-dire" plays on "interdire." In his essay on Jabès and Judaism, Blanchot

defines it as "le temps de l'entre-dire, là ou la Loi, le pur arrêt de l'interdit, vient adoucir sa sévérité." *L'amitié,* 256.

39. *L'entretien infini,* xxvi.

40. *Thomas l'obscur* (new version), 112.

41. *The Writing of the Disaster,* 14. Literary truth has no present because it induces—as its philosophic enemies have often claimed—an oblivion or obfuscation of the real. But such oblivion is full though not a fulfillment. It is the obverse of what in Plato's myth of reminiscence affects the soul as it descends from a prior world to this, and incites anamnesis.

42. *L'arrêt de mort,* 112–13, my translation. In N. or Natalie, one can still discern the influence of surrealistic narratives, especially André Breton's *Nadja.*

43. *Thomas l'obscur,* 117. Since "to give oneself" has a sexual overtone, Anne's will to die cannot entirely avoid that connotation. But the novel implies that the sexual simulacrum is just that: a type of a truth that cannot be incarnated except by this sort of mythical portrayal.

44. *Thomas l'obscur* (new version), 35. My translation.

45. So different, as Levinas has remarked, from the habitations evoked by Heidegger. See Emmanuel Levinas, *Sur Maurice Blanchot* (Paris: Fata Morgana, 1975), especially 25–27, concluding with: "Blanchot ne prêt-il pas à l'art la fonction de déraciner l'univers heideggerien?"

46. *L'entretien infini,* 460.

47. Consider as exemplary the "1807" in his quasi-autobiographical *L'instant de ma mort.* The narrator of this story is saved from a firing squad at the last moment; Blanchot too, as a writer, is marked permanently by the consciousness of death, yet remains unable to convert it into personal or historical significance. The date is marked on the castle in the story; but, in the *histoire événementielle* Blanchot elides, it is the date when Hegel, completing the *Phenomenology,* sees Napoleon in Jena. In Blanchot's "undatable" or immemorial development, then, it may stand for a radicalizing impact on his consciousness, related to Hegel's "refusal of death" (also an acknowledgment of it, but as a perpetually transcended negativity in the dialectic). Hegel's impact, moreover, is not necessarily confined to a single moment in personal space but has its own vicissitude in French intellectual history from Kojève on. The Holocaust, which is specifically called by Blanchot "a date in history," is said to have no keeper, since through its happening "all was lost, including guardian thought" (*The Writing of the Disaster,* 47). Blanchot projects here an end to history very different from Hegel's "absolute knowledge." On the relation or disparity of private and public events, see also remarks on his friendship with Jean Paulhan, "La Facilité de mourir" in *L'amitié,* 17ff.

48. "The horror—the honor—of the name, which always threatens to become a title [*sur-nom*]. In vain the movement of anonymity remonstrates with this supernumerary appellation—this fact of being identified, unified, fixed, arrested in the present." *The Writing of the Disaster,* 7.

49. Paul de Man coined the expression "the rhetoric of temporality" to suggest that time could only be experienced through figures that make up this rhetoric and therefore belong to literary "space." The two major figures are allegory and irony; together they disclose "a truly temporal predicament." De Man's famous description runs: "Irony divides the flow of temporal experience into a past that is a pure mystification and a future that remains harassed forever by a relapse within the inauthentic. It can

know this inauthenticity but can never overcome it. . . . The temporal void that it reveals is the same void we encountered when we found allegory always implying an unreachable anteriority. Allegory and irony are thus linked in their common discovery of a truly temporal predicament." *Allegories of Reading: Figural Language in Rousseau, Nietzsche, Rilke, and Proust* (New Haven: Yale University Press, 1979), 118. These propositions lead Derrida to the following reflection: "Would a radical memory without anteriority [cf. Blanchot's "passé sans mémoire"], an anamnesis which would radically dispense with an anterior past, still be an experience of temporality?" This line of thinking must see time either as a mystery (as a memory that cannot be thought through), or as a void that is the subject of irrational fidelity or of bad faith. "What does a memory without anteriority recall, what does it promise? Is it a memory without origin, genealogy, history or filiation? Must one at each instant *reinvent* filiation?" To escape this predicament, we can assign an anteriority to this memory, but only at the risk of allegorizing a historical fact and so denying it the status of an authentic prefiguration—dooming it to be no more than a phantom, whose interpretive value is limited to disclosing a disjunction within the glimpsed unity. See Jacques Derrida, *Memoires for Paul de Man* (New York: Columbia University Press, 1986), 82–85.

50. See also the essay on Jabès, from which I take (p. 253) "cette rupture du pouvoir violent qui veut faire époque et marquer une époque." Blanchot's "là parle la catastrophe encore et toujours proche, la violence infinie du malheur" shows how close he already is to the concept of a disaster writing. Blanchot's "disaster" is also adumbrated in earlier essays by citing Hölderlin's understanding of a "withdrawal" of the gods, which Heidegger elaborates as "*Entzug.*" This cannot be literalized as an "event," however, without introducing either a mythic speculation or a false mode of temporal reckoning that, seeking a return to essence, an event that is an advent, turns everything else into an inessential non-event. See "Hölderin's Itinerary," in *The Space of Literature*, trans. Ann Smock (Lincoln: University of Nebraska Press), 269–76. I discuss the issue of historical dating, of epochalism, in *The Fateful Question of Culture* (New York: Columbia University Press, 1997), chap. 4, "Language and Culture after the Holocaust."

51. The role of the reader enters here, as a modality of the Other; but since reading at its most intense is also a writing, the theoretical issue of an authenticating (validating) reading is never clarified. Blanchot seems to opt for the notion of an "entretien infini," but without so absolute an intimacy or interiority that it could not find itself outside, estranged, face to face with an extralocutor.

52. On Blanchot and Sade, see especially Françoise Colin, *Maurice Blanchot et la question de l'écriture* (Paris: Gallimard, 1971), 140–43, and Michel Foucault, "La Pensée du dehors," *Critique* 229 (1966).

53. Cf. *L'écriture du désastre* (Paris: Gallimard, 1980): "Écriture (ou Dire) précédant tout phenomène, toute manifestation ou monstration: tout apparaître" (23), and "Vouloir écrire, quelle absurdité: écrire, c'est la déchéance du vouloir, comme la perte du pouvoir, la chute de la décadence, le désastre encore" (24).

54. "De l'angoisse au langage" in *Faux pas* (Paris: Gallimard, 1943), 9–23. The passage is given in my translation.

55. See especially *La Communauté inavouable*, 36–37.

56. The sense of that demanding presence, sort of divine vampire, Blanchot will share with Bataille. The "atheological" mysticism which can be found in both writers requires a separate—close and comparative—study. Blanchot and Bataille meet in 1940

and an intense, lasting friendship ensues. See, especially, Bident, *Blanchot*, 167–80, for a description of the beginning of the friendship.

57. *La Communauté inavouable*, 37.

58. *L'écriture*, 44–45. The last sentence reads in the French: "Lorsque nous sommes patients, c'est toujours par rapport à un malheur infini qui ne nous atteint pas au présent, mais en nous rapportant à un passé sans mémoire. Malheur d'autrui et autrui comme malheur." If "patients" is construed as a noun, it would be the opposite of "agents" or "actants."

59. See *La Folie du jour* (Paris: Fata Morgana, 1973).

60. *The Infinite Conversation*, 172. Descriptions like this suggest something more intense than Hegel's "unhappy consciousness," that "conscience malheureuse" which became the center of Jean Wahl's influential interpretation of the thinker. See his *Le Malheur de la conscience dans la philosophie de Hegel*, first published in 1929. Wahl, who died in 1974, was active at the Sorbonne for some time after the war. We imagine rather the situation of Ahasuerus, the Wandering Jew, or of a Hell without any torment except a time which does not pass, and which subjects us to others without any hope of redeeming them or oneself. The only writer before Blanchot who approaches his sense of "malheur" is Simone Weil. "Tous les problèmes se ramènent au temps. Douleur extrême: temps non orienté: voie de l'enfer ou du paradis. Perpetuité ou éternité." See *La Pesanteur et la grâce*, intro. by Gustave Thibon (Paris: Plon, 1948), 96.

61. For a consideration of Levinas, especially on the concept of time and language, see Susan A. Handelman, *Fragments of Redemption*, chap. 7. On Levinas's more optimistic view of time, see especially 207–8. Blanchot's view is considerably bleaker. Handelman, summarizing *Totality and Infinity*, writes: "Time adds something new to being. The intervals and discontinuities of finite time are the spaces of time's 'It is not the finitude of being that constitutes the essence of time, as Heidegger thought, but its infinity' " (207). See also her authoritative remarks on Levinas's concept of "the word of the other," 217–25.

62. *Le Temps et l'autre* (Paris: PUF, 1979), 68–69. This book, given as lectures at the Collège de Philosophie in its first year (1946/47) was originally published in 1948.

63. *Le Temps et l'autre*, 80. In Blanchot's bouts of metaphysical speculation, there is no significant gendering of sexual difference. Compare the ending of *Le Temps et l'autre* (77–89), its moving and daring theosophical pages on Eros.

64. Levinas, *Le Temps et l'autre*, 71.

65. *L'écriture*, 36. Blanchot, as well as Levinas—to whom he is obviously indebted— is always reinterpreting the master/bondsman relation which had been made the centerpiece of Hegel's *Phenomenology* by Kojève. I leave aside the question of both Levinas's and Blanchot's pacifism: the pacificism that arose after World War I and contributed to a reluctance to engage Hitler could not survive World War II. The moral problem in the political sphere, then, is how to move toward a new kind of pacificism, or ethic of nonviolence.

66. This paraphrase is prompted by 36ff. in *L'écriture*, but also relies on the gist of other passages in the book. The identarian trap is a constant in Blanchot's thought from the 1930s on, and I am not sure his attitude toward it does not change from time to time. There are moments, though, when this inability to "read" oneself, or this "externality," is transformed into a sense of the kind of brilliance that the gods of ancient myth displayed, who radiated beauty and strength without the agony

of a perpetual kenosis of self and consciousness Blanchot depicts in novels like *L'attente l'oubli.*

67. *L'écriture,* 44; my translation.

68. *L'écriture,* 104.

69. In many similar comments Blanchot may be answering Franz Rosenzweig's *Star of Redemption* (1929), in which the Jews are given the special role of pursuing salvation outside of historical time.

70. *L'entretien infini,* 187.

71. Or enigmatic exteriority, the *dehors,* "ce dehors sans intimité et sans repos," which is associated with "malheur" in Blanchot's commentary on Kafka, *L'espace littéraire,* 72. See also *L'entretien infini,* 66, and my remarks on Blanchot's (and Levinas's) concept of "exteriority." Derrida, in his essay on Levinas, elucidates how Husserl contests Descartes, and Levinas both of them, in the latter's shift from phenomenology to the primacy of ethics. "All the difficulties encountered by Husserl could be 'surmounted' if the ethical relationship were recognized as the original face-to-face, as the neither derived nor engendered, nor constituted on the basis of anything other than itself. An absolute outside, an exteriority infinitely overflowing the monad of the *ego cogito.*" Derrida, *Writing and Difference* (Chicago: University of Chicago Press, 1978), 106.

72. See the passage about Israel quoted previously, *L'écriture,* 37. Lacan says interestingly in his *Ethics,* when discussing sublimation and Freud's *Civilization and Its Discontents,* that "ethics punishes the individual relatively much less for his faults than for his misfortunes." The Book of Job moves toward this radical vision of misfortune while still struggling with (through Job's friends) a religious/teleological understanding of it. Blanchot's position, I suspect, reduces the sphere of moral "good luck" (as Bernard Williams defines it) to near zero.

73. Levinas's attitude toward this phenomenal exteriority is very intricate, however: Derrida has exposed its complexity or ambivalence in his essay on Levinas, "Violence and Metaphysics," in *Writing and Difference* (Chicago: Chicago University Press, 1978). Exteriority in the sense in which it is opposed to Hegel's phenomenological perspective owes something to Heidegger's concept of *Existence* as a standing-outside-of (ec-sistence), and endurance (punning on the German "ausstehen") of this outsiderness.

74. *Beyond the Verse: Talmudic Readings and Lectures* (1982), trans. Gary D. Mole (London: Athlone Press, 1994), 109. It might be said that typological (figural) interpretation, founded by Saint Paul and which "saved" the "Old Testament" for Christianity, displays the same transcendent plenitude. The difference has to do with a respect for the literalism of the letter: not only the historical reality of the "figures" recognized by Patristic interpreters but a certain attitude toward the divinely endowed reality of each letter, or combination of letters.

75. Chapter 5 of Bruns's *Blanchot* is a masterly exposition of their mutuality, with very subtle distinctions, which I can only hint at by putting Levinas closer to ethics, Blanchot to poetics.

76. *L'écriture,* 44–45, my translation.

77. *L'écriture,* 67–68.

78. Handelman, *Fragments of Redemption,* 272.

79. The same thought is relevant to the case of Paul de Man, whose essay on Blanchot in *Blindness and Insight* (1971) seeks to make a case for a self distinct from the empirical self.

80. This remark should not be taken to contradict Blanchot's early admiration of Sartre's *La Nausée* or of the latter's "engagement" as a *writer.* The disagreement with Sartre also has to do with Blanchot's rejection of the realistic style in fiction, however probing and intense.

81. In the second part of *La Communauté inavouable* (Paris: Editions de Minuit, 1983), entitled "La Communauté des amants," Blanchot uses Marguerite Duras's *La Maladie de la mort* to project a star-crossed, asymmetrical relationship in which the other is a *dormeuse* (I am also thinking of Valéry's poem) never accessible to the man except in an evasive immediacy ("l'intimité du dehors inaccessible") that makes him unhappily aware both of her absolute fragility (she is "sans défense, la plus faible, la plus fragile et s'exposant par son corps sans cesse offert à la manière du visage") and his inadequate response (he is "sensible à sa propre insensibilité").

82. *L'écriture,* 30.

83. "The renunciation of the first-person subject is not a voluntary renunciation," etc. *The Writing of the Disaster,* 29.

84. *L'écriture,* 46ff. He also calls it "an interruption of being, . . . between man and man there is an interval which should be neither that of being nor of non-being, and which bears the Difference of the word [*parole*]." *L'entretien infini,* 99. Blanchot keeps redefining, often as awkwardly as here, that "Difference," a "rapport du troisième genre," as he also calls it, although this relation is a nonrelation, in the sense that it gives value to an absolute respect for the other in others, a quality of otherness which cannot be reduced to sameness or unity. Such insights, which struggle against the sentimental aura of common moralistic terms coming from the ideology of humanism, seek to define, as does Levinas, "l'autre humanisme." One often feels that Blanchot's enterprise is a revision of Martin Buber's *I and Thou,* where the two contrasted fundamental relations, the I-Thou and the I-It, are called "words" (*Grundwörter*). Blanchot's "Autrui" has no relation to the "I" but is linked crucially to the neutral "Il," which is "le sans 'Je,' le sans nom, la présence de l'inaccessible." *L'entretien infini,* 94–105.

85. *L'écriture,* 37: "puisque je ne puis rien et que je n'existe plus comme moi." Blanchot goes on to say that this "responsible passivity" should be identified with Speaking (*Dire*) because, somehow, it continues giving and remains responsive. But the idea of generosity in "giving" ("le Dire donne et donne réponse") does not fit well the sense of an automatic reflex in "puisque je ne puis rien," which sounds like giving up, not giving.

86. *L'écriture,* 33.

87. Blanchot precedes in this Derrida's inquiry, *De l'esprit: Heidegger et la question* (Paris: Gallimard, 1987). "Toute révolution est spirituelle" is the key notion Blanchot attributes to Ghandi in one of his first texts (1931). See Bident, *Blanchot,* 58.

88. Even were there a change of era, a definitive temporal beginning or end, we could not characterize it except through an abuse of words. See "Guerre et littérature," *L'amitié,* 128–29.

89. His early reading is, of course, much more extensive, and includes an appreciation of Thomas Mann and Virginia Woolf. Also of Jean Paul—although I suspect what impressed him, as it did Nerval, was Jean Paul's own "scène primitive," his "Discourse of the dead Christ from the world's spire."

90. Vivian Liska on Sarah Kofman, in "Last Words: Sarah Kofman between Theory and Memory" (unpublished manuscript).

91. *Robert Antelme: Textes inédits / Sur L'espèce humaine / Essais et témoignages* (Paris: Gallimard, 1996), 68. Cf. *The Writing of the Disaster*, 11: "May words cease to be arms, means of action, means of salvation." The strong placement of "souveraine" recalls Georges Bataille's key use of the word; in this essay I have entirely omitted Bataille's relationship with Blanchot, dating from 1940.

92. On this duality, or double demand, see Françoise Colin, *Maurice Blanchot et la question de l'écriture*, 226. Gillian Rose has argued, especially in the case of Levinas, that the latter has wrongly divorced ethics from politics. Her argument is subtle and difficult; however, Blanchot, on the whole, does not make a generalization of that kind about the Jewish tradition or the philosophical tradition, but concentrates on what might be called the noninstrumental function of language within the temporal space of literature.

93. See the pertinent remarks on refusal in Bident, *Blanchot*, 63–64.

94. *The Writing of the Disaster*, 17.

95. "Parler—il le faut—*sans pouvoir:* sans que le langage trop puissant, souverain, ne vienne maîtriser la situation la plus aporétique, l'impouvoir absolu et la détresse même, ne vienne l'enfermer dans la clarté et le bonheur du jour?" *Paroles suffoquées* (Paris: Galilée, 1987), 16. Kofman is strongly indebted to Blanchot, one of the three people to whom she dedicates her book (the other two are her father and Robert Antelme).

96. "Peu à peu, je découvrais que l'écriture n'est jamais, quoi qu'on puisse en dire, une victoire sur le néant, mais, au contraire, une exploration du néant à travers le vocable." His context is the suicide of Yukel, a Holocaust survivor, which overshadows *The Book of Questions*. See Edmond Jabès, *Du désert au livre: Entretiens avec Marcel Cohen* (Paris: Pierre Belfond, 1991), 68–69.

97. *Le Livre des questions*, 43; "Commentaire de Reb Elar."

CHAPTER THREE: Responding to the Infinity between Us

1. François Poirié, *Emmanuel Levinas: Qui êtes-vous?* (Lyon: La Manufacture, 1987), 63–136 (rpt. Actes Sud, 1996); "Interview with François Poirié," trans. Jill Robbins and Marcus Coelen with Thomas Loebel, in *Is It Righteous to Be? Interviews with Emmanuel Levinas*, ed. Jill Robbins (Stanford: Stanford University Press, 2001), 23–83.

2. See Georges Bataille, *Inner Experience*, trans. Leslie Anne Boldt (Albany, N.Y.: State University of New York Press, 1988); *L'experience interieure* (Paris: Gallimard, 1954), reprinted in *Oeuvres complètes*, vol. 5 (Paris: Gallimard, 1973); Maurice Blanchot, *Thomas the Obscure*, trans. Robert Lamberton (New York: David Lewis, 1973); *Thomas l'obscur* (1941; Paris: Gallimard, 1950); Emmanuel Levinas, *Existence and Existents*, trans. Alphonso Lingis (The Hague: Martinus Nijhoff, 1978); *De l'existence à l'existant* (Paris: Vrin, 1947); *Time and the Other*, trans. Richard Cohen (Pittsburgh: Duquesne University Press, 1985); *Le Temps et l'autre* (1947; Montpellier: Fata Morgana, 1975). On the "communication" between these texts, as well as Bataille's 1947 review essay on Levinas, "From Existentialism to the Primacy of Economy," see Jill Robbins, *Altered Reading: Levinas and Literature* (Chicago: University of Chicago Press, 1999), chap. 6 and appendix.

3. Emmanuel Levinas, "The Poet's Regard," trans. Michael Smith, in *Proper Names* (Stanford: Stanford University Press, 1996); "Le Regard du poète" [1956] in *Sur Maurice Blanchot* (Montpellier: Fata Morgana, 1975).

4. Maurice Blanchot, *The Infinite Conversation*, trans. Susan Hanson (Minneapolis: University of Minnesota Press, 1993), 48; *L'entretien infini* (Paris: Gallimard, 1969). 48. All subsequent references will be given in the text with page references as *IC*.

5. Jean-François Lyotard, *The Differend: Phrases in Dispute*, trans. Georges Van Den Abbeele (Minneapolis: University of Minnesota Press, 1988), 107; *Le Différend* (Paris: Minuit, 1983).

6. Jacques Derrida, "Violence and Metaphysics," in *Writing and Difference*, trans. Alan Bass (Chicago: University of Chicago Press, 1978), 111; "Violence et métaphysique," in *L'écriture et la différence* (Paris: Seuil, 1967)

7. Emmanuel Levinas, *Totality and Infinity*, trans. Alphonso Lingis (Pittsburgh: Duquesne University Press, 1969), 39; *Totalité et infini* (The Hague: Martinus Nijhoff, 1961). All subsequent references will be given with page numbers in the text and abbreviated as *TI*.

8. Ann Smock speaks of the *in*ability in responsibility, with reference to Blanchot's *The Writing of the Disaster*, in "Disastrous Responsibility," *L'Ésprit Créateur* 24 (1984): 4–20.

9. "The Philosopher and Death" in *Is It Righteous to Be?*, ed. Robbins, 127.

10. Jacques Derrida has drawn attention to the syntactical importance of Blanchot's diction, in *Parages* (Paris: Galilée, 1986), 35.

11. See Jacques Derrida, "At This Very Moment in This Work Here I Am," trans. Ruben Berezdivin, in *Re-Reading Levinas*, ed. Robert Bernasconi and Simon Critchley (Bloomington: Indiana University Press, 1991), 15; "En ce moment même dans cet ouvrage me voici," in *Textes pour Emmanuel Levinas*, ed. François Laruelle (Paris: Jean-Michel Place, 1980).

12. "Freedom and Command" in *Collected Philosophical Papers*, trans. Alphonso Lingis (Dordrecht: Martinus Nijhoff, 1987), 21; "Liberté et commandement," *Revue de Métaphysique et de Morale* 58 (1953), reprinted in *Liberté et commandement* (Montpellier: Fata Morgana, 1994).

13. Discussion following "Transcendence and Intelligibility" in *Is It Righteous to Be?*, ed. Robbins.

14. Theodore de Boer, *The Rationality of Transcendence* (Amsterdam: J. C. Gieben, 1997), 49.

15. "The Proximity of the Other" in *Is It Righteous to Be?*, ed. Robbins, 215.

16. Derrida, "Violence and Metaphysics," 104.

17. Lyotard, *The Differend*, 107.

18. Roman Jakobson, "Closing Statement: Linguistics and Poetics," in *Language in Literature* (Cambridge, Mass.: Harvard University Press, 1987), 67–68.

19. For this reason, Jean-François Lyotard notes, the demand of asymmetry, as well as the interpretive demand Levinas's text might be said to issue—"thou shalt not flatten the alterity of this text"—risks turning, at any moment, into persecution. See Lyotard, "Levinas's Logic" in *Face to Face with Levinas*, ed. Richard A. Cohen (Albany: State University of New York Press, 1986); "La Logique de Levinas" in *Textes pour Emmanuel Levinas*, ed. Françoise Laruelle (Paris: J.-M. Place, 1980).

20. Joseph Libertson, *Proximity: Levinas, Blanchot, Bataille and Communication* (The Hague: Martinus Nijhoff, 1982); *The Space of Literature*, trans. Ann Smock (Lincoln: University of Nebraska Press, 1982), 199; *L'espace littéraire* (Paris: Gallimard, 1955). Libertson in fact takes an entirely different view of the passage. Within *The Infinite*

Conversation he sees it as Blanchot's will to restore a dialectical relation between the two poles.

21. Libertson, *Proximity,* 277

22. Thanks to Gil Anidjar for his helpful comments on Blanchot's use of the word *entretenir.*

23. Mike Holland, "Towards a Method," *Substance* 14 (1976): 16.

24. What one imprecisely refers to as the dialogue form in *The Infinite Conversation* is characterized by the flattening out of the difference between the two interlocutors (Christopher Bident, *Maurice Blanchot: Partenaire invisible* [Champ Vallon, 1998], 446). Mike Holland notes that "the speakers have no identity; there is nothing consistent about each one's line of thought." Even with regard to the "dialogues" on Levinas, "a study of the variants between the [original] published texts and their subsequent appearance in *L'entretien infini* reveals that a speech by one 'character' is often omitted so that what he says in the second version is the reply he received in the first" (Holland, 15). This lack of characterological differentiation in itself would not make them un-Levinasian. For Levinas: "It is not difference that makes alterity, but alterity that makes difference" ("The Vocation of the Other," in *Is It Righteous to Be?,* ed. Robbins, 106).

25. It should be clear that at stake here is neither a *mise en abîme* nor the text's self-reflection.

26. Readers of Blanchot offer a divergent range of interpretative responses to this question. Joseph Libertson takes Blanchot to be ventriloquizing Levinas, then giving way to an ambivalent reduction of the Levinasian concepts (*Proximity,* 280). For Leslie Hill, Blanchot speaks in Levinas's voice *to* Levinas, ultimately interrupting the Levinasian interruption (*Blanchot: Extreme Contemporary* [London: Routledge, 1997], chaps. 3 and 4). Gerald L. Bruns refers to Blanchot's "tacit rewriting of [Levinasian] ethics as a poetics of the Outside" (*Maurice Blanchot: The Refusal of Philosophy* [Baltimore: Johns Hopkins University Press, 1997], 111). For Paul Davies, from 1961 onwards in Blanchot, "the experience of the other as neuter is thought alongside Levinas's *Autrui*" ("Difficult Friendship" in *Research in Phenomenology* 17 [1988]: 162).

27. Power, which refers to a relation between existents, is an ontic relation. For Heidegger power could not be latent in possibility, which is an ontological structure.

28. Sarah Kofman has drawn attention to these figures in *Smothered Words,* trans. Madeleine Dobie (Evanston, Ill.: Northwestern University Press, 1998). *Paroles suffoquées* (Paris: Galilée, 1987).

29. Holland, "Towards a Method," 17.

CHAPTER FOUR: Two Sirens Singing

1. See Leslie Hill, *Blanchot: Extreme Contemporary* (London: Routledge, 1997). Hill explains the meaning of the term "extreme contemporary" on the last pages of his book: "Extreme contemporary would be both what addresses us in the present most radically, and in that very gesture addresses us from some other place or time which does not belong to the contemporary, but creates a fissure or caesura in temporality itself" (224). Calling Blanchot and Adorno "extreme cotemporaries" both simplifies this meaning and adds to its complexity.

2. The most important examples are Kafka and Beckett.

3. See Blanchot's use of the expression "contestation de ce qui est" in "Les grands réducteurs," in *L'amitié* (Paris: Gallimard, 1971), 80.

4. Geoffrey Hartman, "Blanchot's Silence: Language after the Holocaust" (unpublished manuscript); Sarah Kofman, *Paroles suffoquées* (Paris: Galilée, 1987), and, most recently and extensively, Michael Rothberg, *Traumatic Realism: The Demands of Holocaust Representation* (Minneapolis: University of Minnesota Press, 2000), 25–106.

5. Maurice Blanchot, *Le Livre à venir* (Gallimard: Paris 1959). The English translations are based on Maurice Blanchot, *The Sirens Song*, trans. Sacha Rabinowitch (Brighton: Harvester Press, 1982), with major changes whenever these were deemed necessary. Significant amendments are explained in footnotes. Subsequent quotations from *Le Livre à venir* refer to the original text in French, indicated as *LV,* followed by the page number.

6. Max Horkheimer and Theodor W. Adorno, *Dialektik der Aufklärung: Philosophische Fragmente* (1944; Frankfurt am Main: Fischer, 1994). The English translations are largely based on *Dialectic of Enlightenment,* trans. John Cumming (New York: Continuum, 1972), with major changes whenever these were deemed necessary. Significant amendments are explained in footnotes. Subsequent quotations from *Dialektik der Aufklärung* refer to the original text in German, indicated as *DA,* followed by the page number.

7. Originally published as "Le Chant des sirénes," *La Nouvelle Revue Française* 19 (July 1954): 95–104.

8. Blanchot, "Le Chant des sirènes" (*LV* 9–18). In the English translation, "The Sirens' Song," 59–65.

9. The Sirens episode is discussed twice in *Dialektik der Aufklärung,* once in the chapter entitled "Begriff der Aufklärung" (*DA* 38–49), more extensively in excursus I, "Odysseus oder Mythos und Aufklärung" (*DA* 50–87). One now knows that the first chapter was written by both authors, the excursus I, which deals primarily with the Sirens' episode, essentially by Adorno alone. See Irving Wohlfarth, "Das Unerhörte hören. Zum Gesang der Sirenen," in Manfred Gangl and Gérard Raulet, eds., *Jenseits instrumenteller Vernunft: Kritische Studien zur Dialektik der Aufklärung* (Bern, Vienna, Berlin: Peter Lang, 1998), 240, n.56. For the sake of simplicity, subsequent references to *Dialektik der Aufklärung* in the text mention only Adorno's name.

10. Homer, *The Odyssey,* trans. W. H. D. Rouse (New York: Mentor, 1937), 141. Translation changed.

11. It is noteworthy that "everything that happens" has been translated very differently in the various interpretations of these verses, depending on the tense—past, present, or future—that is attributed to the verb "happening," *genetaï,* in the description of the Sirens' "knowledge." This variation in the different translations is due to an uncertainty generated by the Greek grammatical form of the verb *genetaï* in Homer's verses: the *aorist,* which in Greek means "unlimited" or "infinite." This tense, which has disappeared from most modern languages, indicates an indefinite time which, according to some grammarians, leaves indeterminate whether the action takes place in the past or in an open-ended present. Others describe the *aorist* as a present mode associated with a future dimension, which has connotations approximating the subjunctive, the time of possibilities and impossibilities, the time of utopias and of the space of the imaginary. Most recent versions, like Rouse's, translate *genetaï* in the present tense; Samuel Butler translates it as "everything *that is going to happen* over the whole world,"

and in the translation used by Adorno the Sirens know "everything that ever *happened*" (*DA* 39). (The references to the *Odyssey* in the footnotes of *The Dialectic of Enlightenment* fail to indicate the source of the translation.) When *genetaï* is read in the past tense, the Sirens become those who record history; in the present tense, they are declaring their omniscient bird's-eye view; in the future tense, they turn into soothsayers or prophets.

12. "Das Epos enthält bereits die richtige Theorie" (*DA* 41). John Cumming translates "die richtige Theorie" with "the appropriate theory," which considerably weakens Adorno's original claim (Adorno and Horkheimer, *Dialectic of Enlightenment*, 34). The German for "appropriate" is "angemessen."

13. Adorno's "Technik" and Blanchot's "technique" are here translated as "technology," although the word has a somewhat too contemporary ring. Adorno quotes a passage from an American review that uses "technology" interchangeably with his German "Technik" (cf. *DA* 48).

14. Sacha Rabinowitch oddly translates Blanchot's "technique" as "material power," (Blanchot, "The Sirens' Song," 60).

15. A striking mistranslation by Cummings turns "von der Erfahrung des Vielfältigen, Ablenkenden, *Auflösenden*" into "from the experience of the multitudinous, from digression and *salvation*." "Auflösend" means "dissolving."

16. It seems at times that Adorno's own apodictic tone and the single-mindedness of his truth-claim suffers from the sort of resistance to the "multiplicity" inherent in the Sirens' song that he deplores in Odysseus.

17. Had Adorno been more attentive to the *aorist* in describing what the Sirens know, he would perhaps have taken into account their knowledge of undetermined, always still open happenings on earth. In that case, the *Dialektik der Aufklärung* would have been less melancholic, its claim to the "right theory" less totalitarian, and the knowledge of the Sirens less archaic.

18. Françoise Collin, *Maurice Blanchot et la question de l'écriture* (Paris: Gallimard, 1971), 117.

19. In the English version "ce plaisir extrême de tomber" is inaccurately translated as "pleasurable dreams of an endless descent." The loss of control implicit in "tomber" is missed here (Blanchot, "The Sirens' Song," 60).

20. The Sirens invite their listeners to return to an earlier stage of human civilization, which Adorno is far from encouraging. The alternative he suggests doesn't present itself as a return to a former, irrational state, but as an alternative enlightenment.

21. Wohlfarth, *Das Unerhörte Hören*, 252.

22. Wohfarth writes: "The negative enlightenment that is prevalent so far has to be replaced by a positive one, an 'identity of identity and non-identity' devised with and against Hegel, which leaves the greatest possible space for the non-identical." See Wohlfarth, *Das Unerhörte Hören*, 242.

23. Wohlfarth, *Das Unerhörte Hören*, 254.

24. In the English version, "tandis qu'Achab s'est *perdu* dans l'image" is translated as "was *overcome* by his vision." The crucial sense of self-loss and of "getting lost in . . ." is missed here (Blanchot, "The Sirens' Song," 60).

25. There are, in Blanchot's account, some residues of the dialectic movement that Adorno recognizes in Odysseus's strengthening of self through the encounter with the other: "After surviving the trial, Odysseus finds himself to be the same person he was

before, and the world finds itself again, perhaps grown poorer, but safer and firmer" (*LV* 16). The stability of the world is thus, for Blanchot as for Adorno, consolidated through Odysseus's triumphant encounter with the Other.

26. This is possibly an indication that Blanchot is actually responding to Adorno's reading of the episode.

27. Wohlfarth, *Das Unerhörte Hören*, 244.

28. For a description of this aspect of the *récit* in Blanchot see John Gregg, *Maurice Blanchot and the Literature of Transgression* (Princeton, N.J.: Princeton University Press, 1994), 199. Gregg makes a convincing parallel with Jacques Derrida's notion of "invagination" and quotes from Derrida's *Parages:* "Every novel contains secretly in-vaginated within it a récit, 'une poche plus grande que le tout' " (ibid.).

29. Adorno's reflections on the transformation from song into narrative are preceded by a historical speculation on the genealogy of language and its transition from magic to referential language, in which the dynamic of the dialectic of enlightenment repeats itself. Mythical language, like the Sirens' song, is equated with *fatum*, with inescapable fate, which referential language undoes. Odysseus misuses the discovery of the difference between word and thing for his cunning tricks. Homer's narrative is an alternative to Odysseus's abuse as well as to the mythical identity of word and thing, embodied in the Sirens' song (cf. *DA* 67).

30. At this point errors in the English translation turn Adorno's words into their opposite. In the German original: "Die Versetzung der Mythen in den Roman . . . verfälscht nicht sowohl jene, als dass sie den Mythos mitreisst in die Zeit, den Abgrund *aufdeckend,* der ihn von Heimat und *Versöhnung* trennt" (*DA* 86). In the English translation: "The translation of myths into the novel . . . does not so much falsify the myths as sweep myth into time, *concealing* the abyss that separates it from homeland and *expiation*" (Adorno and Horkheimer, *Dialectic of Enlightenment,* 78). "Versöhn-ung" means "reconciliation," and occasionally (in a religious or philosophical context) "redemption," but not "expiation," which in German is called "Sühne" or "Busse." The mistake in the translation of "aufdecken" is even more disturbing. That art must *reveal,* not *conceal* the distance separating the present from a time of fulfillment lies at the heart of Adorno's poetics. One can only wonder about the effects of this distortion on generations of readers.

31. The translation of the qualification of this silence in one of the following sentences again turns the meaning of the German into its opposite. The German: "Das Schweigen, dessen Erstarrung der Rest aller Rede ist." This means, literally, "silence that is the rest (the residue) of all speech." In the English translation: "The reticence and composure of the narration are the true marks of eloquence" (ibid., 79).

32. Blanchot, "Après coup," in *Après coup, précédé par Le ressassement éternel* (Paris: Editions de Minuit, 1983).

33. *Après coup,* 99.

34. For a discussion of the various repetitions and modifications of Adorno's dictum, see Michael Rothberg, *Traumatic Realism,* 25–59.

35. Blanchot, *Après coup,* 98.

36. One of the stories Blanchot comments on in "Après coup" is entitled "L'idylle." Although it can be read as a premonition of the concentrationary universe, it is the *récit par excellence* that can no longer be "after Auschwitz."

37. Hartman, "Blanchot's Silence" (see note 4).

38. Jacques Derrida, in *Parages,* shows how Blanchot has "evoked and contested the word *récit,* has claimed and rejected, inscribed and then effaced it." Jacques Derrida, *Parages,* (Paris: Galilée, 1986), 140. Anne-Lise Schulte Nordholt, who quotes this passage, also convincingly discusses the difference between "récit" and "récit-fiction." Nevertheless, Blanchot, in "Après coup," seems to be using the two terms interchangeably. Anne-Lise Schulte-Nordholt, *Maurice Blanchot: L'écriture comme experience du dehors* (Geneva: Droz, 1995), 89–96.

39. Wohlfarth writes: "It is as if there were a secret connection across centuries between the Sirens and fascism. *Das Unerhörte* [the unthinkable] could maybe only happen because the Sirens remained unheard." Wohlfarth, *Das Unerhörte Hören,* 263.

40. For an extensive discussion of the problematic relationship between Adorno's philosophy of history and his "after Auschwitz" statements, see Rothberg, *Traumatic Realism,* 50–51.

41. Blanchot, *Après coup,* 98.

42. "The secret law of the *récit"* is that it "moves towards a point which is not only unknown, ignored and strange" but has "no prior reality apart from this movement" (*LV* 14).

43. Maurice Blanchot, "L'exigence du retour," in *L'entretien infini* (Paris: Gallimard, 1969), 405–18. English translation: "The Exigency of Return," in *The Blanchot Reader,* ed. Michael Holland (Oxford: Blackwell, 1996), 282.

44. Henri Meschonnic, "Maurice Blanchot et l'écriture hors langage," in *Les Cahiers du chemin* 20 (1974): 82.

45. Wohlfarth, *Das Unerhörte Hören,* 274.

46. "A voice comes from the other shore. A voice interrupts the continuous saying of that which has already been said." Blanchot, *Après coup,* 100.

CHAPTER FIVE: A Fragmentary Demand

1. *Martin Heidegger zum siebzigsten Geburtstag* (Pfullingen: Neske, 1959). There were thirty-three contributors in all, including, in addition to those mentioned, Hans-Georg Gadamer, Beda Allemann, Walter Jens, Werner Heisenberg, Ilse Aichinger, Hans Arp, Günter Eich, Helmut Heissenbüttel, and Ernst Jünger. All three French texts (by Beaufret, Blanchot, and Char) were given in the original French, without accompanying translation; Braque supplied a reproduced artwork. On reception of Heidegger in France during the postwar period, see Dominique Janicaud, *Heidegger en France,* 2 vols. (Paris: Albin Michel, 2001), 1:81–184. Beaufret first met Heidegger in Freiburg in September 1946; when Heidegger visited France for the first time, at Beaufret's invitation in 1955, Char and Braque were among those the philosopher expressed a particular desire to meet.

2. See Maurice Blanchot, "Entretien sur un changement d'époque," *La Nouvelle Revue Française* 88 (April 1960): 724–34. The dialogue, together with an unpublished supplement, is reprinted in *L'entretien infini* (Paris: Gallimard, 1969), 394–418; *The Infinite Conversation,* trans. Susan Hanson (Minneapolis: University of Minnesota Press, 1993), 264–81. The phrase "if such exists" (*s'il y en a*), which Hanson renders as "if there is one" (264), will be familiar to readers from many of Derrida's recent texts.

3. On the shifting self-presentation of Blanchot's shorter fictions, see Jacques Derrida, *Parages* (Paris: Galilée, 1976), 10. I examine the specific case of *Le Dernier homme*

in my *Bataille, Klossowski, Blanchot: Writing at the Limit* (Oxford: Oxford University Press, 2001), 229–31.

4. Blanchot, *Les Intellectuels en question* (Tours: Farrago, 2000), 36. On the return to Paris, see Christophe Bident, *Maurice Blanchot: Partenaire invisible* (Seyssel: Champ Vallon, 1998), 373–75.

5. On Blanchot's political activities from the 1930s onwards, see my *Blanchot: Extreme Contemporary* (London: Routledge, 1997). On Mascolo's political association with Blanchot, see "Un itinéraire politique," *Le Magazine littéraire* 278 (June 1990): 36–40, and Blanchot, *Pour l'amitié* (Paris: Fourbis, 1996), "For Friendship," trans. Leslie Hill, *The Oxford Literary Review* 22 (2000): 25–38.

6. Blanchot, "Où va la littérature?," *La Nouvelle Revue Française* 7 (July 1953): 98–107 (98). Though one of the first to be written, the essay does not in fact appear until the beginning of the fourth and final section, under the title "La Disparition de la littérature," *Le Livre à venir* (Paris: Gallimard, 1959), 237–45; "The Disappearance of Literature," *The Book to Come,* trans. Charlotte Mandell (Stanford: Stanford University Press, 2003), 195–201; translation modified.

7. G. W. F. Hegel, *Werke,* ed. Eva Moldenhauer and Karl Markus Michel, 20 vols. (Frankfurt: Suhrkamp, 1970), 13:25.

8. On this tension between the impossibility and necessity of literary criticism, see Blanchot, "Qu'en est-il de la critique?," *Arguments,* January-February-March 1959, 34–37. The piece was subsequently reprinted, with slight changes, in *Lautréamont et Sade* (Paris: Minuit, 1963), 9–14; it appears in English as "The Task of Criticism Today," trans. Leslie Hill, *Oxford Literary Review* 22 (2000): 19–24.

9. See for instance Gerald Bruns, *Maurice Blanchot: The Refusal of Philosophy* (Baltimore: Johns Hopkins University Press, 1997), 148–49. Blanchot himself identifies the parallels (and differences) between his own thinking and that of Schlegel and Novalis in his 1964 essay "L'athenaeum" in *L'entretien infini,* 515–27, *The Infinite Conversation,* 351–59.

10. See Philippe Lacoue-Labarthe and Jean-Luc Nancy, *L'absolu littéraire* (Paris: Seuil, 1978), 79–80, and "*Noli me frangere,*" *Revue des sciences humaines* 185 (1982): 83–92. For Blanchot's (oblique) response to the first of these two texts, see *L'écriture du désastre* (Paris: Gallimard, 1980), 98–99; *The Writing of the Disaster,* trans. Ann Smock (Lincoln: University of Nebraska Press, 1986), 60.

11. See Blanchot, "Notre épopée," *La Nouvelle Revue Française* 100 (April 1961): 690–98; the essay reappears as "Les Paroles doivent cheminer longtemps" in *L'entretien infini,* 478–86, *The Infinite Conversation,* 326–31.

12. Blanchot, *L'amitié* (Paris: Gallimard, 1971), 137, 139; *Friendship,* trans. Elizabeth Rottenberg (Stanford: Stanford University Press, 1997), 117, 119.

13. Blanchot, "Qu'en est-il de la critique?," 37; "The Task of Criticism Today," 24.

14. See Blanchot, "La Parole 'sacrée' de Hölderlin," *Critique* 7 (December 1946): 579–96; with slight modifications, the essay reappears in *La Part du feu* (Paris: Gallimard, 1949), 115–32; *The Work of Fire,* trans. Charlotte Mandell (Stanford: Stanford University Press, 1995), 111–31. I examine Blanchot's reading of Hölderlin and Heidegger in *Blanchot: Extreme Contemporary,* 77–91.

15. There is considerable evidence, though it is rarely explicit, of Blanchot's responsiveness to Heidegger throughout the 1950s. Witness, for instance, the articles "Nietzsche, aujourd'hui," *La Nouvelle Revue Française* 68 (August 1958): 284–95, and "Passage de la ligne," *La Nouvelle Revue Française* 69 (September 1958): 468–79 (col-

lected in *L'entretien infini*, 201–27; *The Infinite Conversation*, 136–51), and "L'étrange et l'étranger," *La Nouvelle Revue française* 70 (October 1958): 673–83.

16. Raymond Queneau (who was a close friend of both Bataille and Blanchot), in a diary entry for December 1950, reports as follows: "Heidegger says he found Bataille's article on Hölderlin very striking and feels great affinity with him [*qu'il se sent très près de lui*]. Sonia [sc. Orwell] wires Bataille to congratulate him. But the article was by Blanchot." See Raymond Queneau, *Journaux 1914–1965*, ed. Anne Isabelle Queneau (Paris: Gallimard, 1996), 737. Oddly, Queneau's editor glosses the anecdote by referring the reader not to the 1946 article but to Blanchot's essay, "La Folie par excellence," which did not appear in *Critique* until February 1951. Bataille recalls the misunderstanding in a letter to Jérôme Lindon shortly before his death; see Georges Bataille, *Choix de lettres, 1917–1962*, ed. Michel Surya (Paris: Gallimard, 1997), 582–83. Blanchot's own reaction to being given the news by Queneau was one of delight: at what the misunderstanding implied about the essential anonymity of writing and what it said about friendship, in particular Blanchot's friendship with Bataille.

17. See Blanchot, "L'attente," *Martin Heidegger zum siebzigsten Geburtstag*, 217–24. Translations from the text in this paper are my own. A complete English version appears in *The Blanchot Reader*, ed. Michael Holland (Oxford: Blackwell, 1994), 272–78.

18. See Blanchot, "L'attente," *Botteghe Oscure* 22 (August 1958): 22–33.

19. See Martin Heidegger, *Vorträge und Aufsätze* (Pfullingen: Neske, 1954), 249–74; *Early Greek Thinking*, trans. David Farrell Krell and Frank A. Capuzzi (New York: Harper and Row, 1984), 102–23.

20. Heidegger, *Vorträge und Aufsätze*, 133.

21. Heidegger, *Der Satz vom Grund* (Pfullingen: Neske, 1957), 209.

22. See Timothy Clark, *Derrida, Heidegger, Blanchot* (Cambridge: Cambridge University Press, 1992), 90–91. Clark points in particular to the similarities between Blanchot's contribution to the Festschrift and Heidegger's dialogue "Zur Erörterung der Gelassenheit" ("Conversation on a Country Path"), first written in 1944–45, but not published until 1959, almost a year after the appearance of Blanchot's first text entitled "L'attente" in *Botteghe Oscure* and, in all likelihood, some time after the writing of the Festschrift piece. Janicaud, in *Heidegger en France* (1:206–7), offers a rather different view of these apparent echoes, closer to that developed here.

23. Blanchot, born in 1907, was almost precisely eighteen years Heidegger's junior. On these dates, and their importance in general for Blanchot, see Christophe Bident, *Maurice Blanchot: Partenaire invisible*, 373–74, and "L'anniversaire—la chance," *Revue des sciences humaines* 253, no. 1 (1999): 173–82. It is perhaps not irrelevant to note here that the author of these lines was born on 21 September . . .

24. See Maurice Blanchot, "Penser l'apocalypse," *Le Nouvel Observateur* 22–28 (January 1988): 77–79. Blanchot explains in the letter that it was indeed his admiration for *Sein und Zeit* that prompted his participation in the 1959 Festschrift; it was only with the publication of Guido Schneeberger's *Nachlese zu Heidegger* in 1962, Blanchot adds, that, like others, he became aware of the full extent of Heidegger's prewar involvement with the Nazi party.

25. See Martin Heidegger, *Sein und Zeit* (Tübingen: Niemeyer, 1986), 261–62; *Being and Time* (Oxford: Blackwell, 1962), 306.

26. Heidegger, *Sein und Zeit*, 250, 258–59; *Being and Time*, 294, 303.

27. Heidegger, *Sein und Zeit*, 262; *Being and Time*, 307.

28. Heidegger, *Sein und Zeit*, 337; *Being and Time*, 386–87.

29. See Blanchot, "Oh tout finir," *Critique* 519–20 (August–September 1990): 635–67; "Oh All to End," trans. Leslie Hill, *The Blanchot Reader*, 298–300. Beckett's *L'innommable* (*The Unnamable*), it will be remembered, is one of the last texts discussed in *Le Livre à venir*.

30. Blanchot, "L'attente," *Martin Heidegger zum siebzigsten Geburtstag*, 218.

31. To the extent that fragmentation is necessarily inimical to all unity, it is clear that there can be no first time for the fragment, which reaches back to that time before time which is the time of something "older, dreadfully old, which was perhaps forever taking place [*de plus ancien, d'effroyablement ancien, qui avait peut-être même lieu en tout temps*]." (See *Celui qui ne m'accompagnait pas* [Paris: Gallimard, 1953], 47–48; *The One Who Was Standing apart from Me*, trans. Lydia Davis [Barrytown: Station Hill Press, 1993], 24.) In this perspective, all Blanchot's writing may be seen as fragmentary, from the early reviews, literary essays, novels, and shorter fiction of the 1930s, 1940s, and 1950s to the more avowedly fragmentary texts of the 1960s and after. As Schlegel was well aware, it is one of the strange characteristics of the literary fragment to know no bounds.

32. Heidegger, *Vorträge und Aufsätze*, 148; *Basic Writings*, ed. David Farrell Krell (London: Routledge, 1993), 355.

33. Heidegger, *Vorträge und Aufsätze*, 171.

34. On the interpretation of λόγος (in Heraclitus) as "the original assemblage of the primordial gathering from the primordial Laying [*die ursprüngliche Versammlung der anfänglichen Lese aus der anfänglichen Lege*]," see Heidegger, *Vorträge und Aufsätze*, 207–8; *Early Greek Thinking*, 66.

35. In 1980 Blanchot proposed a rather different fourfold, based on four sites of fragmentary dislocation: the Outside, the Neuter, Disaster, and Return; see *L'écriture du désastre*, 95–96, *The Writing of the Disaster*, 57–58.

36. Blanchot, *L'arrêt de mort* (Paris: Gallimard, 1948), 78; *Death Sentence*, trans. Lydia Davis (New York: Station Hill Press, 1978), 47; translation modified.

37. Heidegger, *Gesamtausgabe, vol. 9: Wegmarken* (Frankfurt: Klostermann, 1976), 410–12; *The Question of Being* (London: Vision Press, 1959), 80–83.

38. On the "Schritt zurück," see Heidegger, *Vorträge und Aufsätze*, 178.

39. Blanchot, *Le Pas au-delà* (Paris: Gallimard, 1973), 9; *The Step Not Beyond*, trans. Lycette Nelson (Albany: State University of New York Press, 1992), 2; translation modified.

40. See Heidegger, *Vorträge und Aufsätze*, 272–73; *Early Greek Thinking*, 121–22.

41. Blanchot, *L'entretien infini*, 125. Susan Hanson, in *The Infinite Conversation* (88), gives the following version, based on the translation by T. M. Robinson: "They are separated from the *logos* with which they are in the most continuous contact; and the things they meet with every day seem foreign to them."

42. See Blanchot, *L'entretien infini*, 125; *The Infinite Conversation*, 88.

43. See Bident, *Maurice Blanchot: Partenaire invisible*, 16.

44. See for instance Blanchot, "La Bête de Lascaux," *La Nouvelle Revue Française* 4 (April 1953): 684–93; "The Beast of Lascaux," trans. Leslie Hill, *Oxford Literary Review* 22 (2000): 9–18. It may be remembered that it was in response to Char and Heraclitus that, in "René Char et la pensée du neutre" in 1963, Blanchot first formulates in explicit fashion the thought of the neuter that would concern him for years to come; see *L'entretien infini*, 439–46; *The Infinite Conversation*, 298–302.

45. Blanchot, *L'attente l'oubli* (Paris: Gallimard, 1962), 14, 24.

46. On this question of hope without hope, see Blanchot's correspondence with Bataille in *Choix de lettres, 1917–1962,* 589–96.

CHAPTER SIX: Anarchic Temporality

1. Maurice Blanchot, "Littérature et la droit à la mort," *La Part du feu* (Paris: Gallimard, 1949)—hereafter *PF*); "Literature and the Right to Death," trans. Lydia Davis, in *The Work of Fire,* trans. Charlotte Mandell (Stanford: Stanford University Press, 1995)—hereafter *WF*.

2. Jean-Paul Sartre, *Qu'est-ce que la littérature?* (Paris: Gallimard, 1948), 19–20; *"What Is Literature?" and Other Essays* (Cambridge, Mass.: Harvard University Press, 1988), 30.

3. *Phänomenologie des Geist,* ed. Hans-Friedrich Wessels and Heinrich Clairmont (Hamburg: Felix Meiner, 1988), 264 (V.C.a); *Hegel's Phenomenology of Spirit,* trans. A. V. Miller (Oxford: Oxford University Press, 1977), 238.

4. *Qu'est-ce que la littérature?,* 26 / *What Is Literature?,* 35.

5. *Phänomenologie des Geist,* 144–45 / *Phenomenology of Spirit,* 126–27.

6. (Paris: José Corti, 1942); reprinted in *Faux pas* (Paris: Gallimard, 1943), 92–101)— hereafter *FP*. See especially p. 97:

> C'est un fait, la littérature existe. Elle continue d'être, en dépit de l'absurdité intérieure qui l'habite, la divise et la rend proprement inconceivable. Il y a au cœur de tout écrivain un démon qui le pousse à frapper de mort toutes les formes littéraires, à prendre conscience de sa dignité d'écrivain dans la mesure où il rompt avec le langage et avec la littérature, en un mot, à mettre en question d'une manière indicible ce qu'il est et ce qu'il fait. Comment, dans ces conditions, la littérature peut-elle exister? Comment l'écrivain qui se distingue des autres hommes par ce seul fait qu'il conteste la validité du langage et don't le travail devrait être d'empêcher la formation d'une œuvre écrite, finit-il par créer quelque ouvrage littérature? Comment la littérature est-elle possible?

7. And not just literature. Much of Blanchot's work is an exploration of the strange ontological condition in which speech becomes an impossible exigency. *L'attente l'oubli* (Paris: Gallimard, 1962, hereafter *AO*; *Awaiting Oblivion,* trans. John Gregg [Lincoln: University of Nebraska Press, 1997], hereafter *AwO*) is a text made up of narrative fragments and pieces of conversation that deal obsessively (not to say tortuously) with this condition:

> "Express only what cannot be expressed. Leave it unexpressed." (*AO35/AwO6*)
> —"Yes, speak to me now."—"I cannot."—"Speak without the ability to do so."—"You ask me so calmly to do the impossible." (*AO86/AwO44*)
> Wanting to and not being able to speak; not wanting to and not being able to evade speech; thus speaking—not speaking, in an identical movement her interlocutor had the duty to maintain.
> Speaking, not wanting to; wanting to, not being able to. (*AO93/AwO93*)

8. *Unterwegs zur Sprache* (Pfullingen: Günther Neske, 1959), 161–62; *On the Way to Language,* trans. Peter Hertz (New York: Harper and Row, 1971), 59.

9. *Qu'est-ce que la littérature?*, 43 / *What Is Literature?*, 334

10. See "L'expérience-limite" (1962), where Blanchot glosses Bataille's idea that "possibility is not the sole dimension of our existence": "It is perhaps given to us to 'live' each of the events that is ours by way of a double relation. We live it one time as something we comprehend, grasp, bear, and master . . . by relating it to some good or to some value, that is to say, finally, by relating it to Unity; we live it at another time as something that escapes all employment [*emploi*] and all end, and more, as that which escapes our very capacity to undergo it, but whose trial we cannot escape. Yes, as though impossibility, that by which we are no longer able to be able, were waiting for us behind all that we live, think, and say." *L'entretien infini* (Paris: Gallimard, 1969), 307–8—hereafter *EI; The Infinite Conversation*, trans. Susan Hanson (Minneapolis: University of Minnesota Press, 1993), 207—hereafter *IC*). It is this division of time into two temporalities that I'm trying to clarify in what follows.

11. *Phänomenologie des Geist*, 146–47 / *Phenomenology of Spirit*, 129.

12. See "La Mort possible" (1952): "You cannot write unless you remain your own master before death; you must have established with death a relation of sovereign equals. If you lose face before death, if death is the limit of your self-possession, then it slips the words out from under the pen, it cuts in and interrupts." *L'espace littéraire* (Paris: Gallimard, 1955), 110—hereafter *EL; The Space of Literature*, trans. Ann Smock (Lincoln: University of Nebraska Press, 1982), 91—hereafter *SL*.

13. *Œuvres complètes*, ed. Henri Mondor (Paris: Gallimard, 1945), 645—hereafter *OC*.

14. Stéphane Mallarmé, *Selected Prose, Poems, Essays, Letters*, trans. Bradford Cook (Baltimore: Johns Hopkins Press, 1956), 97—hereafter *SPP*.

15. *The Basic Problems of Phenomenology*, trans. Albert Hofstadter (Bloomington: Indiana University Press, 1982), 247–48.

16. *Les Imprévus de l'histoire* (Montpelier: Fata Morgana, 1994), 133—hereafter *IH; Collected Philosophical Papers*, trans. Alphonso Lingis (The Hague: Martinus Nijhoff, 1987), 6—hereafter *CPP*.

17. *Les Imprévus de l'histoire*, 138 / *Collected Philosophical Papers*, 9.

18. *Les Imprévus de l'histoire*, 143 / *Collected Philosophical Papers*, 11.

19. *The Logic of Sense*, trans. Mark Lester (New York: Columbia University Press, 1990), 63.

20. Gilles Deleuze and Félix Guattari, *A Thousand Plateaus*, trans. Brian Massumi (Minneapolis: University of Minnesota Press, 1993), 263.

21. On indiscernibility as a philosophical difficulty see Arthur Danto, *The Transfiguration of the Commonplace: A Philosophy of Art* (Cambridge, Mass.: Harvard University Press, 1981), 1–32 ("Works of Art and Mere Real Things").

22. *Disseminations*, trans. Barbara Johnson (Chicago: University of Chicago Press, 1981), 194–95.

23. *Disseminations*, 221.

24. Maurice Blanchot's *Le Pas au-delà* (Paris: Gallimard, 1973); *The Step Not Beyond*, trans. Lycette Nelson (Albany, N.Y.: SUNY University Press, 1992).

25. See Gerald L. Bruns, "Francis Ponge on the Rue de la Chaussée d'Antin," *Comparative Literature* 53, no. 3 (Summer 2001): 193–213.

26. *L'amitié* (Paris: Gallimard, 1971), 328–29—hereafter *A; Friendship*, trans. Elizabeth Rottenberg (Stanford: Stanford University Press, 1997), 290–91—hereafter *F*.

27. Maurice Blanchot, *La Communauté inavouable* (Paris: Éditions de Minuit, 1983); *The Unavowable Community*, trans. Pierre Jons (Barrytown, N.Y.: Station Hill Press, 1988).

28. *Time and the Other*, trans. Richard A. Cohen (Pittsburgh, Pa.: Duquesne University Press, 1987), 70.

29. "Ethics as First Philosophy," trans. Seán Hand and Michael Temple, *The Levinas Reader*, ed. Seán Hand (Oxford: Basil Blackwell, 1989), 83.

30. (Paris: Gallimard, 1948), 99; *Death Sentence*, trans. Lydia Davis (Barrytown: Station Hill Press, 1978), 52.

31. Maurice Blanchot and Jacques Derrida, *The Instant of My Death and Demeure: Fiction and Testimony*, trans. Elizabeth Rottenberg (Stanford: Stanford University Press, 1999), 3.

CHAPTER SEVEN: The Contestation of Death

1. Jacques Derrida, *Demeure: Maurice Blanchot* (Paris: Galilée, 1998).

2. I will return to this motif elsewhere, notably concerning the fragment "(Une scène primitive?)" ["(A Primal Scene?)"] in *L'écriture du désastre*.

3. "La Naissance et la mort" ["Birth and death"] (unpublished manuscript).

4. "Fidélités" ["Fidelities"] in *L'animal autobiographique—autour de Jacques Derrida* [*The Autobiographical Animal—Around Jacques Derrida*] (Paris: Galilée, 1999).

5. "Mais à mourir, qui est la plus grande besoigne que nous ayons à faire, l'excitation ne nous y peut aider.

Il me semble toutefois qu'il y a quelque façon de nous apprivoiser à elle [la mort] et de l'essayer aucunement. Nous en pouvons avoir expérience [je souligne] sinon entière et parfaicte, au moins telle qu'elle ne soit pas inutile, et qui nous rende plus fortifiez et assurez. Si nous ne la pouvons joindre, nous la pouvons approcher, nous la pouvons reconnoistre; et si nous ne donnons jusques à son fort, au moins verrons nous et en prattiquerons les advenues."

6. "Seul demeure le sentiment de légèreté qui est la mort même ou, pour le dire plus précisément, l'instant de ma mort toujours en instance."

7. Published in *Première livraison*, ed. Mathieu Bénézet and Philippe Lacoue-Labarthe (Paris-Strasbourg: Bourgois, 1978), 1.

8. "A sa place [à la place de lui: 'l'homme encore jeune,' qui est le 'personnage' du 'récit'], je ne chercherai pas à analyser ce sentiment de légèreté."

9. "Vous qui vivrez plus tard, proches d'un coeur qui ne bat plus, supposez, supposez-le: l'enfant . . ."

10. "Son trait décisif, c'est que celui qui l'éprouve n'est plus là quand il l'éprouve, n'est donc plus là pour l'éprouver."

11. "Mourir veut dire: mort, *tu* [je souligne] l'es déjà, dans un passé immémorial, d'une mort qui ne fut pas la tienne . . . Cette mort incertaine, toujours antérieure, *attestation* [je souligne encore] d'un passé sans présent, n'est jamais individuelle."

12. I owe this observation to Etienne Balibar, whom I thank for it.

13. "Certes Socrate n'écrit pas, mais, sous la voix, c'est par l'écriture cependant qu'il se donne aux autres comme le sujet perpétuel et perpétuellement destiné à mourir. Il ne parle pas, il questionne. Questionnant, il interrompt et s'interrompt sans cesse, don-

nant forme ironiquement au fragmentaire et vouant par sa mort la parole à la hantise de l'écriture, de même que celle-ci à la seule écriture testamentaire (sans signature toutefois)." Maurice Blanchot, *L'écriture du désastre* (Paris: Gallimard, 1980), 107.

CHAPTER EIGHT: The Counter-spiritual Life

1. Bataille, "Socratic College," *The Unfinished System of Nonknowledge,* ed. Stuart Kendall, trans. Michelle Kendall and Stuart Kendall (Minneapolis: University of Minnesota Press, 2001), 11; Georges Bataille, *Œuvres complètes,* 12 vols. (Paris: Gallimard, 1970–88), 6:286—hereafter *OC.*

2. Bataille, *Inner Experience,* trans. Leslie Anne Boldt (Albany: State University of New York Press, 1988), 102; *OC* 5:120.

3. Bataille, *Inner Experience,* 102; *OC* 5:120. In his review of *L'expérience intérieure,* Gabriel Marcel took exception to Bataille's attitude toward salvation. See his "The Refusal of Salvation and the Exaltation of the Man of Absurdity," *Homo Viator: Introduction to a Metaphysic of Hope,* trans. Emma Craufurd (Gloucester, Mass.: Peter Smith, 1978), esp. 185–200.

4. See Martin Heidegger, *Hegel's Concept of Experience,* no. trans. (New York: Harper and Row, 1970).

5. See Lev Chestov, *Potestas Clavium,* trans. Bernard Martin (Athens: Ohio University Press, 1968), 40.

6. See Bataille, *Inner Experience,* 59, 119; *OC* 5:74, 138. Note, though, that Bataille says "my method is at the antipodes of 'Yoga.'" "Method of Meditation," *The Unfinished System of Nonknowledge,* 78; *OC* 5:194. Also see Jean Bruno, "Les Techniques d'illumination chez Georges Bataille," *Critique* 195–96 (1963): 706–20.

7. Blanchot, "Inner Experience," *Faux pas,* trans. Charlotte Mandell (Stanford: Stanford University Press, 2001), 39; *Faux pas* (Paris: Gallimard, 1943), 49—hereafter *FP.*

8. See Blanchot, "The Relation of the Third Kind (man without horizon)," *The Infinite Conversation,* trans. Susan Hanson (Minneapolis: University of Minnesota Press, 1993), 66–74; *L'entretien infini* (Paris: Gallimard, 1969), 94–105—hereafter *EI.*

9. In his final *récit,* if indeed it is one, Blanchot speaks of experiencing "a feeling of extraordinary lightness, a sort of beatitude (nothing happy, however)—sovereign elation?" *The Instant of My Death,* bound with Jacques Derrida, *Demeure: Fiction and Testimony,* both trans. Elizabeth Rottenberg (Stanford: Stanford University Press, 2000), 5.

10. I take the notion of "the friendship of this certain, unshakable rigorous No" from "Refusal." See Blanchot, *Friendship,* trans. Elizabeth Rottenberg (Stanford: Stanford University Press, 1997), 111; *L'amitié* (Paris: Gallimard, 1971), 130—hereafter *A.*

11. Blanchot, *The Writing of the Disaster,* trans. Ann Smock (Lincoln: University of Nebraska Press, 1986), 92; *L'écriture du désastre* (Paris: Gallimard, 1980), 145—hereafter *ED.*

12. Blanchot, "The Limit-Experience," *The Infinite Conversation,* 210; *EI* 311.

13. Bataille, *Inner Experience,* 102; *OC* 5:120. Pierre Prévost observes of Bataille, "A une théologie positive, dont il rejetait les conclusions, il opposait une *théologie negative.*" *Rencontre Georges Bataille* (Paris: Jean-Michel Place, 1987), 82. The expression "théologie negative" is used in an unconventional way by Prévost.

14. Blanchot, *The Writing of the Disaster,* 20; *ED* 38.

15. Blanchot, "Master Eckhart," *Faux pas,* 23; *FP* 31.

16. See H. S. Harris, *Hegel's Development: Towards the Sunight, 1770–1801* (Oxford: Clarendon Press, 1972), 230–31 n. For the influence of Eckhart on Hegel see Cyril O'Regan, *The Heterodox Hegel* (Albany: State University of New York Press, 1994), 250–63.

17. In his *Exposito libri Saptientiae,* Eckhart observes, "Negatio ergo negationis, quam li unum significat, notat in termino significato adesse omne quod termini est et abesse omne quod oppositi termini est [The negation of the negation therefore denotes that all is present that belongs to the term and that all that belongs to the opposite term is absent]." *Meister Eckhart: Die deutschen und lateinischen Werke herausgegeben im Auftrag der deutschen Forschungsgemeinschaft* (Stuttgart-Berlin: Kohlhammer, 1936–), II:486, n. 148.

18. Eckhart, "The Book of Divine Consolation," in *Meister Eckhart: The Essential Sermons, Commentaries, Treatises, and Defense,* trans. Edmund Colledge and Bernard McGinn (New York: Paulist Press, 1981), 211.

19. See, for example, Sermon 5b, in Colledge and McGinn, *Meister Eckhart,* 184.

20. Blanchot, "Maître Eckhart," *Journal des Débats,* 4 November 1942, 3. This passage was changed when Blanchot reprinted the article in *Faux pas.* There he writes of "profound experience," not "inner experience." Either way, it should be noted that Eckhart seldom refers to specific experiences in the spiritual life. In the "Councils on Discernment," for instance, he downplays the significance of consoling graces. See Colledge and McGinn, *Meister Eckhart,* 258–59. Some scholars vigorously maintain that Eckhart is a philosopher, not a mystic. See, for example, Kurt Flasch, "Meister Eckhart: Versuch, ihn aus dem mystischen Strom zu retten," *Gnosis und Mystik in der Geschichte der Philosophie,* ed. Peter Koslowski (Darmstadt: Wissenschaftliche Buchgesellschaft, 1988), 94–110.

21. Jean-François Fogel and Daniel Rondeau, ed., *Pourquoi écrivez-vous? 400 écrivains répondent* (Paris: Libération, 1985), 188.

22. Blanchot, "Nicolas De Cues," *Journal des Débats,* 6 January 1943, 3. The column is a review of Maurice de Gandillac's *La Philosophie de Nicolas de Cues* (Paris: Aubier-Montaigne, 1941) and his edition, *Œuvres choises de Nicolas de Cues* (Paris: Aubier-Montagine, 1942).

23. Blanchot, "La Mystique d'Angelus Silesius," *Journal des Débats,* 6 October 1943, 3. The column is a review of Henri Plard, ed., *La Mystique d'Angelus Silesius* (Paris: Aubier-Montaigne, 1943). In his "The Three Creations" Eckhart observes that God "dwells in the nothing-at-all that was prior to nothing." *The Works of Meister Eckhart,* ed. Franz Pfeiffer, rpt. (Kila, Mont.: Kessinger Publications, n.d.), 387.

24. Blanchot, "La Mystique d'Angelus Silesius," 3. Commenting on St. Paul, Eckhart observes, "Best of all is to be one with God. In this union the soul is dead, not only to all outward but also to all inward ghostly acts." Sermon XII, *The Works of Meister Eckhart,* 46.

25. See Prévost, *Rencontre Georges Bataille,* 100–101. Prévost notes that Bataille later became absorbed with Denys the Areopagite. Doubtless Bataille would have read Gandillac's edition, *Œuvres complètes du Pseudo-Denys l'Aréopagite* (Paris: Aubier-Montaigne, 1943), when it appeared.

26. Blanchot, "Nicolas de Cues," 3.

27. Saint Augustine, *Letters*, vol. 2, trans. Wilfred Parsons (New York: Fathers of the Church 1953), 398. Cusa quotes this passage in his *Apologia Doctae Ignorantiae*. See Jasper Hopkins, *Nicholas of Cusa's Debate with John Wenck: A Translation and an Appraisal of "De Ignota Litteratura" and "Apologia Doctae Ignorantiae"* (Minneapolis, Minn.: Arthur J. Banning Press, 1981), 51.

28. Bernard McGinn quotes the passage from homily 101 in his fine study, *The Mystical Thought of Meister Eckhart: The Man from Whom God Hid Nothing* (New York: Crossroad, 2001), 213 n. 27.

29. Colledge and McGinn, *Meister Eckhart*, 208.

30. Blanchot, "Nicolas de Cues," 3.

31. Blanchot, "La Mystique d'Angelus Silesius," 3.

32. For Cusa's muted defense of Eckhart see Hopkins, *Nicholas of Cusa's Debate with John Wenck*, 58–59. Hans Blumenberg offers some illuminating remarks on the debate between Cusa and Wenck in his *The Legitimacy of the Modern Age*, trans. Robert M. Wallace (Cambridge, Mass.: MIT Press, 1999).

33. Blanchot, "Nicolas de Cues," 3.

34. Blanchot, "Inner Experience," *Faux pas*, 41; *FP* 52.

35. Blanchot, "Kafka and Literature," *The Work of Fire*, trans. Charlotte Mandell (Stanford: Stanford University Press, 1995), 23; *PF* 31.

36. Blanchot, "La Poésie religieuse," *Journal des Débats*, 9 June 1943, 3.

37. Blanchot, "On the Subject of *The Fruits of the Earth*," *Faux pas*, 298; *FP* 339.

38. Blanchot, *Lautréamont et Sade*, 2d ed. (Paris: Minuit, 1963), 90.

39. Blanchot, "Glances from Beyond the Grave," *The Work of Fire*, 244; *PF* 238.

40. Blanchot, "Gide and the Literature of Experience," *The Work of Fire*, 224; *PF* 220.

41. Blanchot, "Literature and the Right to Death," trans. Lydia Davis, *The Work of Fire*, 301; *PF* 294.

42. Blanchot sketches his position in "La Puissance et la glorie," *Le Livre à venir* (Paris: Gallimard, 1959).

43. Blanchot, *The Space of Literature*, trans. Ann Smock (Lincoln: University of Nebraska Press, 1982), 96; *L'espace littéraire* (Paris: Gallimard, 1955), 119—hereafter *EL*.

44. Blanchot, *The Space of Literature*, 240; *EL* 322.

45. Emmanuel Levinas, "Reality and Its Shadow," *Collected Philosophical Papers*, trans. Alphonso Lingis (The Hague: Martinus Nijhoff, 1987), 6. Blanchot, "The Two Versions of the Imaginary," *The Space of Literature*, 255; *EL* 343.

46. See Christophe Bident, *Maurice Blanchot, partenaire invisible* (Seyssel: Champ Vallon, 1998), 403–17.

47. Blanchot, *The Space of Literature*, 242–43; *EL* 326.

48. Blanchot, "Une revue peut être l'expression. . . ," *Lignes* 11 (1990): 182.

49. Blanchot's later radicalization of this position, in part a rethinking of experience on the basis of the eternal return, is outside the limits of this essay. See his reflections in *The Writing of the Disaster*, 50–51; *ED* 85. Also see Kevin Hart, *The Dark Gaze: Maurice Blanchot and the Sacred* (Chicago: University of Chicago Press, 2004), chap. 5.

50. Blanchot, *The Infinite Conversation*, xii, trans. slightly modified; *EI* vii–viii. On the theme of a communism beyond communism see also "Le Communisme sans héritage," originally published in *Comité* 1 (1968) and reprinted in *Gramma* 3–4 (1976): 32.

51. That Derrida has been influenced by Blanchot is also evident. See Derrida's

remarks in *Parages* (Paris: Galilée, 1986), 11. In a more subtle way, Derrida draws from Blanchot's notion of contestation in developing his thought of the impossible. Like contestation, the impossible is a ceaseless movement that does not presume a utopia. See Derrida, "Non pas l'utopie, l'im-possible," *Papier machine* (Paris: Galilée, 2001), 360–61. However, it would be misleading to identify Blanchot's and Derrida's senses of the impossible.

52. Hans-Jost Frey, *Interruptions,* trans. Georgia Albert (Albany: State University of New York Press, 1996), 54. Frey is plainly indebted to Blanchot's account of the fragmentary. Also see pp. 26, 31, 40.

53. Derrida alerts us to the need to question the fraternal structure of Blanchot's community in his *Politics of Friendship,* trans. George Collins (London: Verso, 1997), 304–6.

54. Blanchot, *Le Dernier à parler* (Montpellier: Fata Morgana, 1986), 11.

55. Blanchot, *The Infinite Conversation,* 127–28; *EI* 187.

56. See for example Martin Buber, *Moses: The Revelation and the Covenant,* n. trans. (New York: Harper Torchbooks, 1958), 9–10, and *Two Types of Faith: A Study of the Interpenetration of Judaism and Christianity,* trans. Norman P. Goldhawk (New York: Harper Torchbooks, 1961), 130.

57. See Buber, 'Spinoza, Sabbatai Zvi, and the Baal-Shem," in his *The Origin and Meaning of Hasidism,* ed. and trans. Maurice Friedman (New York: Harper Torchbooks, 1966), 93.

58. Blanchot, "Gog and Magog," *Friendship,* 231; *A* 263.

59. Blanchot, *The Infinite Conversation,* 427; *EI* 627; "Paix, paix au lointain et au proche," *De la Bible à nos jours: 3000 ans d'art* (Paris: Société des Artists Indépendents, 1985), 53.

60. See Rabbi Isaac the Blind of Provence, "The Mystical Torah—Kabbalistic Creation," *The Early Kabbalah,* ed. Joseph Dan, trans. Ronald C. Kiener (New York: Paulist Press, 1986), 75–76. Blanchot discusses this in *The Infinite Conversation,* 430; *EI* 630–31.

61. Levinas evokes a "recognition of the Torah *before Sinai*" in "The Nations and Messianic Time," *Beyond the Verse,* trans. Gary D. Mole (London: Athlone, 1994), 97. Blanchot speaks of Judaism as the ground of our relationship with the other, rather than as a religion or a culture. See "N'oubliez pas," lettre à Salomon Malka, *L'Arche* 373 (May 1988): 68–71.

62. Blanchot, *The Infinite Conversation,* 240; *EI* 357.

63. Blanchot, *The Writing of the Disaster,* 20; *ED* 38.

64. Blanchot, *The Infinite Conversation,* 207; *EI* 307–8.

65. Blanchot, "Humankind," *The Infinite Conversation,* 130; *EI* 192.

66. Blanchot, *The Unavowable Community,* trans. Pierre Joris (Barrytown, N.Y.: Station Hill Press, 1988)6; *La Communauté inavouable* (Paris: Éditions du Minuit, 1983), 16—hereafter *CI*.

67. Blanchot continues to insist on this point as late as 1983. See *The Unavowable Community,* 8; *CI* 20. Raymond Carpentier observes that "true dialogue is sacrifice." "L'échec de la communication," in Jean Lacroix, ed., *Les Hommes devant l'échec* (Paris: Presses Universitaires de France, 1968), 20.

Notes on Contributors

Gerald L. Bruns is William P. and Hazel B. White Professor of English at the University of Notre Dame. He is the author of *Heidegger's Estrangements* (1989), *Hermeneutics Ancient and Modern* (1992), *Maurice Blanchot: The Refusal of Philosophy* (1997), and *Tragic Thoughts at the End of Philosophy* (1999).

Kevin Hart is Professor of English at the University of Notre Dame. Recent books include an expanded edition of *The Trespass of the Sign* (2000), *Postmodernism* (2004), and *The Dark Gaze: Maurice Blanchot and the Sacred* (2004). He is the editor of *Nowhere without No: In Memory of Maurice Blanchot* (2003). His selected poems, *Flame Tree*, appeared with Bloodaxe Books in 2003.

Geoffrey Hartman is the author of many works of criticism, including, most recently, *A Critic's Journey* (1999), *Scars of the Spirit* (2002), and *The Longest Shadow* (2002). Daniel O'Hara's *Geoffrey Hartman: A Reader* appeared with Edinburgh University Press in 2004. He is Sterling Professor of English and Comparative Literature (Emeritus) at Yale University.

Leslie Hill is Professor of French at the University of Warwick. He is the author of *Beckett's Fiction: In Different Words* (1990), *Marguerite Duras: Apocalyptic Desires* (1993), *Maurice Blanchot, Extreme Contemporary* (1997), and *Bataille, Klossowski, Blanchot: Writing at the Limit* (2001).

Michael Holland is a Fellow of St. Hugh's College, Oxford, and is the editor of *The Blanchot Reader* (1995). A volume of criticism on Eugène Ionesco is forthcoming from Grant and Cutler, and he is working on a study of Blanchot's fiction.

Philippe Lacoue-Labarthe is Professor of Philosophy at the University of Strasbourg. Several of his books have been translated into English, chief among them being *Typography* (1989), *The Subject of Philosophy* (1993), *Poetry as Experience* (1999), and, with Jean-Luc Nancy, *The Literary Absolute* (1988). Other recent works include *Phrase* (2000), *Heidegger: La Politique du poème* (2002), and *Agonie terminée, agonie interminable (sur Maurice Blanchot)* (2003).

Vivian Liska is Professor of German Literature and Director of the Institute of Jewish Studies at the University of Antwerp. Her books include *Die Nacht der Hymnen* (1993), *Die Dichterin und das schelmische Erhabene* (1997), and *Die Moderne—Ein Weib* (2000). She is currently editing a collection, *Contemporary Jewish Writing in Europe,* and writing another critical study, *When Kafka Says "We."*

Jill Robbins is Professor of Religious Studies at Emory University, where she also teaches in the Comparative Literature Program. She has published two books: *Prodigal Son/Elder Brother: Interpretation and Alterity in Augustine, Petrarch, Kafka, Lévinas* (1991) and *Altered Reading: Lévinas and Literature* (1999). She is also the editor of *Is it Righteous to Be?: Interviews with Emmanuel Lévinas* (2001).

Index of Names

Index of Topics